MANAGERS

MANAGERS

Tales from the Red & Whites

A collection of writing inspired
by Sunderland Association Football Club

Volume Three
by Graeme Anderson, Lance Hardy
and Rob Mason

TALES
FROM

First published in Great Britain in 2018
by Tales From

© 2018 Tales From Ltd

All rights reserved. No part of this publication may be
reproduced, stored in a retrieval system, or transmitted in any
form or by any means, electronic, mechanical, photocopying,
recording or otherwise, without the prior written permission
of the publisher.

The right of each author to be identified as the author of
their work has been asserted in accordance with the
Copyright, Designs and Patent Act 1988.

Printed and bound by Page Bros Ltd

Jacket design by www.stonecreativedesign.com

ISBN 978-1-912249-03-9

Tales From Ltd
107 Jupiter Drive, Hemel Hempstead, Herts HP2 5NU
Registered company number: 9082738
www.talesfrom.com
info@talesfrom.com

TALES FROM THE RED & WHITES

CONTENTS

Introduction		7
The Editors		9
Acknowledgements		11
1	Ken Knighton	12
2	Lawrie McMenemy	48
3	Malcolm Crosby	86
4	Peter Reid	118
5	Gustavo Poyet	202
6	Simon Grayson	244

INTRODUCTION

Welcome to the third volume of *Tales from the Red and Whites*. In this edition Graeme Anderson, Rob Mason and I have interviewed six of the men who have managed Sunderland AFC. Their stories span almost 40 years: from Ken Knighton's five-a-side Wembley winners of 1979 to Simon Grayson's 128-day reign in 2017.

We are delighted that Lawrie McMenemy, Malcolm Crosby, Peter Reid and Gustavo Poyet have also contributed to what we hope will be a popular and vital addition to any Sunderland fan's book collection, alongside *Tales from the Red and Whites, Volumes 1* and *2*.

Malcolm was the last man to lead the club to an FA Cup final; Gus was the last man to lead the club to a League Cup final. Peter took us to seventh in the Premier League in successive seasons (our highest final league placings since 1955) and his seven and a half years in charge is the longest managerial period at the club since the late 1950s.

Lawrie was the club's most popular managerial appointment in living memory before becoming associated with our first-ever relegation to the third flight just two years later in 1987. This is the first time that he has spoken so openly about his time at Sunderland since he left the club.

The three of us would like to send our sincere thanks to Ken, Lawrie, Malcolm, Peter, Gus and Simon for agreeing to be part of this unique volume of work. Each of them gave their time so generously to us so that this book could be written. It has been an absolute pleasure for us to work on this project and we hope that you find it as entertaining and interesting as it has been for us to meet and interview these gentlemen and write about their time at Roker Park and the Stadium of Light.

Thanks also to Adam Leventhal of Tales From Publishing; copy editor Ian Preece; and graphic designers Stone Creative Design.

There are many stories about promotions, relegations and Cup runs that feature, of course, but there are also various revelations of frustrations with the board room, problems with players, potential signings that got away, and, ultimately, sackings; at one time bizarrely following the negative result of a Pools Panel verdict!

As with our previous volumes, there is a lot for supporters to reminisce about, but there is such a lot to learn as well, with answers to long-asked questions, plus several exclusives along the way. In fact, many of these tales have never been written about before!

As ever with Sunderland AFC, there really isn't a dull moment . . .

Lance Hardy
Bawtry, South Yorkshire
Autumn 2018

THE EDITORS

Graeme Anderson was the *Sunderland Echo*'s chief Sunderland AFC writer from 1996 to 2014 and has written more words on the club than any journalist in history. In *Tales from the Red and Whites, Volume 1* he analysed the Niall Quinn and Kevin Phillips strike partnership and co-wrote Gary Rowell's chapter; and in *Tales from the Red and Whites, Volume 2* he interviewed Tony Coton, Martin Scott, Stefan Schwarz and Stephen Elliott. In *Tales from the Red and Whites, Volume 3* his interview subjects are Peter Reid and Simon Grayson.

Lance Hardy is the author of *Stokoe, Sunderland and '73*, which was shortlisted for Football Book of the Year at the British Sports Book Awards in 2010. He is a senior international television producer who has worked at six World Cups and four Olympic Games. He was formerly programme editor of *Football Focus*, *Final Score*, *Match of the Day* and *Late Kick Off* for BBC Sport.

In *Tales from the Red and Whites, Volume 1* he retraced the emotional rollercoaster of Sunderland's 1976–77 season and co-wrote Gary Bennett's chapter; and in *Tales from the Red and Whites, Volume 2* he interviewed Darren Holloway, John MacPhail, Stan Anderson and Tony Towers. In *Tales from the Red and Whites, Volume 3* his interview subjects are Malcolm Crosby and Gustavo Poyet.

Rob Mason is Sunderland AFC's official club historian. He has written for Sunderland's match programme since

1986. In his time as editor, up to 2017, Sunderland won more Programme of the Year awards than any other club. He has also edited the club's magazines *Legion of Light*, *24/7* and *Junior Black Cats*. He has written over 40 books on Sunderland as well as nine on other clubs.

In *Tales from the Red and Whites, Volume 1* he told the tale of The Team of all the Talents and co-wrote Jim Montgomery's chapter; and in *Tales from the Red and Whites, Volume 2* he interviewed Shaun Elliott, Gordon Armstrong and Vic Halom. In *Tales from the Red and Whites, Volume 3* his interview subjects are Ken Knighton and Lawrie McMenemy.

ACKNOWLEDGEMENTS

I would like to thank my mother Sylvia, love of my life Marion and my daughter Amy for their patience and support throughout all three volumes. *Graeme Anderson*

Love and thanks to Mum and Dad for everything, Adelle for the inspiration, and Lijana and Savanna for their support and understanding. *Lance Hardy*

Thank you to my wife Barbara who will now hope I start another book quickly so she continues to have peace and quiet. *Rob Mason*

1

Ken Knighton managed Sunderland longer ago than any living manager, excluding caretakers Ian MacFarlane and Dave Merrington. Knighton had worked with Merrington and manager Jimmy Adamson, but when that pair moved to Leeds Knighton turned down the opportunity to go with them. Instead he remained as first-team coach while long-term caretaker manager Billy Elliott took Sunderland to within a whisker of promotion in 1979. During that summer the board turned to Knighton, who became Sunderland's youngest manager since Robert Campbell in the 1890s.

Knighton steered Sunderland to promotion in his one full season in charge and saw his side proudly sit first in the top flight after scoring seven goals in winning their opening two games after promotion. Constant battles with chairman Tom Cowie eventually saw Ken sacked late in the season, although his side had never been in a relegation position.

After a brief spell in charge of Orient Knighton stepped away from the professional game at the age of 38, forging a second career in telecommunications. Now retired in the south-west Ken has wonderful memories of Wearside but has never been back. Here for the first time, he reflects on his time in charge of The Lads.

KEN KNIGHTON

SUNDERLAND MANAGER
7 JUNE 1979 TO 13 APRIL 1981
MEETS ROB MASON

The last Sunderland manager to win at Wembley doesn't have a statue in his honour at the Stadium of Light. Yes, there is one of Bob Stokoe but Ken Knighton was a Wembley winner six years after Stokoe's Stars of 1973 – albeit at Wembley Arena in the *Daily Express* five-a-side tournament! Six months later Knighton led his side to promotion against newly crowned FA Cup winners' West Ham, before doing something no one has done since – take Sunderland to the top of the top flight.

Visiting Ken at his home in the south-west of England he is keen to show me the only items he has on display which indicate the homeowner has an interest in football, let alone played over 400 games and managed Sunderland to promotion. We chat for hours in his elegant front room before I'm led up to his study where family photographs adorn the desk but on the wall is a large framed photograph of Sunderland's 1979–80 promotion-winning squad. Under it is a small wooden plaque proclaiming the Red and Whites' elevation with Mr Ken Knighton as manager.

It is more than Ken got from the club: 'I bet there's nothing in the minutes of any board meeting where they mention me with regard to winning promotion. Not one mention was given in the first board meeting we had after winning promotion with regard to "Well done for winning promotion." Nothing was ever said. I've got a plaque which was given to me by the supporters' association, along with a framed team photograph, but from the board of directors I got nothing, not even a "well done".'

Knighton's battles with the board, specifically Tom Cowie, meant that even when things were going well on the pitch life was difficult for Knighton. But regardless of that his achievement at Sunderland is something he looks back on as the peak of his career. It is a rare man who rates his biggest game as one where he was manager. Peter Reid, for instance, had some fabulous times as Sunderland supremo but will always point to days when he had his boots on and was winning things as a player at Everton as his greatest moments. Ken Knighton also had an extensive playing career, representing six clubs and once being chaired off the pitch after scoring a goal which kept Sheffield Wednesday up, but after naming the promotion night against the Hammers as his greatest moment I give him the opportunity to pause and think about that, but there is no hesitation: 'Without question it was my greatest moment,' he insists. 'I still feel a tingle down the spine just thinking about it.' A year earlier, when Ken was first-team coach, Sunderland had got so close to promotion they only found they'd missed out in the dressing rooms at the Racecourse Ground in Wrexham where, after winning, they listened to the other results come in to discover they'd lost out on going up by a whisker – as Stoke, Crystal Palace and Brighton all won, the latter at Newcastle. Now, in Knighton's first season as manager, they had chased hard for promotion at a time before the playoffs were introduced and were fourth with a game to play.

With Leicester and Birmingham assured of promotion third-placed Chelsea were a point ahead of Sunderland, but the Blues had completed their fixtures and needed London rivals West Ham to do them a favour. With the best goal difference in the division Sunderland just needed a point to go up, but no one fancied hanging onto a draw in the dying seconds against a team good enough to have beaten Arsenal in the Cup final two days earlier. On the night Sunderland were comfortable winners, goals from Kevin Arnott and Knighton's record signing Stan Cummins seeing off a tiring West Ham and leaving Chelsea crestfallen – in a reverse of the situation in 1963 when, after winning extremely fortunately at Roker in Sunderland's final game, Chelsea won their remaining fixture against Portsmouth 7-0 to pip Sunderland to promotion on goal average.

For all the joy of being in the moment and actually winning the promotion-clinching match Ken's greatest day started and ended badly: 'First of all my abiding memory was one of sadness, because my family couldn't turn up for the game. We'd arranged an end-of-season tour to go to America, and we'd also arranged for supporters to be able to pay to come with us on the flight and stay at the same hotel. That was all booked before West Ham got to the Cup final. My wife and kids as well as my mum and dad were all going that Monday to catch a flight to Heathrow. I was at Roker Park at six o'clock in the morning with three buses of supporters who were dyed-in-the-wool supporters but were going to miss the game where we won promotion because they were going on this trip.

'I went on each of the buses to speak to the supporters to say I was really sorry about how this had happened but told them not to worry because we were going to do it. It was really sad. I had to say "bye" to Carol and my kids ahead of the biggest night of my life in footballing terms. The start of the day had been terrible, to see the coaches going away. I stayed at Roker Park from 6.00 a.m. until after the game, which started at 7.30 p.m.

'The atmosphere building up to that match is something I don't think you could get anywhere else in the country, I really don't. I was in the office and someone came up and said, "There's a chap here who has come from Australia, and he's only come for the game." I had a chat with him and asked when he was going back, to which he said "Wednesday", which was only in two days' time. The gates were closed with a full house more than an hour before kick-off. From the manager's office I was looking out at the queues and thinking, "They're not all going to get in."'

I knew how they felt. At the time I was studying in Sheffield and in the middle of final exams. After rushing out of the exam hall I'd caught a train home and got to my usual Roker End haunt to find queues longer than the length of the pitch. I was panicking that I wouldn't get in but fortunately for me – if not for others – the gates were closed after letting in about ten people after me, with thousands locked out in addition to the 47,000 packed into Roker Park. The ground never held another crowd as big. As the Roker End was two-thirds demolished for safety reasons two years later, Ken's big night was the last truly big night at the full-size Roker Park.

While everyone was able to celebrate afterwards, whether they'd got in or not – or were on their way to the USA for the end of season trip; where the players and staff would relax before a prestige friendly against Fort Lauderdale just 48 hours after the Hammers match – Ken was feeling like the Cinderella of Roker Park.

Knighton's assistant was Frank Clark. 'I remember before the game started Clarkie and me were having a chat and he said, "If we win and get promotion tonight you won't enjoy it after the game." I said, "You're joking, aren't you?" to which he told me to wait and see. Now Clarkie had won a lot in his career and he knew what he was talking about. I remember afterwards going on the pitch, walking around the ground, thanking the supporters. The noise and the atmosphere was so uplifting, and then we got back into the dressing room and I still felt like a million dollars. But then we went up into the boardroom and I looked around and saw all these hangers-on, and people who I had had battles with who were lording it, and I realised Frank was right. That's what he'd been on about. He and I left and went back to Frank's house, and with my wife Carol being away, he, I and his wife had a bottle of champagne there.'

Tom Cowie (he became Sir Tom in 1992) was a self-made man who was Sunderland born and bred. Although he had been a supporter of the club he wasn't football daft like Bob Murray who succeeded him as chairman a few years later. Cowie wanted the best for Sunderland but would have fitted the bill for Len Shackleton's infamous blank page in his autobiography headed 'The Average Director's Knowledge of Football'. Cowie and Knighton rarely saw eye to eye.

Stories abounded of Knighton paying for things Cowie wouldn't fund. Were they true? 'It happened once. That was at Christmas when I said to Tom Cowie – because we were playing on Boxing Day at Roker Park – "What I'd like to do is let the players have Christmas morning with their family and friends, but I want to take them away at about five o'clock just to stay away in preparation for the game the following day." He asked how much it would cost, to which I said, "Look at it this way, how many do you think we're going to get at the game on Boxing Day? Over 30,000? That's going to generate income, and I can do a deal at the Holiday Inn at Newcastle which won't cost much because there won't be many people staying there at Christmas", but he said, "No, we can't afford it." I insisted I wanted to do it, as it was sensible. He said, "If you want to do it you pay for it." So I did it off my own bat. I knew the manager at the Holiday Inn, and he gave me a really good deal for us all to stay there.'

Both Knighton and Cowie had an abundance of experience but were finding their feet in their first roles as manager and football club chairman respectively, Cowie having taken over from Keith Collings six weeks after promotion was secured and the first season back in the top flight was on the horizon. The lack of rapport between Cowie and Ken was there from the start: 'On the morning he was appointed chairman all of the press were there. He came out with a comment which said, "Contrary to what you've heard, Ken Knighton will still be our manager this season." I heard this and thought, "I'm not having that." So, after the press conference, I asked, "Can I just have a word with you?" I said, "We've just won promotion, I've got a three-year contract, and you've just given a statement to the press saying contrary to what you've heard I'm still going to be manager. How do you think that makes me feel?" He replied, "You know everybody thought I was trying to get Cloughie and all these big names." I told him he could have said it a bit better, but he didn't like it at all because I confronted him, and from that day until when I left it was confrontation all of the time. It's very sad, really.'

Indeed, Cowie did try for big names. He attempted to get Brian Clough as well as Bobby Robson and, of course, later attracted Lawrie McMenemy, which proved to be a total disaster. Given the running battle Cowie had with Knighton, goodness knows how he would have got on with Clough. Speaking to Sir Tom at his home in 2009 he told me of his attempts to get Clough for Roker in the mid-eighties – after the Knighton era – 'We had several talks and I was desperate to sign him. I travelled down to Nottingham to see him but you couldn't talk to the man and, in the end, I just thought, "No chance." If he had joined the club I think I'd have fired him about three weeks later.'

Knighton had seen Clough operate when he was a Preston player and involved in Clough's signing of his North End teammate Archie Gemmill, as we shall see, but it was Knighton's purchase of a player from Clough that really taught the young manager a lesson. 'I bought Ian Bowyer from Forest and went to see Cloughie to do the deal. I was with him from 11 o'clock in the morning until five o'clock. Unfortunately, it was when he was on the drink, but I had the best lesson that anyone in football could have had. He was absolutely outstanding, and what he said was, "The battles you can win, win them early. Don't leave it too late."

'I remember the company car I was going to get as manager, and it was one of the directors, Frank Cronin, who was responsible for getting me the car of my choice. He asked what I would like, so I told him I'd like a Vauxhall Vignelli, a really nice car, but he said, "Oh, instead of that let me get you a—" but I interrupted and said, "No, you've asked me what car I'd like. I decide that, and that's the car I'd like." It was only a small thing but if you let them get away with things like that you've got no chance. It was absolutely fascinating spending time with Cloughie, and I'd learned.'

Wearside's wish for Clough was also in Knighton's thinking when he appointed former Newcastle player Frank Clark as his assistant: 'I'd met Frank on a coaching course at Lilleshall, when we'd got on really well. There was a big clamour, when Billy Elliott left, for Cloughie. The supporters were frantic about getting Cloughie, so I got the job and thought the next best thing was to bring in someone who had worked with Cloughie for the last two years. Frank had been really successful and wanted to come onto the management side of things. It sort of fitted in nicely.'

A County Durham lad from Rowlands Gill, Clark played over 450 games for the Magpies so knew the north-east inside out, even if his stripes had been the wrong colour. In fact Frank had been at Sunderland as a junior player before ever going to St James'. A member of the Newcastle side who won the Inter-Cities Fairs Cup in 1969, Clark's last game as a player had been as part of Forest's 1979 European Cup final winning side, a team that included Bowyer (and had future Sunderland boss Martin O'Neill and former Sunderland centre-forward John O'Hare on the bench).

Clark had seen how Clough operated and was behind Ken as he tried to deal with the demands placed upon him by Cowie. A promotion winner in his first season it would have been reasonable to hope for some backing from the newly installed chairman, but mirroring the tale Len Ashurst tells of Cowie making him drive from South Wales for a five-minute meeting – where he was sacked – that could have been dealt with by phone, Knighton explains, 'What he used to do was have meetings with various business people at Roker Park. He'd come in at about half-twelve, have a couple of hours' meeting, and then go back to his office at his business headquarters and ring me and say, "Can you come over and see me? I'd like to have a meeting." I said, "I'm not being funny, but you've been here. Why couldn't we have had the meeting here?" to which he'd insist, "I'd like you to come over here and see me please." It was confrontation all the time.'

Confrontation was nothing new with Cowie. There had been difficulties with his predecessor too. 'At the third board meeting I attended,' remembers Knighton, 'I was sat in the office and the board were having the meeting. One of the directors came through from the meeting and said, "Have you got a key for the door that leads into the boardroom?" I said, "Why would I have a key?" But he said, "I just need to lock the door then." I asked him why, and what he meant, and he said to me that things had been getting out from the board meeting that they'd been having prior to the manager coming in, and they wanted to stop it at source. I said, "Hang on a minute . . ." It was Frank Cronin, but before I could really say anything he'd gone back into the boardroom. I was then called into the meeting. By chance it was my wedding anniversary and the chairman, who was Keith

Collings, said, "We won't keep you long tonight, Ken, because we know it's your anniversary." But I said, "That's OK, because I won't be staying long after the stroke that Frank Cronin has just pulled, more or less saying that I'm listening in to what you've been saying and then letting the press know. If you think that's what I'm about then you can forget it." Then I stood up and walked out, but before I got to the door Keith Collings said, "Mr Manager, we are not giving you permission to leave. I didn't sit down, I just said, "Mr Chairman, I'm going.""

Managers at football clubs can be all powerful but their kingdom can collapse like a pack of cards if the board decides to get rid of them. The person calling the shots one day can be sweeping his belongings into a bin-bag the following day, with his coaching staff often dismissed *en masse* with him. Some managers don't get to be all powerful in the first place, especially if they have to settle for the 'head coach' rather than manager moniker. Gus Poyet and Dick Advocaat, for instance, had to work with director of football Lee Congerton, while Paolo Di Canio had Roberto De Fanti for company.

Following the flirtation with directors of football, Sunderland dispensed with the role when Sam Allardyce came in as manager. Big Sam had been signed as a player for Sunderland by Knighton. That too led to a rumpus with chairman Cowie, who couldn't be budged when Allardyce requested help with a bridging loan when he couldn't sell his house in Bolton: 'I was delighted to sign Sam. He's proved he's a leader. Whenever I signed a player, within reason, then my job as a manager was to get the board of directors to sanction whatever we had agreed. Sam was genuine in what he wanted to do and, again, it ended up being a battle between me and Tom Cowie, and Tom wasn't going to back down. No matter how hard I tried, he'd made his mind up. I couldn't believe that he would behave in that manner. Here we had someone with a genuine problem. He wanted to move to the area and I wanted to do something for him.'

Allardyce had been brought in by Knighton as Sunderland prepared for a return to the top flight, after what was just a third ever promotion. It had taken the famed 1964 promotion team nine games to win a top-flight match, while Bob Stokoe's promotion winners of 1976 went ten games without a win on their return to the highest level. In contrast, with just Allardyce added to the promotion squad, Knighton's men hit the ground running.

'It surpassed our wildest dreams as a start,' smiles Ken, who saw his side score seven times in the first two games to top the embryonic table. Having swept Everton aside 3-1 at Roker on the opening day – on a day marked by Toffees defender Billy Wright scoring an unforgettable own goal from outside the box when he lobbed his own goalkeeper – Sunderland travelled to Manchester City the following Wednesday night.

The season was sandwiched by two hat-tricks. At City John Hawley took home the match ball as Sunderland registered a record 4-0 win in the fixture. Top after two games, inevitably the newly promoted side fell away, starting with a home defeat in the next match – an Allardyce goal insufficient to stop Lawrie McMenemy's Kevin Keegan-inspired Southampton. Later given the chance to strengthen by bringing in former Bristol City striker Tom Ritchie, Knighton watched Ritchie fail to hit the target in his first 11 games. Those fixtures would also be the last 11 matches of Knighton's reign before the sack came. In the very next match Ritchie struck all the goals as Birmingham were beaten 3-0.

'I had a friend who was a reporter,' remembers Ken. 'He rang me before the end of that game and said, "Hello, Ken, I just wondered how you feel?" I said, "I'm sorry?" And he answered, "I just wanted to tell you that Tom Ritchie has scored a hat-trick." I told him to, "Piss off!" Tom Ritchie had experience of playing in the top division with Bristol City and had a good record, but I signed him and he was a disaster.'

Ritchie's hat-trick came under caretaker manager Mick Docherty. Ritchie would score in the next match too. The end of the season would be a dramatic one, Cummins hitting the winner in a famous win at Anfield. Even if Sunderland had lost at Liverpool the way other results went on the final day they would have stayed up. Finishing 17th out of 22 they ended in the same position they were in when Ken got the bullet.

Back to back wins had given Sunderland five victories in ten games as Ken's men sat 14th in mid-March after full-back Joe Hinnigan popped up with four goals in three games. However, a heavy defeat at Bobby Robson's Ipswich, followed by a single-goal loss at home to struggling Wolves and a 2-0 defeat at Stoke brought the end of Knighton's reign.

Bad blood between manager and chairman made the end inevitable. 'I received a letter from Stan Cullis, who was my hero,' recalls Ken. Cullis was a legend as manager of Wolves, where he had won three league titles and the FA Cup twice. 'He'd been my manager when I signed for Wolves as a lad. In the letter he told me about problems he'd had as a manager with a chairman who was very similar to Tom Cowie. He told me, "You can't win. They'll get you, so you've got to try to play better than you are doing." It was in the press that all was not right, and the supporters obviously switched onto that since Tom Cowie and I had that confrontation at Christmas. At one point the fans put creosote on the pitch so it said, "Cowie Out!" Joe Melling, the journalist, told me, "You've got to keep going. You can't let him win because you've got the fans on your side." I knew the fans liked me because of what we'd achieved. Joe said, "You've got to let the fans know what you're up against, for your sake, because he's going to win." It didn't take long because we had a bad run and I knew it was going to happen. It was very sad, really, but the relationship was such that something was going to happen, and he had the power.' Never in the bottom four under Knighton the team were fifth from bottom when Ken was sacked. 'We were going to stay up. I had no doubts about that,' he still insists.

Since being sacked by Sunderland in April 1981 Knighton hasn't been back. Other than staying in touch with his staff Frank Clark and Peter Eustace there had been no SAFC contact with Ken until I approached him to tell his story in *Tales from the Red and Whites, Volume 3*. He had, however, once seen Tom Cowie: 'After I'd finished with football I'd been working in telecoms for about five years and at some point when the kids were away I said to Carol, "Let's have a weekend away." We didn't book anywhere, we just headed out. We ended up at a place called the Chewton Glen hotel in Hampshire. We drove in, looked around and thought it was fantastic, so we went in and asked if they had a room available for that night. They did, and they let us have it at a discount rate. It was a smart hotel and they said they'd park my car for me, so I went upstairs with Carol to see what the room was like. I decided to go back down to reception to check the car had been parked up all right. Just as I walked downstairs I heard the receptionist say, "Oh, good evening, Lady Cowie." I looked around and there were: Lady Cowie and Sir Tom stood at reception. I thought, "I want him to know that I'm here, but I don't really want to get into a discussion. I just stood next to him and looked at him. He looked at me, and I just looked away. There was no conversation and I didn't want any. I just wanted him to know I'd done all right and he and I were sharing this plush hotel. He was obviously a regular there.

'I've never been to the Stadium of Light, and I'm sad about that. I'm getting on a bit, and I have this feeling that I'd like to go back to Sunderland.'

As a manager who won promotion in his one full season, briefly topped the first division table and helped establish his newly promoted side in the top flight before being jettisoned, Knighton has a red and white record to be proud of. There were 24 draws in Ken's 94 games in charge, the others being equally split between victories and defeats. Between his reign and that of Peter Reid, of the seven 'permanent' managers in charge, only Denis Smith could improve on Ken's record, and many of Smith's wins came at what is now League One level.

Compared to some of the more recent big names Sunderland have had as manager it is easy for Knighton's contribution to fade away. Having been in charge for under two seasons and having had a playing career that wasn't on a par with the likes of Peter Reid, Roy Keane or Gus Poyet, for instance, to the younger generation Ken Knighton may just be a name in a list of former Sunderland managers. However, in addition to his promotion win Knighton showed ambition at Sunderland and, prior to Cowie becoming chairman, broke the club transfer record twice in consecutive months. The second of those deals brought Argentinian midfielder Claudio Marangoni from San Lorenzo as an early Christmas present for fans in 1979. Nowadays foreign players are commonplace but back then a player from overseas was rare and a footballer from South America unbelievably exotic.

A story emerged in 2018 that a young Diego Maradona had been desperate to sign for Sunderland in 1977 (when Jimmy Adamson was manager). Sadly, nothing came of that, but in the same era Alex Sabella (who managed Argentina to the World Cup final in 2014) sparkled in the red and white stripes of Sheffield United. Well connected in Sheffield from his time with Wednesday, Ken tried to lure not just Sabella but the man who had signed him, Blades boss Harry Haslam, to Sunderland: 'I tried to get Harry to come on board at Sunderland because he was coming to the end of his time at Sheffield United. I spoke to him about Sabella, who I wanted to sign. What I wanted to do was to bring a marquee signing in for the fans. Someone who could be totally different to what we had in the team but who could provide something that would set them alight. Sabella was the main target, and I tried, but we didn't get anywhere.'

Knighton had already had a false start when it came to a foreign import. A record £250,000 fee had been arranged for forward Božidar Bakota of NK Zagreb in pre-season and the Yugoslavia international was photographed in his Sunderland kit as the club shop started to sell 'Bozo' badges, only for the player's work permit application to fail and the deal to fall through.

Who knows how Bakota would have settled, but Sabella was a class act already attuned to English football. In Sunderland the story goes that Sabella didn't want to sign for the Red and Whites because it was raining when he was shown around and Mrs Sabella didn't like it. Is it true that Sunderland missed out on a player of pure brilliance (he was fantastic, I regularly saw him play for Sheffield United when living in the Steel City) because of the weather?

'No, it never got to that. We never got to the stage where I was talking to him. But I was talking to Harry, who said to me, "Why don't you talk to the Spurs manager Keith Burkinshaw?" In those days you could only have two foreign players in your squad, and Harry said, "I think he's got somebody else who he was looking at." So I rang him and he said, "Look at Marangoni. He's not very old. He's tall and gangly, but he's got a lot to offer." We played in midweek on a Tuesday night. On the Wednesday I flew out to Argentina to watch a game the following day where he was playing. I watched the game and thought he's definitely got something that I was looking for. He was a big lad. You couldn't knock him off the ball and his control was fantastic, while his passing was exemplary. I spoke to Harry and he said, "What do you think?" I told him I was really impressed and he said, "I'm telling you, Spurs would have had him if they were allowed a third overseas player." I brought him on board and he took a long time to settle but, in saying that, we got promoted just by a couple of points, and he scored a goal in a game where we won 1-0 at Fulham which gave us points that ultimately helped us to go up.'

Marangoni mostly looked like a fish out of water at Sunderland. Arriving in December and being thrust into a home second division game with Cardiff must have been a culture shock to him. These days people talk about foreign players needing time to acclimatise to English football but coming in as a 'marquee' player in that era meant you were expected to turn on the style pretty much instantly. However, whereas Osvaldo Ardiles and Ricky Villa at White Hart Lane were looking like the World Cup winners they were, Marangoni looked slow and ponderous on a hard pitch by the North Sea coast. Marangoni wasn't the only Argentinian import to flatter to deceive. At Jim Smith's Birmingham City World Cup winner Alberto Tarantini played in front of Jim Montgomery but had disciplinary problems and only managed 24 games for the Blues.

Supporters expecting silky skills from Marangoni instead witnessed a first touch not as good as some from Silksworth. Marangoni seemed to be on a different wavelength to his teammates. From my regular spot at the back of the Roker End it was easy to see the big picture and to see the balls Claudio was playing and why he was playing them, but his colleagues weren't reading his passes and the lanky Argentine increasingly cut a forlorn figure. From his debut Claudio made 16 successive appearances, scoring three times, but missed the end of the season as Sunderland scrapped to get over the line

'You look back and think, "Did he contribute?"' says Knighton. 'Not as much as I hoped, but he did play a part. After he left us he played back in Argentina and he was the star player for Independiente when they won the Copa Libertadores. He later won further trophies with Boca Juniors, as well as playing nine times for Argentina. It was such a shame it didn't work out better at Sunderland.'

While Claudio's contribution to Sunderland was minimal at best, Knighton's other record signing was a big success. There were no issues of acclimatisation for Sedgefield-born Stan Cummins, who was bought from Middlesbrough. Little Stan had a touch of star quality and the sort of balance and ball control that wouldn't have looked out of place if he had been an Argentinian World Cup winner. Selling manager Jack Charlton – a World Cup winner himself, of course – had managed Sheffield Wednesday when Ken had been his first-team coach: 'I spoke to Jack about him. I'd read an article where Jack had spoken about Stan and, obviously, I'd watched him, as had our scouts. I thought he could provide what we were missing. He had pace and could score goals, so I asked, "What sort of a lad is he?" Jack said he was pretty quiet but would produce the goods. We had to do a lot of haggling with Middlesbrough but we got him on board.'

In the only game Cummins missed in the promotion season following his November debut Marangoni scored the winner at Fulham. Cummins contributed a dozen goals from 26 games, including one on the night promotion was won, and a four-goal haul in a big win against Burnley. Stan would go on to be Sunderland's solitary ever-present back in the top flight, when again he would reach double figures in the goal-charts despite playing as a wide man.

Undoubtedly Cummins was a key player in Knighton's Sunderland winning promotion, as was full-back Joe Hinnigan, recruited from Wigan in just their second season as a league club. His arrival coincided with a 14-game unbeaten run at the climax of the campaign as Sunderland timed their run for the finishing line, not moving into a promotion spot until a 100 per cent three-game Easter which commenced with Cummins hitting what would be the last ever Roker winner against Newcastle.

Promotion was a monumental achievement for a rookie manager who had handled the pressure and made enough correct calls to ensure Sunderland ended the right side of a very tight line. So tight that in the final analysis runners-up Sunderland finished a point ahead of fourth placed Chelsea, who missed promotion on goal difference while The Lads were only a single point shy of champions Leicester.

Leicester topped the table with the same number of points Sunderland had accrued a year earlier when finishing fourth. That 1978–79 season had started with former footballer of the year Jimmy Adamson in charge. The seventies were a decade of lows and incredible highs for Sunderland. Beginning with relegation in 1970 the Cup was sensationally won under Bob Stokoe in 1973. The excitement of European football was accompanied by the disappointment of the cup winners' missing out on promotion. Even after promotion was won under Stokoe in '76 immediate relegation followed despite a gallant late season rally under Adamson. Off the pace in the first year back in Division Two Sunderland saw Adamson leave for Leeds in the autumn of 1978 with The Lads in eighth place and improving.

When Sunderland had won the FA Cup in '73 Billy Elliott was trainer and had played an influential role as caretaker manager prior to Stokoe's appointment. Having benefited from a change of position himself as a player in the 1950s, former England international Elliott was responsible for switching

Dave Watson from his role as a good centre-forward to a great centre-half. Watson would go on to win more caps for England while on Sunderland's books than anyone in history.

Following Adamson's departure his right-hand man, Dave Merrington, took over for eight games before reuniting with Adamson at Elland Road. Merrington left Sunderland in fourth place in December as Elliott was handed the reins. A slow beginning under Elliott was kick-started by a brilliant Cup win over top-flight Everton on a frosty January night at Roker, followed by a sensational 4-1 win at Newcastle the following month, on the day Gary Rowell grabbed his legendary hat-trick.

'It was fantastic,' remembers Ken. 'In those days, if there were any injuries, as the first-team coach I had to go onto the pitch with the "magic sponge". We had a physio in Johnny Watters, but he was more like a doctor, so I had to go on. In that particular game I had to go on when we were 3-1 up, and after I'd come off the pitch I can remember walking behind the goal where our supporters were as I made my way back to the dugout. I had the medical bag, but I just put it down and went . . .' At this point Ken puts his cup of tea down raises two fists and yells, '*Yeaaaa*! Get in there!' He may not have been back to the north-east for decades but derby day has never left him. 'The reaction I got back from them was fabulous, really special. To beat Newcastle was fantastic. I was lucky, I don't think I lost any as a manager.'

Only Len Shackleton and Kevin Phillips can match Rowell's feat of scoring 100 post-war goals for Sunderland – 24 February 1979 was Gary's greatest day in a sequence where the attacking midfielder was top scorer for five seasons out of six. Injury ruled him out of most of the promotion season – itself another tribute to Knighton's achievement in winning promotion without Sunderland's talisman – although the re-signing of the evergreen Pop Robson provided the side with its cutting edge.

Promotion under Knighton was still a year away. Despite winning 12 of the last 16 games in the year of that big win on Tyneside it wasn't enough, as Sunderland were edged out of the top three. There was a groundswell of support for Billy Elliott to be given the job permanently. Liverpool's legendary boss Bill Shankly was even said to have spoken up for Billy, but evidently the Sunderland board thought differently. Eventually, after trying for the biggest names in the game they settled on the untried and youthful Knighton after seeing the coach's contribution to the promotion push and remembering his loyalty when he too could have jumped ship and followed Adamson to Leeds.

'When Jimmy Adamson left to go to Leeds, Dave Merrington – who I got on really well with – asked, "Would you fancy coming with us to Elland Road, as part of the group?" I said that I thought that would be very unfair because I'd come to be a coach at Sunderland and was really enjoying it. It was a fantastic club with great supporters. I thought it would be unfair if we all left – one of us needed to stay – so I told them I'd rather stay. They felt that was fair enough, and it was up to me. I didn't know what was happening or who they were going to bring in, and then Billy Elliott came in and he left me to run the team. All I wanted to do was to coach the first team, so Billy used to leave all of the coaching to me. The directors knew that Billy was a figurehead – a good one because he could see that everything was all right on the coaching side and I think that's why they didn't think to give the job to Billy at the end of the season. I don't think they even thought about giving the job to me. I got it by default, in a sense, because it was absolute chaos.

'I can see it now when we were listening for the other results at Wrexham. We were absolutely devastated not to go up. It was the end of the season and nobody knew what was going to happen. There was talk that Tom Cowie was going to become the chairman. They were going for all sorts of people, and I had a phone call from Bobby Robson. I'd met him a couple of times and he asked, "Can you just tell me a bit about the club?" I told him he knew about the club and that it was fantastic. He said he'd heard that different directors were ringing people and nobody knew what was going on. "That's exactly what it's like," I told him. Everyone was running around like headless chickens because Tom Cowie wanted to be chairman; Keith Collings, I think, was only too pleased to relinquish his role but wanted to have a say. Ted Evans (a director whose brother's wife had left him to marry Cowie) was also getting involved in ringing people. I didn't have a clue what was happening, although Tom Cowie rang me and said, "I'm really sorry about what is going on but it will be resolved." I said that was OK, and I'd just carry on doing what I was doing.

'Bob Cass and Joe Melling were both journalists and were really good pals of mine. They were telling me, "They don't know what they're doing" – because they had tried everything and had been turned down by the people they were after, so eventually they looked at me and thought, "We'll give him a chance." I was the youngest manager in the history of the club.'

In truth, at the age of 35 when he took control, Knighton wasn't quite the youngest manager in the club's history. That distinction falls to Robert Campbell, way back in the 1890s, but in Campbell's day the role was predominantly that of secretary and administrator. While these days you can't imagine the manager tackling jobs such as booking hotels as Knighton did (let alone paying for them) Ken's time as manager was one where he was very much on the training pitch. He was a young tracksuit manager – over two years younger than the eldest member of his squad, Pop Robson. As Knighton celebrated promotion after a year in charge he was still younger than John O'Shea was when he played his final game for the club.

As many managers have found, managing Sunderland is not your typical manager's job. Interviewed elsewhere in this volume by Lance Hardy, Gus Poyet, for example, once told me that unlike everywhere else in the world he had played or managed, in Sunderland there was no place you could go where people didn't want to talk about football. For Knighton taking over Sunderland as a first managerial post at such a young age was a serious challenge: 'A lot of people don't appreciate what it is like to manage Sunderland and/or Newcastle. I remember when Tom Cowie got rid of me and, later, when Lawrie McMenemy came. McMenemy used to annoy me because he'd write things in the paper about what fantastic clubs Sunderland and Newcastle were and how he loved the north-east – but he was down at Southampton. I used to think that wasn't a very nice thing to do because you only have to speak to the managers who have been at Sunderland or Newcastle, and they understand what it's like. At the time I don't think he had a clue what it was like to handle the press up there. It's an absolute nightmare. With Lawrie, I don't know what the press coverage was like in Southampton, but when you go to the north-east after the match you have all these press people around and people firing questions. During the first one I did I realised there were four or five people who didn't say anything, and they weren't even writing anything down. This went on for a while and then Doug Weatherall said, "Right, is that the Sundays out of the way? Can we have the Mondays now?" So the Sunday reporters would leave and then you'd get another set of questions from another set of reporters. On top of that during the week you'd have the local reporters, and then on top of that there was the radio and television. It was non-stop, and you had to be on the mark all of the time otherwise you'd get misquoted or misinterpreted, and I don't think they're so used to that in places like Southampton.'

Modern-day managers will know that Ken's experience is but the tip of the iceberg compared to modern worldwide media demands at the top level. Nonetheless, in the soccer hotbed of the north-east, where you are born either red and white or black and white, it genuinely is a tale of two cities, whether the clubs are experiencing the best or worst of times.

Regardless of his youth Knighton had one big advantage when taking over the hot-seat: 'I was very lucky because I'd had 12 months as a coach out of the limelight with nobody knowing who I was, and because we hadn't moved as a family all of my time used to be spent at Roker Park. I used to live in the place, all the young apprentices used to live on the seafront. I'd had the opportunity to get to know the club and the area.'

Knighton had come to Sunderland in July 1978: 'Dave Blakey had been chief scout at Sheffield Wednesday, where he'd seen me working as youth-team coach. I'd worked closely with him because he brought in some really good youngsters. When Jimmy Adamson got the Sunderland job, Dave went with him then came back for me to be first-team coach.'

Having become manager when he was not much older than the playing squad who liked Billy Elliott, how did Ken establish he was now the boss and not the first-team coach they could have a laugh with? Did the players accept Ken as the Gaffer, or were there difficulties due to his age?

'What had happened to me as a player at Sheffield Wednesday is that one day I was a player and the next day I was a coach, albeit youth-team coach (although I had the reserve team as well). I had to adjust from being a player to being a coach who was in charge of a group of people. That stood me in really good stead. When I went from being coach to being manager at Sunderland I said to myself, "I've got to get a situation where they know I'm no longer a coach, I'm the manager." And it fell into my lap.

'I'd had discussions with the board and arranged a new incentive package. I had a first big meeting with the players. I'd said to them: "Two o'clock, Tuesday afternoon at Roker Park." So at that time we all assembled, and two players were missing. They didn't arrive until 20 to three. That was Jeff Clarke and . . . I forget who the other lad was. They came in, so I said, "Forget about the meeting here now. I'll see you all back here at six o'clock." I said, "If we have a meeting at two o'clock, we have a meeting at two o'clock, not two minutes past two – two o'clock. We've got two players here who've arrived late and they're taking the piss. It's up to you lot to sort them out. I'll see you here at six o'clock." It was perfect, the situation fell into my lap. So I went from coach to manager.'

One player who knew exactly how Knighton could put his foot down was goalkeeper Chris Turner who Ken had wasted no time in signing from Sheffield Wednesday where he had nurtured him. 'Chris was terrific,' recalls Ken. 'When I was his youth-team coach I could see the potential in him and he was mad keen, but there was one time when we had a game on the Saturday and he went out on the Thursday night. He'd had a couple and came in the following morning in a really bad way. I'd heard he'd been out drinking, so I told him, "We're training this morning, Chris, but you're going to be walking around the pitch." He said, "What do you mean?" I replied, "If you think you can go out on a Thursday night, get on the booze and still have a career in football, you're sadly mistaken. So what I want you to do is walk around the pitch while we're training and think about what you've done and how it's going to affect you in the future." I made him walk around the pitch for two hours and kept making sure he was doing it. It was important to get him right, because he was a terrific lad with so much potential.'

Sunderland certainly benefited from that potential when Turner came to Roker Park. An outstanding, agile and brave keeper Turner eventually prised the first-team shirt from Barry Siddall and later moved to Manchester United for a fee which equalled Sunderland's record sale.

Turner wasn't the only person Ken captured from Hillsborough: his old teammate Peter Eustace arrived as first-team coach to join a coaching staff that also included former Sunderland player George Herd. It was an old Sunderland teammate's of Herd who had started Knighton out on his own coaching career at Hillsborough, an opportunity handed to Ken in 1976 by Len Ashurst, who would later have an opportunity in the Roker hot-seat himself: 'When I was a player – and possibly because of the life I had for 12 months before I became a professional footballer, when I was a miner – I thought, "What's going to happen when the time comes that I've got to pack in playing?" I went on all the coaching courses and was a fully qualified coach by the time I was 28. Because of the time you have on your hands as a player I also used to work for insurance companies so that I had more than one string to my bow, but my first priority was to get a coaching job. Len came to Sheffield Wednesday when I was 32 and coming to the end of my career. I wasn't playing regularly for the first team and he said to me, "I've had an offer for you." It was from Chesterfield, I think. He said, "If you want to go you can go, but I'd like you to stay here and go on the coaching staff. But if you're going to be a coach you've got to pack in playing." I was the captain, like I was at all the clubs I played for. Len said that he wanted me, first and foremost, to look after the youngsters. We didn't have a youth-team coach. The one who was there was an ex-teacher with no experience of football. I thought about it long and hard because, having gone into football from the age of 16 until 32, I was still fit and could have carried on playing, but I thought this could be the first step for me as a coach.'

In a lengthy playing career Knighton had worked with numerous coaches, but Ashurst had an unusual surprise in store for the squad at Sheffield with the appointment of Royal Marine Tony Toms as first-team coach. Toms is a one-off. I've been out for a drink with him a couple of times with Len Ashurst, and he's the kind of guy who fills a room. He has an aura around him, and subsequently headed up the private security operation for Madonna and the boxer Amir Khan.

Knighton laughs at being reminded of Tony Toms' impact in the Owls dressing room: 'The funniest thing was – and I was still a player when he came in – he got all of the players in the boardroom and Len explained "Tommsy's" background as an ex-Marine and asked, "Do you want to say anything, Tony?" Tommsy just stood up. He was behind a table and he just put his hands on the surface and did a handstand on the table and did six press-ups like that then sat down and said, "No, not really." He didn't have a clue about football, but he was a good right-hand man for Len. He was a real character.'

Knighton's first taste of being a manager came when he stood in as caretaker boss when Len was sacked in October 1977: 'I was very sad when Len left because I got on really well with him. He'd brought me into coaching. He told me on the Thursday that he was going, that he'd got the sack. I told him I was really sorry about that, and not long after I'd put the phone down it went again. It was the chairman who said, "Len's leaving the club and we'd like you to be caretaker manager." I asked, "Does Len know this?" And he said, "I think he does." I told him I'd ring him back. So I rang Len and told him what had been said and what I'd been asked, because I didn't want Len to think I'd done anything behind his back, as it had come completely out of the blue. Len said, "No problem. If they want you to do it, you do it." I had one game, which we won – strangely enough against Chesterfield. We won 1-0 with Arthur

Cox as their manager, after which I went home and heard that Jack Charlton had got the job. They hadn't told me anything at all about it. I went in on Monday as normal and Jack was there with all the press men. It was a fantastic coup for Sheffield Wednesday.'

Knighton's team for his one match in charge of the Owls included Turner in goal and Rodger Wylde at centre-forward, a man Ashurst later brought to Sunderland. Ken stayed with Wednesday until the end of the season under Big Jack, who brought in Ian St John as part of the coaching staff – although TV demands as part of ITV's *On the Ball* (which pre-dated his success with Jimmy Greaves on *Saint & Greavsie* in the mid-eighties) meant the Scot couldn't be at Saturday games. Having previously won promotion with Boro Big Jack would take Wednesday up from Division Three to Two in 1980, just as Knighton was taking Sunderland from Division Two into the top flight.

Knighton was only 33 when he took charge of the Owls. Seventeen years earlier he'd been working as a miner: 'I had played for the school team and we had won the Yorkshire Schools Championship. We were just a village team and there were six of us who eventually became professional footballers, which was incredible. Five of us were signed as apprentices when we left school, but I was the odd one out so I had to get a job. Of the other five, only one was successful, and that was a lad called Ian Butler. He and I played for Hull City together, further down the line. I started work down the pit, which was the best thing that ever happened to me. I came from a mining family and left school when I was 15. My dad was a miner and I ended up working down the pit for 12 months at Denby Grange Colliery. I was playing for my local village team from the age of 14 against men. I was getting kicked about but it made me, really. We'd just play anywhere, but mainly I suppose I played in what they'd now call midfield. I was playing for a team called Kexborough Rovers and for Wath Wanderers. I had a knock on the door from a Wolves scout because Wolves then had a team who played in the Northern Intermediate League, based near Barnsley. I played for them and then went down to Wolves for a trial and became one of their first two apprentice professionals. Before that it was always groundstaff, and then me and a lad called Bobby Thompson signed as apprentice professionals.

'I was a mad Huddersfield Town supporter. Me and my dad used to go to every home game. That was when they were in the old First Division. I'd be passed down to the front. That was my team in the old Leeds Road days, so to be leaving the pit to be paid to play football was something of a dream.'

Having moved to Molineux in July 1960, Ken's debut came in February 1965, a week before his 21st birthday in a 2-1 defeat away to Liverpool. Bobby Woodruff got Wolves' goal in that match at Anfield and would score a hat-trick of headers as Wolves won 3-0 on Ken's home debut . . . against Sunderland.

As a young player Knighton needed to be versatile to get games: 'Midfield was definitely my best position. At Wolves I was a wing-half but most of the first-team games I did play were as a left-back. I don't understand that. When I went to Oldham I went as a left-back but ended up playing mostly in midfield.'

Knighton played a total of 16 games for Wolves, who were relegated at the end of his breakthrough season. 'As a player I was very lucky. I made the move from Wolves when I was 22 because I really wasn't getting very many first-team games. It was different in those days. You'd have a squad of about 42 players – a first team, second team and third team. At Wolves you'd have England internationals in the reserves. I moved to Oldham, where Ken Bates was chairman. It was a very forward-looking club, and then I moved on to Preston, where I was a teammate of the old Sunderland wing-half Jim McNab. Later I played for Blackburn, where there was a lot of history, and after that my time at Hull City was really exciting. At one point it looked as if we were going to get promotion to the First Division.'

In total Ken played 359 league games. One of his greatest moments came with the Owls in April 1974 when supporters chaired him off the pitch after he hit a winner against Bolton that kept Wednesday up: 'It was my best moment as a player. That was a great day for us. Sheffield Wednesday are a big club who could have got relegated to the old Third Division. We'd played Middlesbrough the week before and lost 8-0. I was injured for that defeat but got fit for the Bolton game. I wasn't a prolific goalscorer but managed to score the winner. What was nice was I'd been invited to the supporters' club that evening to present some trophies. I was the local hero that night.'

Internationally Ken was never capped, although at youth level he was called up for an England get-together. In 1969 he toured Tahiti, New Zealand, Singapore, Hong Kong and Thailand with an FA party skippered by Jimmy Armfield. Ken even got on the scoresheet in the opening match of the tour, a 4-1 win in Tahiti in which Tony Hateley scored a hat-trick.

During Knighton's time as a footballer he always had one eye on what he would do when his playing days were over. He had many lessons in playing for managers as varied as Jimmy McIlroy, Eddie Quigley, Johnny Carey and Terry Neill, but he got one of his clearest insights thanks to having a telephone when his next door neighbour didn't.

As Sunderland manager Knighton learned from Brian Clough when he conducted the transfer of Ian Bowyer, but he had already seen how Cloughie went about ensuring he bought a player he wanted: 'I'd met him before when I was a player at Preston North End, when Cloughie was at Derby. In our team was Archie Gemmill. We lived in a place called Lytham. There was a lad called Graham Hawkins, who was a player, me and Archie, who had three semi-detached houses and lived in a row. Preston were selling Archie, who said to me, "Look, I don't know what's going to happen but do you mind if I give them your phone number?" Typical Archie, he didn't even have a phone. That was in the early seventies. The phone went and a voice said, "Can I speak to Archie? It's Harry Catterick from Everton. I asked him to hold on and dashed round to Archie's and told him Harry Catterick was on the phone. But Archie said, "I don't really want to go there. I'm told there might be another club interested, and I want to find out who that is." I went back to the phone and said, "I'm really sorry but Archie is out at the moment. I'll get him to ring you back later." I went back round to Archie's and asked, "What's going on?" He just said he'd rather wait because there was another club interested. Later I was sat at home when I saw a car pull up and chap called Stuart Webb got out. Webby was secretary of Preston when I first joined and he had joined Cloughie at Derby. He came to the door and said, "I've got Brian Clough in the car and we want to know what the situation is with Archie. We know other clubs are buzzing around." I told him I'd had a phone call from Everton and he said, "If they ring back can you put them off?" I knew Stuart and so I said, "Yes, that's fine." When the car pulled away I went around to see Archie, who I knew had never had a move like this before. His wife came to the door and I asked if Archie was all right and then I heard this voice saying, "Tell him to come in." It was Cloughie. Brian stayed the night, slept on the sofa and signed Archie the following the morning. I sat down and talked to him for an hour and he was absolutely electric – fascinating. While others were ringing up he'd driven up from Derby to make sure he got the player he wanted. Doesn't he deserve all the accolades he had?'

Ken, unlike Brian who devoted his life to football, got out early, leaving the game after just one more managerial job in the league, regardless of having promotion at Sunderland on his CV. Six months after leaving Roker Ken took the job as manager of Leyton Orient (then known as just Orient). It was a position he held for six months to the end of the season as Orient were relegated before he walked away from the professional game at the age of just 38. His old Sunderland backroom team of Frank Clark and Peter Eustace became the next two occupants of the Orient hot-seat, the pair staying at Brisbane Road for a dozen years between them.

'It was a conscious decision because I didn't want to put my family through what we'd gone through twice,' says Ken. 'At Orient it was such a hard job. There were very few supporters coming in on a regular basis. It was a small club. They had players like Stan Bowles and Billy Jennings, who were coming towards the end of their careers and saw Orient as a chance to earn some money for two or three years. I had to trim the squad and get rid of those players because they weren't interested and weren't putting a shift in. I was bringing young players in and it was a battle. At the end of it Orient were very good about it. I got on very well with the chairman and they paid me up. I got an opportunity to work for Plessey's as a sales manager. The sales director in London was a mad keen Orient supporter so I was very lucky to get a shoo-in that way. I thought, "Let's do it." The chap who recruited me, the Orient shareholder, asked me what I was going to do when I left Orient. When I told him I didn't know he said, "Why don't you come to our place?" I told him I didn't know anything about telecoms, but he said to me, "You've built teams and you've worked with them, and that's what it's all about." So I was able to transfer the skill.

'I'd prepared for the future by getting my coaching badges when I was a player, but I'd also worked part time in sales when

I was a player, so I was prepared for life outside of football. I then got a phone call from Dagenham. They were semi-professional then and just trained a couple of nights a week. I thought that'd be nice, and it was terrific. I really enjoyed it. We got through to the third round of the FA Cup for the first time in the club's history in 1984–85. To do that we beat a league club, in fact we beat two: Swindon after a replay and Peterborough. I had a clause in my contract that I would get a percentage of the gate if we ever got through to the third round of the FA Cup. They'd put it in there but I never thought it would happen, but when it did I was sat there watching the draw thinking, 'Come on, something like Spurs away... We got Carlisle United away; 4,500 turned up and we lost 1-0!'

There was also a brief spell in charge of non-league Trowbridge, which ended in January 1988, but contrary to what the internet might tell you there was never a spell scouting for Manchester United. 'That's untrue but I did do a bit of scouting for David Pleat,' explains Ken.

'I worked in telecommunications for 22 years. I retired when I was 62. I worked for Plessey before going to Cable & Wireless. It was terrific. I knew very little about telecoms but I like to think I knew about people. I could recognise ability and knew how to manage and motivate people. I built about three teams from scratch and they all did really well. We were successful as a team so I was able to take what I had as a manager of a football team into the role of being the manager of a telecoms team.'

Regardless of a solid and extensive playing career and the pinnacle of managing a promotion-winning Sunderland team, evidently Ken Knighton succeeded in staying in touch with the real world. After stepping away from the game as a still young man, those life lessons learned as a miner before he became a player stood Ken in good stead. Like his predecessor Jimmy Adamson Knighton came from a mining community and feels his working-class roots helped him connect with the crowd as manager of Sunderland. He notes, 'I'd also observed that Jimmy Adamson seemed to have alienated himself from the fan base and I felt you shouldn't be like that. You can't be aloof. You have to get the fans to feel a part of the club and you have to feel part of the fans.'

Like a lot of Sunderland managers, Knighton came to appreciate that, as Bob Stokoe famously said, 'Until you've seen football on the north-east coast, you've never seen it.' Ken says, 'Sheffield Wednesday was a big club but Sunderland rose above all of that. Roker Park was magical for me. I used to love playing there, so to go up there and eventually become manager was really, really special. When I was appointed I went around the supporters' clubs in the north-east to speak to the fans before the season. I got a fantastic reception.'

These days Knighton is probably the least well known of the post-war Sunderland managers who actually won anything, which is why I was keen to ask Ken to tell his story in this volume of *Tales from the Red and Whites*. Although he resides in the southwest and still hasn't been to Sunderland since he was sacked this is a man who, like Niall Quinn, saw Sunderland get under his skin: 'Absolutely it did. I'm very sad at the demise at the club and hope that the new owners succeed in turning them round.' Knighton's reign was an exciting one with promotion followed by the flying start in the top-flight, the ambitious signing of Marangoni and that mostly forgotten Wembley win. Winning a five-a-side tournament in Wembley Arena doesn't compare with winning an 11-a-side match over the road, but back in 1979 it really was quite a big deal and a trophy of some prestige.

'I remember it vividly because I had a school mid-term exam the next day and I wasn't allowed to stay up to watch it! Typically, we then won it, but there's no footage anywhere,' says my co-author Lance Hardy. Thankfully Lance passed his exams and these days through his senior role in TV football coverage is responsible for beaming tournaments from around the world into our living rooms as they happen. In 1979, however, there was no such thing as the internet, social media or mobile phones. For those of us not having to be in bed early in readiness for an exam it was a case of putting *Sportsnight* on BBC 1 knowing Sunderland had taken part but having no idea how they had gone on.

'It was taken very seriously,' remembers Ken. 'It was a tournament where we were representing the club and our supporters. Whatever you take part in, if it's a trophy it's a trophy, and you want to win it.'

Following a 3-0 victory at Luton at the weekend Sunderland took a team perfectly suited to the short-form game to Wembley for the Wednesday-night competition: Stan Cummins, Kevin Arnott, the late Mick Buckley, Shaun Elliott and Chris Turner lined up with youngster John Cooke as sub. As the highlights unfolded on TV it was seen that Sunderland had breezed past Ipswich and West Brom, winning each game 2-0, with Arnott notching three of the goals.

That set up a semi-final with Newcastle United. Braces from Arnott and Cummins left TV audiences in the northeast suddenly eager to get to work the following morning (or dreading it) as the bragging rights were red and white in a derby no one in the region knew had even taken place until it suddenly came on the telly. Hammering Newcastle would have been joyous enough, but there was equally the realisation The Lads were in the final.

Facing a Brighton team that included Mark Lawrenson Chris Turner kept up his record of never conceding a goal in the tournament, while Arnott maintained his feat of scoring in every round. Buckley also got on the scoresheet as an overall score of 10 goals for and none conceded evidenced a comprehensive triumph. Sunderland had won a Cup at Wembley – one you can still see on display at the Stadium of Light today.

While in modern times there would be worries of injuries in the middle of an important season, winning at Wembley did the promotion charge no harm at all: three days later Bristol Rovers were walloped 5-0 at Roker.

The five-a-side tournament was far from the only distraction. The season marked the club's centenary, a home game against an England XI coming three weeks before the trip to Wembley, while a month earlier Knighton's side had put five past touring Paraguayan side Olimpia Asunción and, in the run up to the promotion clincher against the Hammers, Tommy Docherty brought his QPR team to Wearside for a testimonial for his son Mick.

That Wembley Cup win is largely forgotten by many, as is Ken Knighton, but as the manager of promotion winners and the last man to take Sunderland to the top of the top-flight table – however briefly – Knighton is a manager with a record many would envy. Of all Sunderland's promotion winning managers only Roy Keane can emulate Knighton's claim never to have been even a brief part of a relegation season. Ken Knighton wasn't as big a name as Roy Keane – who is? – but he thought big. Bringing in Marangoni as a marquee record signing was a brave move. Like many a manager before and since, Ken found that his most difficult opponents weren't the opposition but the board. His place in red and white history should not be forgotten or underestimated and so his place here in *Tales from the Red and Whites, Volume 3* is one that is fully warranted. Clearly he was a Knighton in shining armour.

EPILOGUE

Following Knighton's dismissal Sunderland stayed up under caretaker manager Mick Docherty. Next in the hot-seat was Alan Durban, who was gradually building a promisingly effective if largely unexciting side during almost three years in charge in the early eighties, before he too was sacked by Tom Cowie. Following one game with Pop Robson as caretaker manager Sunderland's record outfield appearance maker Len Ashurst was installed as manager. Ashurst took Sunderland to Wembley in the League Cup final but couldn't stop them going down, after which he was dismissed less than 15 months after being appointed. Frank Burrows looked after the shop during the close season until Sunderland sensationally appointed Lawrie McMenemy, one of the biggest personalities in the game, as their next and very highly paid boss . . .

2

Lawrie McMenemy's arrival at Sunderland was greeted with delight. The Roker club's response to relegation had been to capture one of the biggest personalities in the game. McMenemy had brought unprecedented success to Southampton, winning the FA Cup, promotion, reaching the League Cup final and taking them to their highest ever league position as runners-up to Liverpool in the top flight. Prior to his time on the south coast McMememy had won league titles with the other three clubs he had managed: Grimsby Town, Doncaster Rovers and Bishop Auckland, so he had a track record of success. At Sunderland, though, that track record of success would be spectacularly and sadly derailed . . .

LAWRIE McMENEMY

SUNDERLAND MANAGER
11 JULY 1985 TO 16 APRIL 1987
TALKS TO ROB MASON

In a book studying six Sunderland managers why make Lawrie McMenemy one of the choices? Perhaps only Lawrie and I thought it was a good idea. 'A lot of people think I shouldn't have done this interview, but you've given me enough time to say things which probably has got things off my chest,' says McMenemy in 2018, over three decades after his sudden and controversial departure from a tumultuous time at Roker Park. Certainly any number of other managers would have been more popular reads. Is there any Sunderland supporter with a good word to say about McMenemy? I'm not about to try to rewrite history here and try to make out McMenemy did well at Sunderland. Lawrie agrees with everyone else that he didn't succeed at Sunderland by any stretch of the imagination, reflecting, 'At the end of the day you are the manager, you are getting very well paid, and if it doesn't work out you have to put your hands up and say, "I failed."'

Nothing went right in Lawrie's time at Sunderland between 1985 and 1987. He went from hero to zero, his arrival having been rapturously received, only for his reportedly astronomical salary to become a bone of contention as his side struggled badly. In the current era Jack Rodwell took a similar sort of stick as a highly paid player who did not do well, but for a manager to stay out of the limelight as Rodwell did was not a possibility. Eventually McMenemy took off in the dead of night, leaving his Sunderland reputation in tatters while elsewhere in the country he remained a respected figure in the game, going on to manage in international football. Even now every Sunderland supporter around at the time has a firm opinion of the McMenemy era, but exploring how the man himself views it is the challenge of this chapter.

The relationship between manager and chairman is always key. In the other chapter I've written for *Tales from the Red & Whites, Volume 3* the confrontational relationship between 1980 promotion-winning boss Ken Knighton and chairman Tom Cowie is illuminating. A little over four years after Knighton was sacked, and with Alan Durban and Len Ashurst having occupied the hot seat in the intervening period, McMenemy was tempted by Cowie's exceptional offer to come to one of the big two clubs in his native north-east. 'The timing was right,' he says. 'And also, I can't deny it, there was the fact that he made such a fantastic offer. The figures given in the newspapers weren't correct, but it was a lot more than I was on. When you've got a family and you're in the football business you know it's not for life.'

Appointed not just as manager but to the board as 'managing director', McMenemy had a vastly different viewpoint to every other manager in Sunderland's history as to the machinations in the corridors of power. Where other managers would be wheeled in for the last couple of items on a board meeting agenda – and Knighton had been the subject of insinuations that he was listening in to sections of board meetings he was not welcome to be party to – in McMenemy's case he was part of the board. 'Being the manager, normally you only come in at the end of the meeting, do the football bit, have a cup of tea and then that's it. Being a managing director you're in it from the beginning, you're not used to it and you'd rather be out with the lads or the staff rather than watching all this going on.'

There to bolster Cowie's position in the most acrimonious of boardrooms, as director Barry Batey and Cowie conducted open warfare, once Cowie stepped down as chairman – remaining for a while technically as a director but without attending board meetings – Bob Murray stepped into the breach, and had to deal with the enormous financial problems that threatened to swamp the club.

Just as most managers want their own players, rather than those associated with the usually failing last guy, new chairmen tend to want their own appointment as manager. Murray 'inherited' McMenemy, one of the biggest names (and biggest earners) in the game. As Sunderland struggled on and off the pitch in 2018 the club's cloth was cut accordingly with the appointment of an up and coming manager from St Mirren in Jack Ross.

In contrast, having McMenemy in charge a third of a century earlier, as Sunderland slipped towards the first of their two relegations to the third tier, was like having a Pep Guardiola or José Mourinho at the helm, in terms of the wage packet. Understandably, this counted against the manager when people contrasted the outlay with the outcome. McMenemy, of course, had been offered his salary having established himself as a successful manager and personality within the game – one who three years after Bob Stokoe had led Sunderland to the FA Cup had emulated that feat with Second Division Southampton, who had beaten Manchester United in the final. They could easily have met Stokoe's Sunderland in the semi, the Saints ending the Cup run of Malcolm Allison's Crystal Palace, who had knocked Sunderland out at Roker Park in the quarter-final.

Without the wall-to-wall media coverage football has now, in some cases in forms of media not even in existence in the seventies, it was easy for the average fan to just think of McMenemy as that big Geordie on the telly who had won the Cup with Southampton. He actually had a track record of sustained success, but became one of a line of managers for whom their time at Sunderland was as much a blot on their CV as they were on the club's. Howard Wilkinson and Martin O'Neill are others who spring to mind, although I, for one, think that O'Neill would have got it right if given the time.

As well as winning the only major trophy in Southampton's history, McMenemy got the Saints promoted, took them to runners-up in the top flight – their highest ever position – and reached the League Cup final. Before then he won league titles with the other three clubs he managed: Grimsby Town, Doncaster Rovers and Bishop Auckland. Prior to becoming a manager, as coach he helped his previous club Gateshead to their league title too. If everything McMenemy touched turned to gold before coming to Sunderland, on Wearside nothing worked for him: 40 of his 90 games in charge were lost, with only 28 won. Ironically, before becoming Sunderland manager Roker Park was a ground he had done well at. As Bishop Auckland manager in 1966 he had brought his side to face Blyth Spartans at Roker in FA Cup first-round second and third replays, eventually winning 4-1 after a 3-3 draw. As Southampton boss he brought a star-studded side including Dave Watson, Kevin Keegan Mick Channon and Charlie George to win 2-1 in front of over 41,000 and knock Sunderland off the top of the top flight in 1980. Under Ken Knighton, early in the season, that was the last time Sunderland topped the table.

Optimism and anticipation were overflowing when 'Big Mac' got the Sunderland job in the summer of 1985. Big-name players were signed and a crowd well over twice the size of the previous home gate turned out to see the opening game of the season. Sunderland, though, were outplayed by a Blackburn side managed by the man the players attribute much of the success during the early years of Peter Reid's reign to: Bobby

Saxton. Sunderland lost without scoring and that would be the case for the next four games as well.

Here were Sunderland – a top-flight club the previous season, when they had also reached the League Cup final – propping up the old Second Division with not even a goal, let alone a point after five games. It didn't get much better under Lawrie. Relegation was avoided on the last day of the season but only delayed by a year, as the last club to have only ever played top-flight football sunk to the Third Division for the first time in its history, the manager having jumped ship late in the season. It was a terrible time. The gate for McMenemy's last match was even lower than the sub-10,000 attendance that had seen the last home game before his appointment. Those that were there for that ill-fated meeting with Sheffield United played merry hell after the match, protesting outside the main stand.

Lawrie doesn't need reminding of this. As Sunderland kicked off the 2018–19 season, having returned to the third division for a second time, he is 82 and reflects, 'I'm not looking to make excuses. I'm trying to talk as an old man when it doesn't matter what people say to me now at my age, but if any supporter looks at the club and thinks about it, wasn't it Gus Poyet who said the club had a problem around it? My question would be, "Why? Why?" I was only there two years but I'm not the only manager there who has failed, and I'm not the only manager that failed who had success at other places. Is it a problem with the area? Is it because Newcastle thrived as a city as Sunderland lost the shipyards and the pits?'

Let's look at the bigger picture here. I said at the beginning I wasn't going to rewrite history. I'm not pretending things were anything other than terrible during McMenemy's time at Roker Park. Lawrie acknowledges this himself more than once in this chapter, and I'm a Sunderland supporter who saw all of the home games and most of the aways while he was in charge. I didn't go home with a smile on my face very often but, as McMenemy says, he's not the only manager to have struggled at Sunderland having succeeded elsewhere.

Until we get to the bottom of this the club are likely to have more lows than highs. At the launch of *Tales from the Red and Whites, Volume 2*, an evening at the Stadium of Light with seven of the 11 players featured in that book, a recurring theme was uncovered when they spoke. Time after time a former player would remark, 'Sunderland were struggling when I came to the club.'

More than 30 years since leaving Sunderland, Lawrie laments, 'I keep looking at Sunderland's results, hoping that they're going to do well. There must be something wrong over 50 years for a club of that size to see clubs like Bournemouth and Brighton in the Premier League when they are in the third division. It's not right. Sunderland, Newcastle and Middlesbrough should all be in the top flight. It would be great for the area. Newcastle have had good years up near the top, Middlesbrough have had their moments, but why can't Sunderland do it?'

While Newcastle have played in the Champions League and Middlesbrough reached a European final recently enough to have brought on Lee Cattermole as a sub in that match, all Sunderland have to show for the four and a half decades since winning the Cup is the two seventh-place finishes under Peter Reid and the lost Cup finals of 1985, 1992 and 2014.

McMenemy doesn't pretend to have the answer to the conundrum, but he is keen to pose the question that has clearly perplexed him all these years. He does have a theory regarding the backdrop to his own era, pointing to the 1984–85 miners' strike, which came to a close earlier in the year he returned to the north-east. Then, of course, what is now the Stadium of Light was the site of Wearmouth Colliery, the biggest and deepest in the Durham coalfield.

'Forget football,' says McMenemy. 'I think that must have affected the people of the area who didn't deserve that stress and uncertainty about the future when, by looking over the bridge at Newcastle, they saw an area and a city thriving a bit more. I'm asking the question: is that the reason?'

Certainly times were incredibly tough as Prime Minister Thatcher's policies tried to rip the heart out of the coalfields. On the other hand, during the depression of the thirties Sunderland won the league title, Charity Shield and FA Cup in the space of a year. It was during that year that Lawrie McMenemy was born, in July 1936. He was born in Gateshead, then part of County Durham (as was Sunderland, but not Newcastle). Lawrie grew up in the area, and like most at that time didn't have two-bob to rub together, so he knew the culture of the north-east, and even after a lifetime in the south his voice is unmistakable and has never lost its north-east twang.

Growing up in Gateshead it was nigh on impossible not to become enthralled with football, but did he watch Newcastle, Sunderland or Gateshead, who were still in the Football League then? 'I couldn't afford to go to any. I only went to Newcastle with a lot of others to stand in the car park and to get in when they opened the gates ten minutes from the end. You came up the stairs to the top and they would lift you up and pass you over their heads and you'd sit on the little wall by the running track. If you were lucky you saw nine minutes of football. I couldn't afford to pay to get in but I did see Jackie Milburn.'

Like all north-east youngsters McMenemy harboured dreams of playing himself: 'Newcastle started a thing called "the Ns" – just the capital letter. When you got signed up by them as a kid you thought, "Oh, fantastic!" but then you realised they had signed hundreds of lads. There was no time-factor on you signing – for most it just fizzled out and you ended up going to a local club. In my case I went to Gateshead. That was when the Callender brothers, Tommy and Jackie, and people like Johnny Ingham were there.' The Callender brothers deserve to be remembered. Between them they played 910 Football League games for Gateshead with another 75 in the FA Cup, a record for two brothers at one club.

It was with Gateshead that McMenemy began his coaching career, combining his work in the education department of the local council with working under Newcastle United's fifties Cup heroes: 'The two managers who were at Gateshead when I was coach were Bobby Mitchell and Jack Fairbrother. They were smashing fellas, both different sorts of characters, but they weren't coaches. They had been brilliant players: Bobby Mitchell was a fantastic left-winger who played for Scotland; and Jack was just an eccentric type of goalkeeper. Bobby was more interested in the greyhounds that ran around the track at Gateshead then, but their names were enough for them to be at Gateshead. It was a brilliant experience for me, as I was doing what they should have been doing.

'Over the years I've seen criticism which we all get, but at Sunderland it was said I was a five-minute wonder because I'd won the Cup at Southampton and that's all I did. But what the Southampton directors had found out was that when I was at Gateshead as player–coach we won the league, which was the North Regional League then – but you can only win the league you're in. At Bishop Auckland we won the league and Cups, at Doncaster I'd won the league and I'd won it again at Grimsby. Now, OK, we'd had ups and downs in between, but winning the league with every club I'd managed was on my CV. At Southampton we didn't win the league but we were second in the top flight one year, three points behind Liverpool, and we won the FA Cup, got promoted and got to another Cup final in the League Cup in 1979, as well as getting into Europe a few times. Later on I worked with England, managed the B team, where we won six and drew two of my eight games, and then with the under-21 team we won the Toulon Tournament twice, I think, in my time. I then managed Northern Ireland. Add to that I'm in the Hall of Fame of League Managers for managing 1000 games – and there's not many in that – so while I failed at Sunderland I thought being described as a "five-minute wonder" was a bit harsh!

'Anybody who has been in management a long time knows that one of the strengths is starting at the bottom. I'm quite amused when I see people like Thierry Henry, who was a wonderful player, saying he wants to pack in TV to start managing in the Premier League. People like Cloughie started at Hartlepool, and Bill Shankly's first three clubs as manager were Carlisle, Grimsby and Workington. Nearly all the ones who have had any success started at the bottom and it helped in the long run.'

As a young coach without a stellar playing career behind him McMenemy worked his way up from the very bottom, starting when he finished his National Service – a stint that involved him being on duty at Buckingham Palace as a member of the Coldstream Guards and effectively ruining his budding career as a footballer by damaging his foot playing for the army in Germany: 'I came back from the army and had a job with the education department in Gateshead, where I was putting on a sports course. You could take your preliminary badge locally in those days, and then there were coaching courses on at the youth club, connected to the education department, so that was my first experience of coaching. The next stage was to get a full badge, for which you had to go residential for a week. In our area it was at Houghall Agricultural College in Durham. I went there and the main man running it was called George Wardle, who ran Crook Town as well. I had a good week and got the badge, after which he contacted me to say that Bishop Auckland needed a manager. It would be the first one the club had ever had, because up to then the committee had done everything. Bishops were called "amateur" but the lads used to get their expenses. I used to go in two nights a week when we trained. I'd signed two or three from the Newcastle/Gateshead area. They used to come to my house at tea-time after their jobs and get in my car, and that's where they made a few bob because I was driving them over but they could claim travelling expenses, so they got a little envelope.

'We won the league, the League Cup and the County Cup, and they let me manage, so I just got on with it. There were people like Jimmy Goodfellow [Sunderland born who played nearly 500 league games] and Dave McClelland [4 league games] who both turned professional eventually, and I had a famous old player called Seamus O'Connell who had won three amateur cups and played for Chelsea when they won the league in the same season.'

O'Connell hit eight goals in 11 games as Chelsea won the title, including a debut hat-trick in a 6-5 defeat to Manchester United, but kept playing for Bishop! 'His family were in the cattle business in Cumbria and he didn't want to turn professional and he didn't have to,' explains Lawrie. 'He was past his best and had made his name many years earlier, but I got him to play and we enjoyed the trips through in the car as much as anything. There were legends in the team like Bob Thursby, the captain, who had played for England at amateur level.'

Manager McMenemy was still in his late twenties, and learning all the time, when he came into contact with the man who would become his mentor: 'The thing that changed everything was in, I think, my second year there. I'd got settled in and I contacted Alan Brown at Sunderland, who agreed to send a team over for a pre-season friendly. As I remember it he sent virtually the first team. It was obviously good for us because we got a lot of people through the gate. Whatever I'd done I'd obviously caught his attention and he kept his eye on me.'

'Bomber' Brown, as his players at Sunderland knew him, is a figure in the club's history notorious with many supporters. In both 1958 and 1970 he was manager when Sunderland suffered the first two relegations the Wearsiders had ever suffered. The first of those ended the proud boast that Sunderland were the only club never to play anywhere but at the highest level, a record that stretched back to their entry into the Football League in 1890.

However, Brown's players remain fiercely loyal to him to this day, even though almost all were cowed by his tough disciplinarianism. Charlie Hurley, Jim Montgomery and Len Ashurst are among his 1964 promotion winners who remain admirers, while Monty's Cup-winning teammate Dennis Tueart is another who always waxes lyrical about Brown's coaching abilities if not his man-management. Hurley and Ashurst, of course, followed Brown into management – as did no fewer than five other members of Brown's '64 team! Brian Clough was another to play for Brown and regard him as a managerial mentor. When Roy Keane managed Sunderland it was Clough who he looked up to rather than Sir Alex Ferguson (who he also played for), and Roy was always keen to learn about Clough's mentor Brown.

Asked if it is a fair comment to say Alan Brown was the biggest influence on his career, McMenemy answers with an emphatic, 'Absolutely!' Elaborating, he adds, 'He was way ahead of his time. From a football point of view. He brought in shadow play when nobody had ever heard of it. He was terrific. He didn't look for publicity and he wasn't too good with the media. He just didn't have a mix-and-mingle type of nature but he loved the job and he was a wonderful man.'

Brown resigned after winning promotion at Sunderland in 1964 following a dispute with the board over whether he could purchase the club-owned house he was living in. Taking over at Sheffield Wednesday he led them to the 1966 FA Cup final. Ten days before a quarter-final against Blackburn Rovers, 'the Bomber' had a mission.

'Once he moved to Sheffield Wednesday I got a call from him as he was travelling to Newcastle from Sheffield to see a game between the English and Scottish Leagues,' remembers Lawrie. 'We were living in Cromer Avenue in Low Fell, so it was on his way. He came in and we got the kettle on and had a sandwich ready and then he said, "Do you mind leaving the room?" He said this to me, not my wife Anne! It was because he wanted to tell my wife he was going to ask me to join him at Sheffield on a full-time basis, but he told her, "There's no point doing it if you don't want to go." She said yes and then I came back in and he offered me the job.'

Having taken McMenemy out of the north-east Brown hailed from himself, Bomber showed a side of his nature not commonly known on Wearside: 'When we moved he didn't even ask he just said, "Listen, I'm going to lend you some money because you're going to have to buy a house, and you can't afford it." We got a house which was newly built. Obviously I paid him back as soon as I could, but he never pushed for the money back. That was the sort of man he was.' Told the story of why Brown had resigned from Sunderland over housing matters McMenemy notes, 'I didn't know that, but it shows the strong principles he had. When I joined him at Hillsborough he had just had Sheffield Wednesday in the Cup final the previous season. It was after that he had a clear out of staff. He kept a bloke called Jack Marshall – "Jolly Jack" we called him. He'd had a bit of management experience and was a great number two as the man between Alan Brown and everybody else. He was the one who would be chirpy in the dressing room, as Alan wasn't like that. The players would treat the manager with total respect. They wouldn't muck around as they'd be too frightened to do anything like that. Alan had a different type of humour to everyone else, which sometimes the players wouldn't pick up on, but Jack was brilliant being the number two.'

At Hillsborough McMenemy would work in tandem with – and even lodge with – a man who would later have a spell as caretaker manager at Sunderland following the resignation of Bob Stokoe. Lawrie explains how Brown's Sheffield restructuring shaped up: 'There was me and another big fella called Ian MacFarlane, a Scotsman who had been coaching at Bath. He put the two of us together. It was a terrific experience because we alternated. We would be with the first team for a month and then with the reserves for a month, then change over. He wasn't someone who would say, "Do this, do that and this is what you should do" but his influence just rubbed off on you – I just looked at Alan Brown and picked up off him. Ian and I were working our socks off and gaining great experience. We all got on well. Eventually he said to us both that by now we should be looking to get into management.'

Brown's interest in his protégés continued after he had left Wednesday. In February 1968 Brown returned to Sunderland. In this day and age managers tend to bring their retinue of coaching staff with them. Had that been the case in the late sixties maybe McMenemy and MacFarlane might have become Mackems much earlier. As it was they remained at Sheffield under new Owls boss Marshall, but it was only a matter of time until both moved into management: 'Alan Brown obviously put our names in and I remember the two of us driving all the way to Carlisle to be interviewed. On the way back we were passing fields between Carlisle and Newcastle and big Ian said, "One day one of us is going to own all of this", so we had a laugh about it but neither of us got the job, although later he did go to Carlisle.'

That interview took place in October 1968 when, ironically, the man who got the Carlisle job was Bob Stokoe, who would later bring MacFarlane to Sunderland and succeed McMenemy as the man dubbed 'the Messiah' returned for his second stint at Roker some 14 years after winning the Cup.

After losing out to Stokoe at Carlisle, McMenemy didn't have long to wait for a post. On 1 December 1968 he became the new manager of Doncaster Rovers, where he took over from George Raynor, a man who had managed Sweden to the 1958 World Cup final as well as managing Juventus and Lazio as part of an incredible CV.

Five months after becoming a Football League manager McMenemy had a league title to his name as Rovers won the Fourth Division (now League Two): 'The chairman at Doncaster said I was a wonderful young man and then two or three years later we got relegated and he said I was useless, but within a week of me losing the job I got the job at Grimsby after the chairman there contacted me. He was called Paddy Hamilton and was a wonderful Irish fella. He had a big business in Grimsby but he also had a branch of it in Doncaster, so he'd seen what I'd done there. I'd learned a lot obviously and we won the league.'

Taking over at Blundell Park in the summer of 1971 Lawrie got off to a flying start: 'My first game was a derby match with Scunthorpe and we had about seven and a half thousand, but by the end of the season we got over 22,000 for the last game. We had a great time there. We loved it. There were tremendous people on the board.' Beating Scunthorpe 4-1 on the opening day with a hat-trick from a Scotsman called Matt Tees who would score 29 times that season, the Mariners scored three or more in over a third of their fixtures in that campaign. McMenemy's signings that year included former Sunderland forward Alan Gauden and Lew Chatterley, who he would later bring with him to Wearside as a coach.

At Sunderland McMenemy brought in big-name veterans, as he had at Southampton, but while that approach was successful on the south coast it dismally failed to replicate at Roker. Had this policy of bringing older heads in been one he had employed at Grimsby and Doncaster? 'I wasn't able to bring too many players in at Grimsby and Doncaster because you were restricted by finance, but you would have a look at what you had got and who were the experienced ones and who the lads listened to. I tried to get teams that were a mixture of what I call violinists and road-sweepers. It was a balance where one could do what the other one couldn't.' Bill Shankly used to take the same approach, the Liverpool legend also employing a musical analogy, explaining that a football team, 'Needs eight men to carry the piano and three to play it.' Enlarging on the theme Lawrie continues, 'What you have to learn as a manager is not to get too many of one and not enough of the other. Balance in your team is essential. Now and again you'd get a road-sweeper who thought he was a violinist and you'd have to bring him to one side and remind him. Sometimes you'd have a violinist who would talk down to the road-sweepers and then you'd have to remind him that without him you wouldn't be able to play. That was management. There is a complete difference between coaching and management. What I found going to all those coaching courses in 20 odd years of management was that all the managers could coach but not all of the coaches could manage. That's without a doubt – definite.

'I managed in all the four divisions as well as international level. In the lower divisions you were 90 per cent a coach and ten per cent a manager. The higher up you went . . . I had Peter Shilton, Mick Mills, Dave Watson, Jim McCalliog, Mike Channon, Kevin Keegan, Peter Osgood, Alan Ball, I could go on and on. They didn't need coaching, they needed management – big time! So you were ten per cent a coach and 90 per cent a manager.

'All teams, no matter how good they were, needed a method of play. I smile a bit now when the papers are full of facts and figures: percentages of how many times each player passes the ball, for instance, and then they'll say, "Oh, he's gone three at the back." I did that years ago at Southampton when it suited me because I had three blokes who could play central, but I also had full-backs who could go forward. With three at the back I had a spare man who would slot in whenever one of the full-backs went forward. The first time we did it was at Everton. Mark Dennis said to me, "Ron Saunders wouldn't let me go forward" but I told him to get forward and he was brilliant. It was brought in, it suited them and we were successful with it.'

McMenemy had moved from Grimsby to Southampton in the year Sunderland won the FA Cup under Bob Stokoe but, again, it was Stokoe's predecessor Brown who played a role in landing him the opportunity. Coincidentally someone else who recommended him was the manager defeated by Stokoe's Stars at Wembley, Leeds boss and former Sunderland centre-forward Don Revie: 'Alan Brown had put a word in and, although I didn't know it at the time, Don Revie had as well. In those days every summer coaches and managers would gather together at Lilleshall for a coaching week that the FA ran. You mixed and mingled and met people. On an afternoon you might have a First Division manager doing a session then the next afternoon you might have someone from abroad. We were the ones who ran around. You weren't taking badges or anything, everybody had done all that, but you were meeting people that you wouldn't have met normally. You could be a Fourth Division fella having breakfast lunch or tea with someone from the top flight. It also gave some older managers a chance to meet up with some younger ones. Ted Bates used to go regularly from Southampton and it gave him a chance to meet me, otherwise I would have just been a name to him.'

Just as McMenemy joined Southampton in the year Sunderland won the FA Cup so did Bates. In Bates case, though, that had been in 1937 – and he'd been there ever since! The grandson of an England double international at cricket and rugby and son of a county cricketer and professional footballer, Ted Bates had played over 200 games for Southampton, turning out in every position, including goalkeeper. Having also served the Saints as coach and manager when he stepped aside for McMenemy he was the longest-serving manager in the league.

'He'd been manager for 18 years and, like a lot of managers then, he had a plan that when he got to a certain age he'd retire, and that's what happened. I got invited to go for interviews at Southampton. The mistake I made was I took on the title of Team Manager designate. I just shrugged it off but the reason they did it was because Ted had been there for so long and before that he'd been a coach and before that a player. Over the years Ted had been manager they had brought in younger people at times to be his assistants. They had been looked at to see if they could possibly take over but none of them had passed the test in the board's eyes, so they were giving themselves an "out" if I didn't make it.'

McMenemy made it so fully at Southampton that he now has the freedom of that city, as well as the MBE and an entry in the *Guinness Book of Records* as one of the 20 most successful post-war managers (obviously not for what happened at Sunderland). At Southampton he also has an honorary MBA from Solent University which now has a Lawrie McMenemy Centre for Football Research.

Later a director of the Saints, McMenemy's legacy to them is more than the entries in the record books. 'I started the academy at Southampton,' he says. 'Ted, bless him, because we were the best club in Hampshire he knew we'd get all the best kids, so he didn't have scouts anywhere else. We wouldn't get kids from Scotland because you couldn't sign them until they were 16, but by that time Rangers and Celtic would know about them if they were any good, but in England you could sign lads at 14.

'Brendan Foster got me up to Gateshead to open a stand at the International Stadium. While I was there I saw that there was a big warm-up area underneath the stands, so I arranged to hire that for two nights a week. It coincided with Jack Hixon and his two lads who had been Burnley's scouts – and Burnley were full of Geordies – finishing at Turf Moor. I heard about this so I got onto them and signed them up. Jack was the main man. One of them scouted around the Scottish borders all the way down to Newcastle. Jack had an office in the Central Station at Newcastle and he looked after the Newcastle and Gateshead area and the other one did Gateshead to Middlesbrough. They would go to school games and bring in the best kids two nights a week to Gateshead and in the school holidays they would bring the best kids down to Southampton.

'I did the same at Bristol with a Geordie fella who used to play in Bristol and hired a gymnasium, and in London I got asked to go and present some medals with David Peach at a place in Kent. There was a fella who would hire a couple of ex-players so people would pay a few bob for their kids to play. It was a bloke called Bob Higgins, who is in trouble now.'

In July 2018 Higgins was found guilty of indecently assaulting a young trainee with the possibility of a retrial to follow in 2019 on 48 other counts of the same charge which a jury did not reach verdicts on. Such people have no place in football and modern day FA safeguarding procedures thankfully make it much more difficult for anything untoward to besmirch the game and damage young lives. Thankfully also the positive side of youth football is that opportunities are provided for those with the right combination of talent and attitude.

'Newcastle and Gateshead produced Alan Shearer and also Tommy Widdrington and Neil Maddison who made the first team,' continues Lawrie. 'Bristol eventually produced Gareth Bale and also the full-back Jason Dodd, while we got Steve Williams, Austin Hayes, the three Wallace brothers and Dennis Wise from London. It was totally productive and I carried that on all the time I was there.'

Leaving Southampton Lawrie looked unsinkable, but then so did the *Titanic*, which, as Jimmy Tarbuck once joked, was the other thing apart from McMenemy that should never have left Southampton. When Lawrie's appointment as Sunderland manager was made on 11 July 1985 I, like every other supporter, was thrilled to bits with the news. Only the arrivals of Martin O'Neill and Sam Allardyce have ever pleased me as much, even allowing for the fact that Big Sam isn't everyone's cup of tea (he gets results and had England not come calling there's not a black cat in hell's chance the club would have sunk as it has).

McMenemy looked as firmly planted in Southampton as the dry-docked HMS *Victory* is in nearby Portsmouth, so how come he came to just relegated Sunderland? 'What had happened for me is that one day I got a knock on the door and Tom Cowie was stood there. How he found my house I don't know because we lived in a little village. He'd been in London but had made his way there. I invited him in and put the kettle on. He said that he didn't want to leave until he'd signed me up. The timing was right for him because things had changed at Southampton. The old board were wonderful gentlemen but were dying off. They all had companies in the area and there were younger ones on the board. This coincided with chairmen of top-flight clubs getting together more.

'I'd wanted to sign a player and mentioned it at a board meeting. I'd tell them how much the player would cost and they would say yes or no money wise, but they would never ever question the ability of the player. This time, though, I started being asked questions such as, "Are you sure he can tackle?" I'd never had that before, and we hadn't had many wrong-uns signed. Twelve years at a club like Southampton was a long time, and it was becoming not monotonous but repetitive.'

Cowie was desperate for a big name to come to Sunderland. Previously he had met with Brian Clough and Bobby Robson. Cowie had decided there was no way he could work with Cloughie after Brian kept him waiting and then, in his inimitable fashion, informed the chairman that directors would not be allowed to travel on the team coach. Robson had agreed to take over at Sunderland but was then talked out of it by Ipswich. For McMenemy the timing was right and the chairman who made Ken Knighton pay out of his own pocket for a night's pre-match accommodation for the team found the money to offer a top salary for a top manager. If only it had been plain sailing after that but in 'typical Sunderland' fashion anything that could go wrong did go wrong.

The run-around from Bobby Saxton's Blackburn on the opening day of the season wasn't the start of the story. That came in the first training session. "We went down to Seaburn where we were training on the beach. I said to the lads, 'Right I'm not going to do a lot of talking, you've all heard I'm here let's get straight down to it. I need to get to know you so hope you've had a good summer and let's get started. They were doing their warm up with the trainer and they were jogging around. I said to the physio, 'If I point to a player you tell me who he is. It wasn't as if Sunderland were up the road from

Southampton and I used to watch them regularly. They were totally at the other end of the country and I knew names but until I got in there I couldn't get to know their nature.

"As they were running around I noticed one who was limping a bit so I asked who's that there? That's a bad start, he's limping. The physio just said, 'Cartilage' and I thought, "Bloody hell, he's good. The only bloke I knew who could recognise something from distance was Bob Paisley who had an art of doing it. I said, 'How the hell do you know that?' and he said 'He had it at the end of last season.' I said 'Hang on a minute, he had a cartilage problem at the end of last season and he's been away all summer why he hell didn't he get it done? The physio said we told him he needed it but he'd said 'Not in my f****** time and walked out the door and went back home for the close season. That was my first session."

By now Lawrie is in the moment and continues, "You're asking me about losing games at the start of the season and he was one of the top players of a club I had taken over. He had said two fingers to the club, saying not in my time when he knew he needed an operation! When he came back they had to put him in and get the operation done. When he came back he was never as good as he thought he was, I remember taking the player off in one of the last games of the season. I did it on purpose because he was the supporters' hero and I made a point of bringing him off. He knew, and as he walked by me he called me a four letter word. I'd never had that sort of thing even in the early days at any of my other clubs but that was one of the things that happened that supporters wouldn't know in terms of dealing with players. The club was out of order in letting him go. It could well be that the previous manager Len Ashurst had gone by then. Len knows the game and the player wouldn't have listened to any of the staff. The board should have been told and he should have been brought to task. The dressing room at Sunderland was completely different to what I'd been used to for so long. You had to work out who was who and what was what. It wasn't the best dressing room. There were players in there I wouldn't have had in the club but you can't just say here's a week's pay off you go because they're under contract."

It was in the sixth game of the season when Wearside finally celebrated a point from a 3-3 draw at home to Grimsby as if it was something to be proud of, after five goalless and pointless games. After the fifth of those matches where defeat at Millwall meant McMenemy's Sunderland had a goal difference of -10 was Lawrie already thinking, 'What have I let myself in for?' or when the breakthrough came with that 3-3 draw against Grimsby was he believing 'Here we go' and expecting to be on an upward curve from then on, especially as it was followed by a draw at Leeds and then back to back wins?

"Any manager has got to think positively. You couldn't keep losing games. Over my career I'd had spells where you went through a bad patch, through injuries or whatever. There was so much expectation but things weren't done early enough. We hung on in the first season and then I was up against it a bit."

Seven players made their final appearance for the club as Stoke were beaten 2-0 to ensure Sunderland stayed up, four points clear of the last relegation place as Carlisle, Middlesbrough and Fulham went down. At the final whistle Lawrie appeared by the touchline to wave a white handkerchief to what was the second highest league gate of the season, only marginally fewer than had witnessed his first game. "When I came and did that it was a form of apology. I was saying 'Sorry, I know it could have been better.' We were totally relieved to have stayed up and determined to do better. You never know until things crop up. I knew certain players who I wouldn't want around but if they are on contracts you can't just say 'There's the door' and not everybody wants to take them.

Sunderland's second season under McMenemy started with debuts for a new goalkeeper and striker in the shape of Iain Hesford and Dave Buchanan. The exodus included captain Shaun Elliott, England Under 21 full-back Barry Venison, former Liverpool forwards Howard Gayle and Dave Hodgson, Scottish international striker Ian Wallace and the on loan Tony Ford and Andy Dibble, the latter being a goalkeeper who had excelled in helping to keep Sunderland up.

A 2-0 opening day victory at Huddersfield was made even better when the Terriers best player that day, Steve Doyle, signed for Sunderland under a month later. By the end of September Sunderland were sixth after six games – albeit their one league defeat being a 6-1 hammering at Saxton's Blackburn. By the end of the following month The Lads were fifth as Buchanan – plucked from Blyth Spartans after making his league debut for Leicester on the same day as Gary Lineker (New Year's Day 1979) and scoring when Lineker didn't – scored his fourth goal in as many games and was looking the part.

If McMenemy was like the *Titanic* leaving Southampton then Sheffield United was the iceberg. Many people recall that it was losing at home to the Blades late in the season that sunk Lawrie, but it was also a defeat by the same 2-1 scoreline in the away game at Bramall Lane that was the beginning of the end, where the *Titanic* was struck. Sunderland actually led at half-time in that match in Sheffield, Gary Bennett – a player who still thinks highly of Lawrie – having given The Lads the lead moments before the break. However, an 89th-minute winner by the home side's David Frain, after future Sunderland loanee Peter Beagrie had equalised, did the damage.

The fateful return match was an eerie re-enactment of the previous meeting, as Beagrie again equalised before the Blades inflicted a late winner, this time former Newcastle man Peter Withe scoring five minutes from time. The game remains one of the lowest points in Sunderland's entire history. Unlike in recent seasons, where fans have watched performances every bit as bad and barely raised a protest – the result of being punch-drunk with too many failures – back in the day there was hell on. Everyone around at the time remembers the scenario but how does the man at the centre of the storm recall events?

'We didn't win and after the game there were a hundred or two hundred demonstrating in the car park and they scratched three cars: Eric Gates', mine and Bob Murray's. I think that upset Bob Murray because he thought they were going at him then. I tried to ring him on the Sunday but I couldn't get him, so I rang the other director, Gordon Hodgson. He was a Tom Cowie man, he worked at Cowie's. He was a very nice man who was a good solid fella. He knew better than anybody the problems I was facing. He always had to support Tom Cowie, which he did. I rang him and said, "Look, there's a board meeting coming up next week but I think we should bring it forward." He said, "I agree, but you should have a word with Bob Murray." I spoke to Bob who said he'd have a word with Gordon Hodgson. We had a board meeting where there was just three of us. Bob Murray said, "I think you should go" and I looked at Gordon and said, "What do you think?" He said, "I've got to agree." That was on the Monday, I think, and I think it came out on the Wednesday. What Murray did that time he got together with me and Gordon Hodgson was say, "If you don't go, I go." So there was no choice. The club needed him as chairman and he knew that.'

Murray was in his first year as chairman. He was trying to deal with the ongoing battles in the boardroom and fighting to keep the club afloat financially. He knew the club could not afford to keep McMenemy on and has a different view of events at this time to Lawrie. This, though, is McMenemy's standpoint. As he goes on to explain, he thinks Sunderland could have stayed up but he acknowledges he could and should have handled things differently. Instead he drove to his Hampshire home in the dead of night and the first thing people knew about it was when they read of his departure in the *Sun*: 'That was one of the mistakes I made. Hands up! I let a friend of mine, Alex Montgomery, have the story. He was a London-based reporter and I let him know what I was going to do. I can understand why the northeast reporters were annoyed because I knew how the media worked. Wallop! They were giving me it 100 per cent because in their eyes I'd done a runner. Looking back that was a mistake. Hands up. Mistake. What I did was gather up Anne and other members of my family, packed our car and drove south early in the morning. By the time the rest of the media found out, I'd gone. Looking back, I can understand that wasn't fair to them. They'd get stick from their editors, so naturally they went, bang, two feet into me. A lot of what they said was over the top. For instance, I didn't want to go.'

Whether McMenemy wanted out or not the club wanted him gone. Results hadn't been good enough after almost two seasons, gates had tumbled to the absolute hardest of the hardcore, and even they had signalled they had had enough by the vehemence of the protests after the last loss of Lawrie's reign.

As a supporter I felt it was time for Lawrie to go, but I wouldn't expect many managers to not have a deep well of resolve that convinces them that, given a bit more time, they would be able to turn things around. At Southampton the club had stuck with McMenemy when they got relegated at the end of his first full season, after which he repaid them. In the light of things going pear shaped at Sunderland does Lawrie feel that he could have turned the situation around as he had with Southampton?

'Because of the way it happened I got slaughtered and I just had to shut up and get on with it. Obviously any manager with experience would want to stay up. I did think I would have been able to keep them up as I had done the previous season, and look at it again in the summer. I had another year left. Your question originally was, "Do I think things would have changed if I'd stayed on?" I can't be certain, but I knew it had to change, and that was my target.'

The simple facts are that at the time of McMenemy's departure, prior to the Sheffield game, Sunderland had won three of the last five home games, had lost three home games in five months and had never been lower than sixth bottom. It was a record that was a million miles from being great but it didn't mean the team were glued to the bottom of the table, as they have been in recent seasons. Of course there are lies, damned lies and statistics, and another way of looking at it was that after the beating by the Blades just one point had been taken from six games, and the way the team were playing an upturn looked beyond them.

Bob Murray called upon Bob Stokoe to return to the club and try to keep them up – but 3-2 defeats would haunt him, defeat by that scoreline occurring in four of the nine games he oversaw, beginning with the first at Bradford. Stokoe's Roker return, oddly enough, was against Leeds. Instead of what would have been a poetic 1-0 win the match ended 1-1 after goalkeeper Hesford – experiencing a season comparable with that of Jason Steele and Lee Camp in 2018–19 – was beaten from 40 yards. Two encouraging wins sandwiched another 3-2 loss before a healthy point in the penultimate match at Millwall saw Sunderland go into the final league game fifth from bottom, albeit level on points with the two teams immediately beneath them. Disaster struck against a mid-table Barnsley with nothing to play for: 2-0 up against a side managed by Allan Clarke (who had played against Stokoe's Sunderland at Wembley 14 years earlier) Sunderland somehow managed to lose 3-2, missing a penalty for good measure in a game where former Sunderland striker Rodger Wylde equalised for the Tykes.

Finishing third from bottom Sunderland still had a lifeline. In what was the first year of the playoffs the third-bottom side took part with the teams finishing third, fourth and fifth from the league below. So it was that The Lads faced Gillingham, where they lost the first leg by the now familiar 3-2 scoreline. When that result was reversed at Roker – where Sunderland again missed from the spot – the match went to extra time. With each side scoring once more the score was level on aggregate, with Sunderland being relegated simply because the extra time had been played on Wearside, as the Gills scored the decisive 'away' goal.

'As even Bob couldn't keep them up maybe the ability just wasn't there, or the players weren't bothered. It's very sad but I hope I see them get back up again,' says Lawrie, now that Sunderland in 2018 find themselves at the same level they slipped to in 1987.

Relegation to the third tier of English football for a club of Sunderland's stature was an enormously sad chapter in their long and proud history. Bob Stokoe magnanimously accepted blame, although he had only been parachuted in for the closing stages of the season. Bob Murray appointed Denis Smith, who got Sunderland out of the third tier immediately and back into the top flight just two years later. The drop into the third tier was meant to be a one-off, before Sunderland slumped there once again in 2018 after back-to-back relegations where the common denominator was CEO Martin Bain under the ownership of Ellis Short. As *Tales from the Red and Whites, Volume 3* is published all Sunderland supporters are hoping that Jack Ross, under the club's new ownership led by Stewart Donald, can emulate what Sunderland did under Denis Smith and make Sunderland's stay in the third tier as brief as possible.

The hope and even expectation on Lawrie McMenemy's appointment was that Sunderland would be promoted to the top flight and eventually become a force there. Eric Gates, Frank Gray, David Swindlehurst, Alan Kennedy and George Burley, for instance, were all established top-class players, but as a group found it hard going in a struggling side. How frustrating was that for McMenemy, who had brought them to the club hoping the same formula that had proved successful in red and white stripes on the south coast would also work on Wearside?

'I was disappointed because, in my own mind, I thought I was doing what I'd done at Southampton, mixing old heads and young legs. I knew them as players but I didn't know them as personalities, but you think as a manager you can get the best out of them and pull them together. I remember a conversation I had with Alan Kennedy, who came in to the dressing room one day. I remember him talking to me about a young kid – Gordon Armstrong – who was playing on the left side with Alan Kennedy behind him. I was expecting Kennedy, as a senior experienced international player, to help this kid in front of him, but Alan's point was, "How the hell do you think I can play when I've got a kid in front of me?" He was looking at it from his point of view and felt he needed more help, but I was hoping it would work like it did at Southampton, where Alan Ball, bless him, was helping a young Steve Williams. They would have a go at each other on the pitch verbally, because Steve was strong minded, but he and other young players would give nothing but 100 per cent praise to Alan Ball for the help he'd give them, even though it might come out harshly. I was expecting Alan Kennedy to do an Alan Ball and help the young'un, but it worked the other way as Alan Kennedy wanted more experience in front of him to help him. The other lads weren't bad lads at all but they didn't do for us what they had been doing for the clubs they were at before.

'Maybe it was my mistake. You take a gamble. It worked out for me at Southampton, but it could well be because I'd been there that long when I brought them in. My first one was Peter Osgood. I brought in people like Alan Ball, who was at the end of his career and I got him very cheap. I said, "Bally, you're here to get us promoted." He did and when we got to Wembley for the second time in 1979, in the League Cup, his eyes lit up. He couldn't believe he was going back to Wembley at that stage of his career. When we qualified he was up all night. He never went to bed. They were all out celebrating. They rang me from a place called Bedford Place, not far from the Dell. "Come and join us, boss," they said, but I was entertaining the other manager. I got the bloody bill the next day but I didn't mind because Bally was lovely. He loved the game and everyone around him benefited. He knew if he'd had a bad game, but he was such an influence with young players.'

While signing veterans, including Sunderland FA Cup hero Dave Watson just as he turned 33, McMenemy had tremendous success with his old heads and young legs policy at Southampton, at Sunderland it was a different scenario: as well as the old heads not succeeding, the best young legs were sold off – in the shape of future England international Barry Venison and Nick Pickering, who had already won a full cap before McMenemy arrived. The sale of two of the best young full-backs in the country, as a trio of veterans in Kennedy, Burley and Gray were brought in, has long since bemused many observers, so what was Lawrie's thinking in selling Venison and Pickering?

'I think I had to prove I could bring money in as well. Nick Pickering was a very quiet lad and obviously a good player. Barry was ambitious and rightly so.' Venison asked for a transfer and reputedly wrote to every top-division team asking if they were interested in him as he neared the end of his existing contract. 'He went to Liverpool. Once he knew they were interested in him there was no way he would want to stay because it was a step up for him and it proved good for him. I've got nothing against them. They were good lads but it was hard for the club to turn any money down.'

Money was in extremely short supply during the era, with the huge pay packet Cowie had dangled in front of McMenemy a constant subject for discussion. Acknowledging it was a lot of money, Lawrie also argues that he brought money into the club through other means in addition to the transfer market: 'Over the couple of years I was there I was able to bring in up to £250,000 worth of sponsors that weren't there before. Tom Cowie's name was on the shirts before, but I went to him and said, "Look, I've done something with Vaux and they'll put their name on the shirts." To be fair to Cowie he said, "Bring them in." Tom's name was on the shirt but he wasn't putting the money in, and he backed off. Obviously I got well paid but I repaid £250,000 worth of it through that.'

One of Sunderland's biggest problems during McMenemy's time was a similar problem to when Sunderland were relegated to League One in 2018 – the inability to field a convincing goalkeeper. Starting with Seamus McDonagh, who infamously complained the goals were different sizes at each end in a match at Grimsby (and later returned to Sunderland as goalkeeping coach under Martin O'Neill), McMenemy tried Bob Bolder, youngster Cameron Duncan and Andy Dibble in his first year before signing Iain Hesford in his second season, when Bobby Mimms and young Duncan also got a few games. 'I didn't remember all the names until you brought them up,' admits Lawrie, 'but what I do remember is I was sat with Cloughie one day and it cropped up then that you've got to have a good goalkeeper to have a good team. That's when I finished up getting Peter Shilton for Southampton. What a difference he made. He was totally single minded and 100 per cent on the game. He wasn't a lively character in the dressing room, but to have him in the dressing room was terrific.' If only a Shilton – or at least a steady and reliable long-term number one – had come in to replace the brilliant Chris Turner, who had just been sold to Manchester United for a club record fee before McMenemy arrived, then just perhaps things might have turned out better for Lawrie. Things could scarcely have been worse.

Tom Cowie, having brought McMenemy to the club, bailed out at the end of Lawrie's first season. While he technically remained on the board for a few more months he wasn't seen at Roker Park, where the boardroom remained in turmoil as new Chairman Bob Murray fought to establish a harmonious board, something he eventually did after McMenemy's departure. While Lawrie was at the club, however, he was party to boardroom turmoil that was a world away from the genteel atmosphere of he had worked in during the bulk of his time in Hampshire.

'Tom Cowie had left and one of the massive things he had done which made my job totally difficult was that he had wanted me to be a director. I didn't ask to be a director, I didn't want to be on the board. Why would I? He gave me some silly title of Managing Director, or whatever. Looking back, I think it was because he had already had problems in the boardroom with Barry Batey.' Batey was a high-profile director of the era at the centre of the power struggle that dominated what was going on behind the scenes both before and after McMenemy's time in the Roker hot seat.

'I didn't want to take on being a director and would rather have concentrated totally on football as I'd always done,' continues Lawrie. 'The fact that money was talked about was wrong on their behalf. They should never ever tell people what salaries are unless it is a limited company and you have to publish figures. Barry Batey didn't help himself. He revealed the players' salaries to the press! Then he expected to get on the bus with the players! The atmosphere was incredibly wrong and totally different to whatever I'd had at Southampton, where the board were "olde worlde" gentleman. I mean, the chairman George Reader refereed the World Cup final!'

Not only did Reader referee what was effectively the 1950 World Cup final – the 1950 World Cup was differently organised to every other tournament and the decisive final game of the competition Reader took saw host nation Brazil only need a draw with Uruguay to take the trophy; but they lost 2-1 before a world-record crowd of 199,854 at the Maracanã – but he had actually played a handful of games for them in the league way back in the 1920s. Southampton had signed him after he scored against them when playing for Exeter. Reader's colleagues on the board in Hampshire were a group of characters evidently from another world to the self-made local businessmen on Wearside. 'People like Sir George Meyrick owned half of Bournemouth and had a castle in Anglesey,' continues McMenemy. 'He only went to two away games, Arsenal and Ipswich, and enjoyed a few drinks there because he went to Eton with the Hill-Woods and the Cobbold family. Another director owned a brewery in the area. Another one owned a company called "Feathery Flake" and wore a monocle and a pressed carnation. When they were on a plane once, he wasn't well, so the doctor sat next to him – they called the director, by the way, Mr Charles Chaplin. The plane took off and they called for the stewardess . . .' At this point Lawrie does an impression and says in a very posh voice, '"Have you a glass of water?"' continuing, 'The stewardess came back with a glass as the doctor was getting the tablets out and he pulled the carnation out and stuck it in the water. That's the sort of directors we had!

'When we got relegated I was running around the track two days later on my own and I saw the chairman and Sir George and I thought to myself, "Aye-aye, this is it" but the chairman just said, "Manager: sort it out" and walked away. Sir George looked at me, winked, smiled and said, "Get rid of the pain in your side." What he meant was Terry Paine, who was a legend but who didn't help me one little bit.'

Terry Paine played over 700 games for the club and was part of England's 1966 World Cup-winning squad. 'He was a good player but not in my time. His legs had gone, but he'd been at the club 18 years. Ted Bates had signed him as a schoolboy. John McGrath – who I knew from Newcastle days – would say that Paine would say on a Friday, "Right, I'm off up to see Ted and pick the team." He felt he should have got the job when I got it, so he certainly wasn't going to help me. The club stood by me and got him out. Things like that happen in football.'

While the boardroom at Southampton sounds like an old boys' club, consisting of very rich men enjoying a jolly time, at Sunderland there was anything but jollity and enjoyment. 'I famously remember a meeting where everything that Barry Batey said Tom Cowie said the opposite,' recalls Lawrie. 'Barry thought he was representing the man on the terraces. He was down to earth and had a real north-east accent. Then you had Tom, who was a successful businessman with a different accent and sounded very posh in comparison. You had Geoff Davidson, the secretary, who was probably on edge, and Bob Murray sitting quietly, weighing all this up, and Gordon Hodgson, who was a Cowie man. No matter what happened there was Cowie and Hodgson on one side, Bob Murray biding his time, and Batey questioning every single thing. I listened, and everything Batey said Cowie would say to Geoff Davidson, "Don't put that in the minutes" or "Ignore that comment." That made Batey even more wild. Geoff Davidson was sat with the pen in his hand, not sure if he should put it down, and I'm sat there thinking, "What the hell?" and then at the end Cowie said, "Meeting closed", got up and was walking to the door when Batey came out with a mouthful of abuse, to which Tom turned around, looked at Geoff Davidson and said, "Put that in the minutes", walked out and shut the door! That didn't help me one little bit as a manager.

'Managers would ring each other about different things and get together now and again at managers' meetings. The usual thing would crop up where people would say, "I bet you wish you were back at Southampton." But anybody of any experience – I'm talking about Cloughie and Bobby [Robson] and seniors like Shankly, Paisley, Bill Nicholson, Joe Mercer – they'd all been through it. They'd had their good times and their bad. None of the managers I've talked about ever had as many problems to deal with regarding the boardroom, especially as I was called "managing director", which went against me big time. I wasn't a proper director like directors I knew. Directors should be helping the manager and letting him get on with it. You couldn't write a play about it.

'It wasn't a happy time. It was the worst time in my career, really, for my family as well. We did go through having an awful lot of stick. I think managers can learn to take it, but when it affects your wife and kids as well . . .'

There was, though, a family bonus from Lawrie's stint at Roker: 'There was a person on the office staff at Roker Park when I was there called Martin Long. He was assistant secretary, or something. He worked with Geoff Davidson. A good thing about my time at the club was Martin started courting my daughter, and they've been married now for about 26 years.'

One of Lawrie's kids who was in the eye of the storm was son Chris, who was coaching at the club. 'He'd started coaching at Southampton with the big youth policy I set up,' says Lawrie.

'There was an opportunity for him at Sunderland and I gave him it. Lew Chatterley used to regularly point out that professionally our relationship was manager and coach rather than father and son. Full marks to Bob Stokoe when he came in, because he said to Chris, "I'm keeping you on." But then he made his own way and finished up managing Chesterfield for a while. Sean Dyche is a big pal of his, because he played at Chesterfield when Chris was there, and speaks so highly of him. I remember, once, I was abroad somewhere and Chesterfield won a Cup tie and drew Liverpool away. At half-time I found out the score when someone told me it was 0-2. I said, "You mean 2-0?" and was told, "No. Chesterfield are winning!" It finished up 3-3, which was fantastic – even though they got stuffed in the replay. Kevin Keegan had him at Newcastle and he had a little spell with England under-21s. He's been in Spain for about 12 years now. He's got a company called Primero Property.'

While Chris weathered the storm inside the club after his dad left – which can't have been easy, to put it mildly – family has always been as important for Lawrie as it is for anyone: 'I had the opportunity to go to Man United at one stage, and I didn't because we didn't want to unsettle our children's education, plus the board at Southampton didn't want me to go. The timing of it was wrong, but if ever I wanted to do well it was back in the north-east because I grew up there, I learned about football there and everybody loved the game. I'd love to have achieved there what I did at other places. Looking back, I feel sorry for the supporters. I'm sorry I didn't bring what people wanted. I'm not making excuses. I had two years and I didn't succeed. The area is built on football. It was a release for the working man to go to the match on a Saturday afternoon and shout his head off. I was brought up on that. It's not like other areas of the country where it isn't as important and never was. That's why I wanted to succeed at Sunderland more than anywhere, and that's why it hurts still to this day that I didn't succeed.

'I think that they can say what they like about me, but stop for a little bit and think, "Hang on, the managers of the last 20, 30, 40 years . . . apart from Bob winning the Cup, what's happened to the club? Why has it not done better? It has the support. It has a big ground. What's the reason?" To be fair, they're in the third division now – I'm not going to get the blame for that, am I? Don't blame me for that one, please.'

EPILOGUE

Following McMenemy's sudden departure ambitious new chairman Bob Murray turned to the legendary Bob Stokoe to try to rescue a season which ended in playoff heartbreak and a first-ever relegation to the Third Division. The appointment of Denis Smith was a master-stroke, as Smith ensured Sunderland were promoted immediately. Within a further two seasons Sunderland were back in the top flight but were unable to stay there with Smith sacked at on the penultimate day in December 1991. Stepping into Smith's shoes came Malcolm Crosby . . .

3

'Some are born great, some achieve greatness, and some have greatness thrust upon them,' Shakespeare wrote. And while the Bard wasn't talking about Malcolm Crosby when he penned that, there's no doubting which of those three categories the former Sunderland manager would fall into.

The unassuming backroom boy was thrust centre stage with the board's sacking of Denis Smith in December 1991 – suddenly finding himself taking charge of a major English football club having never aspired to or coveted the opportunity to do so.

If fate had dealt him a winning hand, it was his misfortune never to be able to make the most of it. He was sacked barely a year after taking over, having never fully received the backing of a cash-strapped board unconvinced he was the man for the job long-term.

One thing that couldn't be taken away from Crosby, though, was the fact that in his brief tenure he steered Sunderland to an FA Cup final – one of only four managers in the club's history to have done so, and the last to achieve that feat. In this chapter, he meets Lance Hardy who, like Crosby, can look back on that curious 1992 FA Cup final and say, 'I was there.'

MALCOLM CROSBY

SUNDERLAND MANAGER
30 DECEMBER 1991 TO 1 FEBRUARY 1993
MEETS LANCE HARDY

If I had five pounds for every Sunderland fan who has asked me over the last few years if I will one day write a book called *Crosby, Sunderland and '92* I would have, well, quite a few fivers. I guess that is because for my generation 1992 was our *Stokoe, Sunderland and '73*: I was only five years old when Bob Stokoe ran across the Wembley pitch in jubilation after the 1-0 win over Leeds United; I was in my early twenties by the time Malcolm Crosby almost engineered another FA Cup final fairytale for the Red and Whites 19 years later.

Interestingly, there were several similarities between those two FA Cup runs: Sunderland were struggling at the wrong end of the Second Division on both occasions; each season was played out against a backdrop of economic hardship in the north-east (albeit for different reasons); and Stokoe and Crosby had taken over at the helm at Roker Park at the end of the previous year, and just before the FA Cup run began (in Stokoe's case it was a matter of weeks; in Crosby's case it was a matter of days!). Unsurprisingly, the Rokerites were regarded as massive underdogs in both 1973 and 1992. Obviously, the big difference between the two FA Cup final appearances is that one ended in glory, and the other ended in defeat. Furthermore, the Boys of '73 remain massive heroes to this day, while the starting XI from '92 could make a good quiz question, at least outside the north-east.

But these facts shouldn't deflect from the sheer flavour of romanticism that swept through Sunderland again throughout that dark winter and early spring of 1992 when, just for a moment, a repeat Roker triumph in the greatest Cup competition of them all looked as though it could be possible.

Personally, I would say the biggest similarity between 1973 and 1992 was that the nation took the Sunderland manager to its heart; whether it was Stokoe with his fierce passion and trilby, or Crosby with his gentlemanly manner and unique caretaker-manager status. Indeed, my head still shakes in disbelief and the hairs can often still stand on the back of my neck when I recall watching Desmond Lynam introduce Crosby as 'the caretaker manager of the FA Cup finalists, Sunderland' on BBC One just before his post-match interview with Barry Davies at Hillsborough. These are the things that dreams are made of . . .

To further put Crosby's achievement into context: 1992 was the first time since 1976 that Sunderland had got as far as the last 16 in the competition, never mind the quarter-finals, the semi-finals, and the final. The thrill that the whole Cup run produced was immense. As I said, it was my generation's 1973 . . .

Living and working in London by that time, I went to Sunderland's two quarter-final matches, the semi-final and the final in 1992, and worked on the fifth round and fifth-round replay at BBC Television Centre. I will certainly never forget that whole Cup run. I lived every minute of it. Tickets weren't easy to obtain, they never are, and so it was that I found myself in the Norwich end for the semi-final and the Liverpool end at Wembley, having previously experienced a great evening, followed by a lively exit, from the away end at Stamford Bridge – and enjoyed the night of all nights in the Fulwell End for the replay, Gordon Armstrong's last-minute winner providing my generation's Vic Halom moment.

Twenty-six years later, it is therefore a great thrill for me to interview Malcolm Crosby – one of only four men to lead Sunderland to an FA Cup final – on a hot summer's day in the garden of his home in rural Oxfordshire.

Appropriately, one of the first subjects we discuss is 1973. Crosby (who was a player at Aldershot at the time) was there that day, in the Leeds end, when Ian Porterfield scored the only goal of the game and Jim Montgomery made the famous save that is still replayed every year on FA Cup final day.

'On the Friday night we drew at Stockport County and got promoted from the old Fourth Division,' Malcolm remembers. 'After a night out in Manchester, I travelled on to Watford, got off the Aldershot team coach, got the train, met my mate, and watched Sunderland win the Cup. The memories that stick out are obviously the goal and the save. The rest of the time Sunderland were pretty much outplayed and chasing the ball, from what I remember, but it didn't matter because at the end of it we won the Cup and that is the most important thing.

'It was probably one of the best weekends I have ever had in my life!'

I wondered if Crosby, who was a professional from 1972 to 1984, had come up against any of the 1973 Sunderland FA Cup winning team during his playing days.

'I think I played against Bobby Kerr, when he was at Hartlepool United, later in his career, but he would be the only one,' Malcolm replies.

Kerr had two seasons at Hartlepool in the early 1980s. By that time Crosby was also nearing the end of his own playing career, which included 294 appearances for Aldershot, 103 appearances for York City, and loan spells at Wimbledon and Wrexham. It was quite a return for a 16-year-old hopeful who had travelled over 300 miles from South Shields to attend a two-week trial at the Recreation Ground in 1970.

'Yes, it was a long way to go,' Malcolm says. 'I didn't even know where it was! My father worked on the railways, and I thought I knew the country quite well because I was very keen on the railways, but I had never heard of Aldershot.

'I was born in South Shields, I played for the town team, and I had a trial at Darlington when Ray Yeoman was manager. I did well in that trial. They said they were going to have me back, and they said they would get back in touch with me, but that was the only trial I ever had.

'I was always a Sunderland fan and a South Shields fan,' Malcolm adds. 'I went to a few FA Cup games as a Shields fan, including Crewe away [in 1965] and QPR away [in 1970], and I went to Roker Park a lot in the late 1960s. It was the Charlie Hurley era. I will never forget the corners! When Charlie started coming up the field, it used to be quite exciting.

'I was asked to go down to Aldershot, but I wasn't really chosen. They picked three players from South Shields, but they wanted four, so they could put two in each hotel room. I made the numbers up, and I was the one they kept on! So I was very fortunate. I would say there were about eight or nine players in the town at that time who were probably better than me, and I was always surprised they didn't go on to make a living from football.

'Aldershot's ex-manager was from the north-east. His brother lived in South Shields, and he was the one who recommended me. Jimmy Melia, the ex-Liverpool player and future Brighton manager, was in charge at that time. He was so enthusiastic and luckily he took a liking to me.

'I was offered an apprenticeship, but I had a marine engineer apprenticeship in South Shields lined up as well. So I came home, thought about it, and decided that I wanted to try the football, which was a big risk because after two years I could have been looking for another club. Fortunately, I was offered a professional contract, and I stayed there for ten years. Two years before, another local lad, Joe Jopling, who did very well at Aldershot, got a good move to Leicester City when he was only about 20. Unfortunately, he suffered a bad injury and ended up coming back to Aldershot. I was a right-winger and Joe was a left-back, and he would be a bit easy on me in training; he kept letting me go past him all the time, so I think I must have looked quite impressive,' Malcolm laughs. 'We played together for many years.'

During Crosby's early days at Aldershot he had a loan spell at Southern League side Wimbledon. Dave Bassett, the Football League and the Crazy Gang era were all still around the corner, but goalkeeper Dickie Guy – a hero in the FA Cup matches against Leeds United in 1975 when he saved a penalty from Peter Lorimer at Elland Road – was there in a side managed by the man who led Colchester United to their celebrated FA Cup fifth-round win over Don Revie's side in 1971, Dick Graham.

'I loved it there,' Malcolm says. 'We didn't have a reserve team at Aldershot and so it was good to play in the Southern League. I felt it brought me on, because it is tough when you are a young player up against men. I was only 11 stone, but I was prepared to wade in; that is the way I played. So I ended up playing in midfield and I loved it. I got into the Aldershot team and I felt pretty comfortable.'

Crosby only made one permanent move as a player after joining Aldershot, and it was to prove pivotal in his later career as a coach. He moved to York City in 1981 where, within a few months, he would meet future Sunderland manager Denis Smith.

'I was actually having my testimonial year at Aldershot when I got asked to sign for York,' Malcolm explains. 'It was difficult, because after being at a club for ten years you feel as though you belong there. I was quite brave and quite daft to move in my testimonial year, but I felt that I needed the experience of playing for another club, so that is what I did.

'I will never forget that we had gone seven games unbeaten and we came in one day to find out they had sacked the manager, Barry Lyons. I now understand that you can get the sack for anything at any time! But, back in 1981, I couldn't understand it at all. Denis Smith came in on loan from Stoke City, and then at the end of that season he got the manager's job.

'Den brought Viv Busby in and they completely transformed us. They were very good together, and we ended up having a very good team. We won the Fourth Division title with over 100 points, and we had some fantastic FA Cup ties against Arsenal and Liverpool. I was on the bench for a couple of those big games. We beat Arsenal on what was like an ice rink – I don't think they were too happy about it – and we drew with Liverpool twice in two years.

'After we won promotion [in 1984], Den said to me, "If you want to carry on playing you can move on a free, but I would like you to take the youth team, play in the reserves, and on occasions you may play in the first team."

'So that is what I did,' Malcolm continues. 'I actually brought Marco Gabbiadini through as an apprentice at York! When I took the job on "Gabbas" was already there, and he was the same size as he is now! His mother and father were brilliant people, and they would make him a lovely packed lunch. He would come in with his packed lunch, and he had eaten most of it by half-past nine! You could see why he was a big, strong lad! He was very good for such a young player; a big, powerful kid, obviously. It was clear that he was going to move on, and Den did well to take him to Sunderland when he went there.'

Denis Smith and Viv Busby took over at Roker Park in the summer of 1987 following Sunderland's first-ever relegation to the third flight. By that time, Crosby had left York and was coaching in Kuwait.

'I got offered a job with Bobby Campbell, who later managed Chelsea,' Malcolm explains. 'It was a good job financially, but I wanted the experience as well. I played quite a few first-team games – about a dozen or so – in the First Division out there. It was a lovely place and all the clubs had tennis courts, swimming pools, fantastic facilities, but the club I was at [Al Qadsia] was poorly run. Bobby got the sack, and after he left I was stuck there. Luckily, Geordie Armstrong, the ex-Arsenal player, was there at the time as well. He got a job at Al Salmiya and asked me to join him as his under-18 coach, and I absolutely loved it. We did really well. We won the league! Obviously, George had been a great player, and he was a top man, as well as the fittest bloke in the world, God rest his heart. [Armstrong collapsed and later died at the age of just 56 while coaching at Arsenal in 2000]. I had an offer of a new deal in Kuwait, but I met up with Den and Viv when "Buzza" opened a pub in Durham in 1988. Sunderland had just won promotion back to the Second Division. I had a chat with a couple of Sunderland directors that night, and that was essentially my interview for the youth-team job! So I went to Sunderland. I wanted to go to Sunderland.'

It is sometimes said that football is cyclical. Well, Crosby was now employed in the same role at Roker Park as Ray Yeoman – the man who gave him his first trial at a Football League club at Darlington in the late 1960s – had been at Sunderland back in 1973.

It would have been an exciting time to have worked with the Sunderland youth team. Gary Owers and Richard Ord had just broken into the first team, while the likes of Brian Atkinson, Kieron Brady, David Rush, and later, Michael Gray, Craig Russell and Martin Smith were coming through.

'Yes, I had some really good kids and some good players at Sunderland,' Malcolm says. 'Brian Atkinson was local. He was a good professional, but he didn't like me to start with because he said that I made him train too hard! When I took over I told them that we would be training most afternoons, and Atky replied, "We never did that with Chris McMenemy [the previous Sunderland youth team coach]!" I said, "Well, I'm not Chris McMenemy!" Four months down the line, he told me that I was right.

'David Rush came out of Notts County. He was unhappy there. He was just non-stop. I used to think, "How does he not stop running?" He would wear centre-halves out. They just couldn't handle him.

'Mickey Gray was the other one. He came to us from Manchester United after he had been released. [Gray was a young left-winger during his spell at Old Trafford – but he was born in the same school year as Ryan Giggs.] He was a great player for Sunderland, as we know.

'Even the ones that didn't make it to the top as professionals were top lads: players like Warren Hawke, who ended up in Scotland with Greenock Morton and Berwick Rangers; Paul Williams, who was such a good athlete; and Anthony Smith at left-back.

'The sad one was Kieron Brady. He had so much talent. If he looks back, he would probably say that he wished he had been more professional, because he wasn't a good professional, unfortunately. I once saw Kieron playing for the youths at York. Sunderland kicked off, little Stephen Brodie rolled the ball to him, and he flicked it up and volleyed it over the goalkeeper from the halfway line. He was such a wonderful talent. He could have been one of the best players to have played in this country. He really could, he had that much ability.'

Kieron Brady remains a cult hero among Sunderland fans of a certain age. Anybody who watched the team in the early 1990s will have their own personal memories of him, such as Crosby's above. My own particular favourite was seeing him nonchalantly flick the ball over his head with the back of his heel before bringing it to rest on his knee at Bradford City when Sunderland were awarded a throw-in during an exciting late surge into the playoffs in March 1990. He scored the only goal of the game that day too, and was just as brilliant three days later at Bramall Lane when he starred in a 3-1 win over promotion-bound Sheffield United. Most famous of all was another man-of-the-match display from him at home against West Ham United in a 4-3 win at Roker Park the week before the Bradford game.

Former Sunderland captain Michael Gray has since described Brady as the most talented footballer he ever played with. However, the Republic of Ireland youth and under-21 international only played for Sunderland 40 times in four years. His short career was cruelly cut short due to a rare vascular condition in his right leg. He was forced to retire at the age of just 22.

'Kieron had to finish and it was terrible,' Malcolm recalls. 'He took us to the High Court because of that, and it was the worst thing I have ever had to go through. It was all very sad.'

Brady lost his case for clinical negligence against Sunderland AFC. A recovering alcoholic, he is now highly respected for his work regarding anti-discrimination and equality matters, alcohol awareness, and mental health. He also had a part to play in the 1992 FA Cup run, albeit far less of one than he could have done. More on that story later . . .

'The only thing we didn't have at Sunderland at that time was a decent training facility,' Malcolm says, looking back to when he joined the club in 1988. 'It was actually embarrassing, but that was the case at most clubs back then. We trained near Cleadon village, and we only had a couple of pitches, so anybody could just walk in and have a kick-about while we were there. We later had the place in Whitburn, but we still only had two pitches, although there were changing rooms there. When you look at the facilities around today, I don't think players know how lucky they are, they really don't. Sometimes I think they're spoilt nowadays, and I worry that some take it for granted and don't appreciate what they have. We had to clean the bath, clean boots, put the kit out. It wasn't a bad thing at all. It gave us a bit of character, really.

'It was just another time,' Malcolm adds. 'Den had Viv, physiotherapist Steve Smelt, and me. That was it. I can't even remember if we had a kit man! I think I used to do the kit with the youth kids. They sorted it all out, and then I brought it back to a lady who washed it. Then we put it out together. So everything has changed massively; players walk into a training ground today and everything has been done for them. Sunderland's facilities now are first class.

'Den and Viv created a very good atmosphere. Buzza would take most of the training sessions; they would be lively and bright, and players used to enjoy all of that. Denis was a bit more serious; he would do the functional work with the team. The two of them worked very well together, and they were great with me. I would tell them all about the really good young lads who were too good for the youths; a couple of good examples would be Brian Atkinson and Kieron Brady. I would make a recommendation, but they already knew about them, really. A lot of that was due to Jim Morrow, the youth development officer. He was very good at his job, and he was the one who was out there looking at them. We brought some really good players through at that time, actually.'

Brian Atkinson, Kieron Brady, and Warren Hawke had all broken into the Sunderland first-team squad by the time the club won promotion to the First Division in 1990 via the playoffs. David Rush was soon to follow as well.

'It was absolutely fantastic to see them all get a chance to play in the top division in the 1990–91 season,' Malcolm says. 'I remember the playoff final against Swindon Town at Wembley. Colin Calderwood smashed Gabbas after about a minute. It was a bad tackle, and nowadays he would be sent off straight away. Gabbas struggled the whole game as a result.

'As a team, we were awful that day,' Malcolm adds. 'Luckily, we still went up because of what they had been up to [Swindon Town were found guilty of financial irregularities that summer and were subsequently relegated], but it was always going to be hard for us, and I don't think Den was given enough money to get a better team together for the challenge we faced in the top division.

'Bob Murray [the Sunderland chairman] maybe had his reasons for it, but I think if he had put more money in and got some better players we could have stayed up. We signed Kevin Ball and Peter Davenport, but we needed four or five new signings to add to a team that had finished the previous season sixth in the Second Division. You see it now: whenever a team goes up, they have to spend fortunes on better players so they can compete. So that was hard on Den and Viv.'

Sunderland were relegated straight back down to the Second Division. Early in the following season, Denis Smith sold Marco Gabbiadini to Crystal Palace for £1.8 million. It allowed him to sign John Byrne – a player he had been after for a while – and Don Goodman. But Sunderland were stuck in the lower half of the table, and by the end of the year they had fallen into the bottom six. Viv Busby was released by the club in early December [Crosby briefly replaced him as first-team coach] and then following a 3-0 defeat at Oxford United a few days after Christmas, Denis Smith was sacked.

'I wasn't too happy about it at that time,' Malcolm remembers. 'Because what happened was I came in one morning after taking the reserves and Jim Morrow told me that Den wanted a word. He told me that Viv had left and I was now the first-team coach. I felt bad about that because if I had been Viv I might have thought I had something to do with it, and I had nothing to do with it. I didn't know what had gone on. After that, of course, Den and I didn't have too many games together before he was gone too. Our first match was Wolves away and we lost 1-0. We had two players sent off [John Byrne on six minutes and Gordon Armstrong on seven minutes], and the referee was an absolute joke. We then beat Leicester and Portsmouth, lost to Tranmere and, admittedly, we were awful at Oxford. That is when I was asked to take over. I found it all a bit strange after what Den had done for the club. We weren't even halfway through the season, and I felt he should have been given more time, really. When I look at that run of results again now, I don't think they look that bad, to be honest with you. Losing at Oxford was a bad result but, for me, it wasn't a sacking offence.

'So I wasn't too happy about it, and I didn't really want to stay. I didn't think we had been treated properly. We had been given five games together, and that wasn't really an opportunity for us in my view. I was a different type of coach to Buzza. I did more functional work. To this day, I think Sunderland should have given Den and me more time. We should have got at least ten games or so to work together.'

Crosby was appointed caretaker manager of Sunderland on 30 December 1991.

'I was 37 years old at the time and so for me to be put in the position of managing Sunderland was a big ask,' Malcolm says. 'But I was Sunderland daft, so what was I going to do?

'I am sure that Bob Murray had somebody in mind for the job. He was a very well organised chairman. I didn't think for one minute that I would be the manager on a permanent basis. It felt to me that I was just going to keep it warm for somebody, and I think that had I lost a couple of games at that time then he would have done something about it.

'Unfortunately for Bob I got off to such a good start that I think it put pressure on him, probably because the fans gave him that pressure.'

Malcolm adds with a smile, 'What was it again? Four wins from my first four games?

'I was manager of the month in my first month! I have a great little story about that to tell you. I have the commemorative Barclays Manager of the Month plate up on my wall, and one day one of my daughter's friends came over and asked me, "When did you work in the bank?" It was very funny.'

Sunderland's start to 1992 under Crosby was extraordinary. Barnsley were beaten 2-0 at Roker Park on New Year's Day, before Port Vale were defeated 3-0 at home three days later in the FA Cup – Brian Atkinson, Peter Davenport, and John Byrne scoring the goals. When Millwall were thrashed 6-2 the following Saturday, and promotion hopefuls Derby County were dismissed 2-1 at the Baseball Ground a week later, there was only going to be one place that the Barclays award was going to go.

'I brought Brian Atkinson into the side,' Malcolm says. 'That was the biggest change I made. What he did was give me energy. Atky was strong for a young player, and he had good ability; he could see things, he could break things down, he could pick a pass out. Paul Bracewell kept him right so it was good.

'Roger Jones came in as my assistant. Roger is a great fella, but he wasn't a coach. He did more administrative, office work, which meant that I could get out on the field. I was fortunate because I had a top professional in Paul Bracewell as captain, and basically he became like an assistant coach for me. I would go through everything with him. Brace was fantastic, both on and off the pitch. But I thought he was trying to do too much, running from one wing to the other when he played, so I told him to just stay in the middle of the pitch. He did that for me, and he found that he had more energy. He was a great player for me that season.'

Due to Sunderland's new £900,000 club record signing from West Bromwich Albion, Don Goodman, being Cup-tied, Crosby had to skilfully chop and change his team for the FA Cup matches, eventually settling on a 4–4–2 formation with John Byrne and Peter Davenport up front, and David Rush coming into the team on the right side of midfield. Goodman would always return to the action in the league games, and regularly produced the goods with 11 goals that season.

'I have to say that Don Goodman was brilliant with all the players during the FA Cup run,' Malcolm says. 'He was a great support to them all. Obviously, he was very disappointed not to be able to play, but he never once showed it, and that is all I could ask for from him. He was missing out on the packed house, and then coming back into the side for away matches at Grimsby, or somewhere like that, so it wasn't very easy for him. Don and Byrney were very good together too. They were a real handful for defences.

'But it worked out for us because Peter Davenport used to put everything he had into those FA Cup games for us, but then he didn't have that much left for the league games in between. Full credit to Peter. He really shone in those FA Cup games. He was more of a Premier League player, to be honest – clever, good movement, but probably not the most physical of lads – so when he played against those top division sides, he gave them big problems.'

A bad winter meant postponements galore in the early rounds of the FA Cup. Sunderland had to wait until early February to play Oxford United away in the fourth round.

'The weather was very bad for a while,' Malcolm remembers. 'The Oxford match was postponed a lot. We got down to Nottingham at one time and then had to turn back, but then we got it played. We didn't want to get knocked out down there. It was a big game for us, especially because of us getting beaten 3-0 at Christmas, and then Den getting the sack afterwards.

'I have to say, the players were fantastic that night. We organised ourselves well. We decided that if we won the toss, we would kick up the hill and against the slope. All these things get taken into account. We won 3-2 [John Byrne, Paul Hardyman, and Brian Atkinson scored], but it should have been 3-0. We were 3-0 up and we got caught twice when we took our foot off the gas in injury time. It was a great performance to go down there and win. It was a big win for us.'

Suddenly, Sunderland were in the fifth round of the FA Cup for the first time in 16 years. First Division West Ham United were to be the visitors to Roker Park, and the *Match of the Day* cameras were there for the first time since 1985. Cup fever was beginning to build . . .

'The first match against West Ham was played on an awful day,' Malcolm says. 'It was an awful game as well. The conditions made it like that.'

John Byrne equalised for Sunderland in the second half in a 1-1 draw that was played in exceptionally windy conditions. The goal earned a replay at Upton Park. It was to be there – 11 days later – that the FA Cup run really took off.

Byrne scored twice in the first half to put Sunderland 2-0 up. Two goals from Martin Allen drew West Ham level. But Tony Norman had a great game in goal, producing a tremendous one-handed save from Tim Breacker late in the second half, before Kieron Brady, on as a substitute, delivered a cross which was flicked on by Byrne for the onrushing David Rush to strike home and put the Rokerites through to the quarter-finals.

'What a game! Tony Norman was outstanding for us that night. He was absolutely fantastic. But for the lads to score three goals down at West Ham takes some doing as well. The players should take all the credit for it. It was a fabulous result,' Malcolm says.

The quarter-final draw took Sunderland to Chelsea on a Monday night. The match was shown live on Sky Sports in what became a forerunner to the *Monday Night Football* show which is now a regular occurrence in the satellite television sport schedule. The Blues were managed by Ian Porterfield, and had Bob Stokoe working as his chief scout in the north of England at the time. Clive Allen gave the home side the lead but, with just eight minutes remaining, Sunderland equalised. John Byrne's looping header from Paul Bracewell's cleverly lofted pass seemed to be in the air for about ten seconds before it dropped into the net. The away end – positioned about 50 yards behind the goal line at Stamford Bridge in those days – erupted as the goalscorer came over to celebrate with us.

'We were very good at Chelsea,' Malcolm says. 'That was the one game where I felt that we were really, really professional. I thought we controlled the game, but we were losing 1-0 for a long time until Byrney got us a deserved equaliser right at the end. It was another great result for us, and another tremendous performance by all the players.'

The 1-1 draw at Chelsea ensured an all-ticket replay at Roker Park. By this time the capacity at the old stadium had been significantly reduced to just over 26,000, but nobody who was there that night will ever forget it. It almost rivalled the Sunderland versus Manchester City FA Cup fifth-round replay in 1973 for atmosphere, celebration and volume. In terms of drama, it may just have pipped it!

An injury to Gary Bennett in the first match meant that Kevin Ball came into central defence to partner Anton Rogan. Otherwise, Sunderland were unchanged. Peter Davenport gave the home side a deserved first-half lead, but Chelsea's response was relentless and Tony Norman produced another man-of-the-match performance, sometimes helped by his woodwork, to keep the Rokerities in the lead as the second half went on and on. Eventually, the equaliser came, Dennis Wise poking the ball home with less than five minutes left. You could hear a pin drop in the Fulwell End.

Then, just as it seemed that our Cup dream might be dying, after all, Gordon Armstrong produced the goal of a lifetime, from Brian Atkinson's last-minute corner, to power a header past Dave Beasant into the Roker End net from the edge of the penalty box. Cue scenes of mass jubilation and a semi-final at Hillsborough against Norwich City.

'It was a great game,' Malcolm says. 'Chelsea were really on top in the second half, and had it gone into extra time you would have fancied them to win it. But that is when we got ourselves a little bit of luck. I say that for the following reasons: 1) we did well to get ourselves a corner; 2) we were going into extra time if we didn't score from it; and 3) to score a goal like that at that stage of a game is a real killer. Teams don't normally come back from that. That is what happened that night – it just totally killed Chelsea. It was a wonderful goal and it was all about the two of them, Atky and Gordon, practising and practising and practising after training,' Malcolm reveals. 'They used to do that corner all the time, and I would always say to them, "What are you two doing? You will never score from that! A header from the 18-yard line? No chance!" But they had the courage at that time in that game to do that. It was all down to them. It was just as they did it on the training ground, and it came off at a vital moment in a massive game. When it went in, it was just a *"Wow!"* moment, wasn't it? It was a truly, truly great goal.

'That night was very special. Old stadiums always seemed better than the modern ones when they were full for night games, and to win a match like that under the lights at Roker Park was just fantastic, it really was. That gave the players a big lift. We played a lot of night games, which always makes it feel like there is double the crowd anyway, but it was down to the players' mentality how we got those big results. I could only guide them. They were the ones that scored the goals, stopped the goals, and won the games. They will always get the credit when people ask me about it because I knew that we weren't a great team – but there was such a strong spirit, and so much energy.'

The FA Cup bandwagon kept rolling on. Sunderland had reached the semi-finals of the competition for the first time since 1973, and just like in 1973, the match would be played at Hillsborough.

But successive league defeats at home to Denis Smith's new club, Bristol City, and away at relegation-threatened Newcastle United, now under the leadership of the recently appointed Kevin Keegan, followed, and by the time Sunderland played Norwich City in the FA Cup semi-final the Rokerites were down to 21st in the Second Division table, only just above the drop zone themselves on account of a loss of form in the league and an abundance of games in hand.

'When you get involved in an FA Cup run like that it really affects your league performances because the players are mentally and physically drained,' Malcolm explains. 'I could see it, but I didn't have enough in the way of options to make massive changes. The players were good socialisers, that is for sure, but if you were to have looked through every team in that league at that time they would all have been the same. So maybe they could have recovered better, but sports science didn't exist back then. The players just found something extra in the FA Cup, that is the truth, and I think we paid the price for that a little bit in the league games, certainly those that immediately followed the Cup ties.'

The Sunderland players found something extra again in the FA Cup semi-final, defeating Norwich with a lovely well-worked move in the 34th minute involving David Rush and Brian Atkinson down the right that resulted in a pinpoint cross which was finished off from close range by a header from John Byrne. It was the only goal of the game. Sunderland, incredibly, were going to Wembley again.

'Yes, that was another good goal: down the line, pull back, header,' Malcolm recalls with a smile on his face. 'Norwich were actually a really good team [the Canaries went on to finish third in the inaugural Premier League season 12 months later, after leading it for large parts of the campaign]. They had a really good strike force, but we hardly gave them a kick. It wasn't a great game, but then not many semi-finals are. When you go into a semi-final, you just have to be prepared to try to win it. Norwich hardly had a chance. It wasn't the best game in the world, but who cares if you are a Sunderland fan?

'The biggest disappointment was that due to the Hillsborough disaster a few years before, we weren't allowed to go back onto the pitch after we had won,' Malcolm adds. 'We were desperate to go back out because all the Sunderland fans were still there celebrating. Obviously, we totally understood the reasons, but it did take a little bit away from it.'

Two days short of the 19th anniversary of Sunderland's famous 2-1 FA Cup semi-final triumph over Arsenal in 1973, when Bob Stokoe was brought to tears on the pitch at Hillsborough, this was the moment when it all began to finally sink in for Crosby, the man who was still officially called 'the caretaker manager of Sunderland'.

'There were plenty of "pinch yourself" moments during that season, without a doubt, but probably the biggest pinch of them all would be the semi-final,' Malcolm says. 'To think that we had reached the FA Cup final at Wembley when most of the season we had been under pressure to just stay in the Second Division was incredible, really, and a fantastic achievement. The players were on their knees at times – at West Ham away and Chelsea at home, in particular – and how they ended up winning those games was a credit to them, it really was. But it was totally down to their individual characters and their collective character. I like to look back on it all and think that I set the team up well, but it is the players who do the hard work. They did it, and they deserve the credit. They always managed to find something extra in the Cup.'

Those same players now had to find something extra in the remaining ten Second Division fixtures. There was no doubt about it, Sunderland were now in a relegation battle as well as the FA Cup final. And, as a result of their Cup exploits, Sunderland now had to fulfil those remaining ten league fixtures in just 25 days – then prepare for the FA Cup final.

'The fixture list was relentless,' Malcolm says. 'We just didn't have the energy to compete, and I would also have been taking too big a risk if I had brought in some of the young kids to help us out, because we desperately needed to get results. Getting wins in those games became harder and harder and harder because of all that. We played nine league games in April alone – *nine!* [it was ten matches in total including the semi-final] – when you would normally play four, maybe five. But whoever I spoke to wouldn't want to talk to me about the next league game, it was all about the FA Cup, and that included my players. So that was difficult as well. The Cup had taken over, but you just can't stop the Cup taking over at a time like that because it just happens when you are involved in it. Everybody was thinking about Wembley, and the players were just like the fans, really. The fans weren't as excited about playing Cambridge United as they were when we played Chelsea. That's understandable, and the players were exactly the same. By that stage I just had to keep us up, and that became a very hard task, but there was nothing we could do about it because the league season had to finish before the FA Cup final. Those were the rules. Of course, no team would have to do that today.'

Equally unsettling to Crosby was the constant speculation about his own future. Despite leading the Rokerites to Wembley he was still the caretaker manager.

'Every day in the newspaper there were stories that somebody was coming in,' Malcolm recalls. 'I was trying to do the job, and I was reading that Tom, Dick or Harry was going to be the new manager next week, so that wasn't very helpful. It does bother you but, again, there is not much that you can do about it.'

Among those names regularly mentioned in connection with the Sunderland manager's job during Crosby's time as caretaker manager were Dave Bassett, Joe Jordan, Brian Little, Bryan Robson and Neil Warnock. In the end Sunderland won two, drew four, and lost four of their remaining league fixtures. They stayed up by five points, one point and two places above Newcastle.

'Luckily we just scraped through. In an ideal world, we would have won the FA Cup, and stayed up, and Newcastle would have got relegated! As it was, we both stayed up – just,' Malcolm says with a smile. 'Actually, I got to know Kevin Keegan very well later on. I worked for him when he was the England manager, and I went to Euro 2000 with him, and he is one of the best fellas I have ever met in football.'

On the morning of the penultimate league match of the campaign, away at Blackburn Rovers, Crosby was finally announced as Sunderland's new manager. It had taken Bob Murray four months to offer him the job, and it finally came less than a fortnight before the FA Cup final. The sting in the tale for the 17th permanent boss in Sunderland's history – Jack Ross is number 35 by the way! – was that the contract was only for one year.

'When I was offered a one-year contract, everybody close to me told me to tell Bob Murray to clear off,' Malcolm remembers. 'But I loved being at Sunderland. I was a Sunderland supporter through and through. So I think he knew that I wasn't going to turn it down.

'I didn't think the way Bob did it was very good,' Malcolm continues. 'Obviously, I was absolutely delighted to be named as Sunderland manager, but at the same time we hadn't discussed a contract or anything like that. So the whole thing was a bit strange. It wasn't done fantastically well, to be honest with you. I think it should have been done up in Sunderland. I would really liked to have been announced at Roker Park rather than in some hotel near Blackburn!

'I have got nothing against Bob. I don't think he wanted me as manager when he first gave me the job, and I understand that, when I look back, because I was only 37 years old, and he obviously had another manager in mind. But if you get those kind of results like we did, and you get to Wembley like we did, then there is going to be a lot of pressure to appoint me – and that is what happened. I just feel that I was made the manager just because we got to Wembley. I know that was quite a good achievement in itself, but was it what the chairman really wanted? Only he would be able to tell you that. Personally, I think that it probably wasn't what he wanted, if the truth is known.

'Hey, it's all history now – but it's good for a book!'

The newly announced Sunderland manager now had an FA Cup final to prepare for in ten days' time.

He had been dealt a severe blow when popular right-back John Kay, an ever-present in the FA Cup run, was badly injured in the league run-in against Swindon Town and subsequently ruled out of playing in the big occasion. As well as facing a dilemma regarding the absence of Kay in his defence against Liverpool, Crosby was now also given the added headache of who to replace him with at right-back. He decided to give the number-two shirt to midfielder Gary Owers, who had only just returned to the first team himself after a three-month injury lay-off. The fit-again Gary Bennett was selected to partner Kevin Ball in central defence, with Anton Rogan moving over to left-back. This meant that there was to be no place in the starting line-up for one ever-present member of the FA Cup team.

'Paul Hardyman had a good spell for me, but then he took a dip before the FA Cup final, and that was one of the reasons why I left him out, which was a hard decision to make,' Malcolm says. 'I played Anton Rogan at left-back. I possibly made a mistake by not playing him at centre-back, but I thought that I was going to need somebody to get forward as well as defend against Liverpool – and Kevin Ball wasn't great at going forward; he was a centre-half or a sitting midfield player.

'So that was the reason why I went the way I went,' Malcolm adds. 'I thought Bally and Benno had decent pace between the two of them, and I thought they might be able to do all right handling Dean Saunders and Ian Rush. I also thought that both Gary Owers and Rogey could bomb along for me from the full-back positions, and Owersy did that in the first half and he did it really well.

'The other option would have been to play Bally at right-back and leave Owersy out, and then play Benno and Rogey as centre-backs, and Paul Hardyman at left-back. It was hard on Paul

Hardyman. He came on later in the game, of course, and so he got a taste of it, but it was very disappointing for him, obviously. Then again, as the manager, I had to make that decision.'

The midfield, attack and goalkeeper all picked themselves.

But the decision about which players were to be on the Sunderland bench – Paul Hardyman and Warren Hawke were selected on the day – is another case of what might have been regarding the hugely talented one.

'There is another sad story regarding Kieron Brady and the FA Cup final,' Malcolm reveals. 'He had been a substitute in almost every game in the Cup, but when we got to the final Steve Smelt told me that Kieron had put something like six pounds on in weight. Kieron was prone to being a bit heavy, and so about a month before the final I pulled him into the office and I told him, "Lose at least half of it and you will either be playing at Wembley or you will be on the bench." Do you know what happened? He put more weight on! If you're six pounds overweight it will show on a footballer, but if you put even more on it is definitely going to show. That is the reason I didn't put him on the bench. That told me what sort of professional Kieron was. I had actually told him that he would be playing in the FA Cup final if he lost some weight, and without a doubt he would have come on had he been in anything like decent shape. So that was very sad. He had been given a wonderful opportunity in advance, but he just didn't bother, and that was such a shame.'

Sunderland lined up as follows: Tony Norman; Gary Owers, Kevin Ball, Gary Bennett, Anton Rogan; David Rush, Brian Atkinson, Paul Bracewell, Gordon Armstrong; John Byrne, Peter Davenport.

The Liverpool team was: Bruce Grobbelaar; Rob Jones, Steve Nicol, Mark Wright, David Burrows; Ray Houghton, Jan

Molby, Michael Thomas, Steve McManaman; Dean Saunders, Ian Rush.

The attendance was 79,544. The best chance of the first half fell to John Byrne, a player who had scored in every round of the FA Cup so far and was on the verge of equalling a record that was last achieved by Peter Osgood of Chelsea in 1970 if he could find the net again in the final. He was Sunderland's sure-fire bet in front of goal that season, but when his chance came at Wembley, in front of goal, early in the first half, he inexplicably mis-kicked!

'John Byrne was so talented,' Malcolm says. 'He should have done even better with his talent and played at an even higher level, in my opinion. He had a great run in the FA Cup with us and, without doubt, that FA Cup run is what he is best remembered for – he scored in every round and when he missed that sitter in the final in front of goal that would have been it! Whether we had gone on to win the Cup or not, he would have made history had that gone in. Incredibly, it was probably the easiest chance of them all that he had as well!'

Liverpool switched Steve McManaman from the left-flank to the right-flank at half-time, and the decision to do so was to prove critical.

'I would say that we were probably the better side in the first half,' Malcolm says. 'My last words in the dressing room to the team at half-time just before they went back out were: "Go ten minutes, and you'll win this game." I felt that if we could get Liverpool frustrated, and stay in the game, then we could win it on a set-play, or whatever.

'Then within about a minute or so we were a goal down!'

It was McManaman who created the opening goal, from down the right wing, and Michael Thomas who struck a superb volley that flew past Tony Norman to give Liverpool the lead. I was sitting right behind him when he hit it!

'Once they went 1-0 up it was very hard for us; you could see a release from Liverpool as soon as they had scored,' Malcolm reflects. 'There was a better team on the pitch against us and when they went 2-0 up it was even harder.'

When Ian Rush scored the second goal on 68 minutes it was essentially game over.

'Whatever team I had put out that day it would have been hard for us to win the game,' Malcolm admits. 'The players did fantastically well to get there in the first place, and that is what should be remembered, really. If we had got beaten 6-0 by Liverpool in the final, I couldn't have had a go at them, because getting there in the first place was such a miraculous achievement.'

With the 1991–92 season finally completed, and his one-year managerial contract signed, Crosby could now look forward to the forthcoming campaign.

However, he was to get an early taste of what was to come five minutes into a summer break on a Spanish island.

'Fair play to Bob Murray,' Malcolm says. 'He said that we could go anywhere in the world after the FA Cup final. So I put it to the players, and they all wanted to go to bloody Magaluf, where everybody goes.

'On the first night out there, John Byrne, who I had known at York when he was just a kid, pipes up – after a few drinks – that he wants to leave the club. When we got back to Sunderland he told me that he could go to Millwall and join Mick McCarthy. He was gone by September. I think we got £250,000 for him.

'Paul Hardyman also decided to go and play for Bristol Rovers,' Malcolm adds. 'I said to him, "Do you know the size of this club compared to Bristol Rovers?" But he was from that part of the country and he just made up his mind to go. He later told me it was the worst decision of his career.'

But the biggest loss of all for Crosby was his captain, Paul Bracewell.

'The situation with Brace was a really frustrating one for me,' Malcolm explains. 'He wanted two more years at Sunderland, and I wanted to give him two more years, but Bob Murray wouldn't do it. He offered him one year. Then Kevin Keegan offered him two years at Newcastle, so he went there. You only have to look at the club records to see how big a loss he was for us. I never replaced him. But look what happened to him at Newcastle – he was their captain, and their best player, and they won the Championship. He spent three seasons there before, ironically, he came back to Sunderland! To this day I don't know why the chairman dug his heels in about it. If you have appointed a new manager then surely you should support him? I wasn't asking the earth to offer a two-year contract to Paul Bracewell, our FA Cup final captain, who everybody loved at Roker Park. I thought the world of him, and he wanted to stay, and letting him go to Newcastle backfired. I had to get on with it, but he was a big miss. I wanted him to be part of my staff as well as a key player.'

The issue of one-year contracts was also causing problems for Crosby in his attempts to create the backroom staff he wanted.

'It was disappointing and frustrating for me to only be offered a one-year contract because it is not easy to plan when you have only got a year,' Malcolm explains. 'I would have liked to have been given two years, and I think I would have made a good job of it because I would have been able to have brought the right people in to join me. Unfortunately, it is hard to bring the right people in on one-year contracts, because a year is no good to anybody. I really wanted to bring George Armstrong in as my assistant. The reason I couldn't get him was because I couldn't get him a two-year contract. Understandably, he said that he couldn't move from Arsenal, where he had been for years, up to Sunderland on a one-year contract. So it was very difficult. I knew I needed the right man with me and George Armstrong was that man. I think the players would have respected George, and we would have been much better off as a result, but I didn't get the support to bring him in.

'I brought Bobby Ferguson in, which was a big mistake. He was a good coach, but he was a lot older than George, and he didn't have the energy any more.

'I made another big mistake in bringing Terry Butcher in. Bobby Ferguson wanted me to bring him in as a player. [Butcher replaced Crosby as Sunderland manager in February 1993.] My other frustration was that I wanted to change the team after the FA Cup final, and I had a chance to do that when I received a great offer for Gordon Armstrong from Ian Branfoot at Southampton for something like £750,000. I told Bob Murray that I would like to let Gordon go – not only for Sunderland, but also for Gordon to have an opportunity to play in the Premier League. But Bob kept putting the price up and up, and in the end Ian told me he just couldn't pay that much. So that stopped me bringing in two or three players that I really wanted – people with experience, such as Danny Wilson at Sheffield Wednesday, who I hoped I could bring in as a replacement for Paul Bracewell.

'I wasn't really allowed to make too many changes,' Malcolm adds. 'We weren't a great team – our league position told you that – and I needed to bring in three or four players to liven the place up a bit, but unfortunately that didn't happen. You live and die by your recruitment. I needed to have much more money to spend to make a difference, but it wasn't there for me to spend. The example I gave about Gordon Armstrong and Southampton is a good one. I think it would have done him the world of good and it would have done Sunderland the world of good as well.

'I did bring in John Colquhoun, who had played for Hearts. He was doing fantastic for me, but then he got a really bad back injury, and was out injured. I also signed Shaun Cunnington, who had been a top player at Grimsby Town. I paid decent money for him, and the chairman backed me on it, but then this lad who never got injured was now out injured as well. Having said that, in the end, he was the one who got a vital couple of goals that kept Sunderland up.'

By that time, Crosby was long gone. He was sacked as Sunderland manager on the first day of February 1993. It was less than nine months since he had led the team out at Wembley. Ironically, his last match in charge of the team – an away fixture due to take place at Tranmere Rovers – was postponed. The Pools Panel selected a home win! The decision to sack Crosby afterwards became part of football folklore.

'After Tranmere was called off, I went to Crewe to watch another game,' Malcolm says. 'Ironically, Terry Butcher was the man who dropped me off at the station. It took me about six hours to get back home afterwards. I think I eventually got back to the training ground at about 11.30 at night. Then, on the Monday, I got the sack. So I think the board must have taken the Pools Panel verdict quite literally!'

Sunderland were placed 16th in the Second Division at the time. They had gone out of the FA Cup at the fourth-round stage at Sheffield Wednesday after an injury-time mistake by Tony Norman had gifted Mark Bright the winner the week before.

Within days of Crosby's sacking, Terry Butcher was appointed as Sunderland's player-manager.

'The last thing I wanted was for Sunderland to end up in a relegation battle, but bringing Terry Butcher in as player-manager was a big risk as far as I could see,' Malcolm says. 'The rest is history, isn't it? He nearly got them relegated. They were so close to going down that season. They went to Notts County needing a win to make sure they stayed up and lost 3-1, and only results elsewhere saved them.'

'It nearly ended in disaster,' Malcolm adds. 'He just got it totally wrong, and that disappoints me because when I was in charge I tried to do things the right way, and that was very hard at that time because every day I was fighting against what Kevin Keegan was able to do up at Newcastle.'

It is now almost 50 years since Crosby left South Shields to attend that two-week trial at Aldershot, with the prospect of a career in marine engineering waiting for him at home. But when he got his chance he decided to give football a go instead. In the 25 years since Crosby lost his job at Roker Park he has built up an impressive curriculum vitae as a coach. When you add his time spent at York City, Sunderland and the two Kuwaiti clubs to the list, the 64-year-old has now worked in a coaching capacity at no fewer than 14 clubs, as well with England under Kevin Keegan.

There was also one brief stint as manager of Gateshead in 2015 (under the chairmanship of his good friend and former Sunderland vice-chairman Graham Wood); the only time he has managed a club on a permanent basis since his time at Sunderland.

Importantly, he has not lost his sense of humour either: 'The only thing that really annoys me about what happened at Sunderland after all these years is that had I known that I was going to get the sack after a Pools Panel result I wouldn't have bothered going to bloody Crewe that day, that is for sure!'

EPILOGUE

Sometimes football clubs enter periods which can only be described as drift and decline. Like a glacier inching towards the ocean, the speed of movement might not be obvious but the direction of travel is. Sunderland had been in decline since the latter stages of Denis Smith's reign, and neither his sacking nor a subsequent FA Cup final appearance under new boss Malcolm Crosby could disguise or alter the underlying trend. That drift and decline accelerated and gathered pace, first under Terry Butcher and then under Mick Buxton, until the point was reached where suddenly the club was on the precipice and looking all but certain to drop into the third tier of the game.

In 1987 Crosby's predecessor, Denis Smith, had taken Sunderland out of the Third Division and up to the top flight with a commanding and demanding managerial style which left no one in any doubt who was in charge at Roker Park.

In 1995, with the club staring into the abyss again, the manager who would save them from the drop and take them back to the top division was a man of similarly strong and single-minded character.

4

Peter Reid is the longest-serving Sunderland manager of the past 60 years.

His time at the club saw immense change off the pitch – Sunderland AFC moving home for the first time in almost a century and swapping the outdated Charlie Hurley training ground for the state-of-the-art Academy of Light.

On the pitch, the changes were no less seismic - unlikely escape from relegation, a promotion, relegation, epic playoff final, record-breaking points total, two superlative seasons in the top flight, another relegation escape and a surprisingly swift sacking, weeks into a new campaign.

Dull it wasn't!

More than two decades on from his appointment, the Reid era is still talked about with sentiment by fans who recall a time when Quinny and SuperKev's irresistible double-act thrilled them.

There were dark times too, as Reid acknowledges: times when he made unpopular decisions, struggled against relegation or suffered personal abuse.

But even his harshest critics would accept he gave Sunderland fans many of their happiest moments and since he was shown the door in 2002, the club has not gone close to reaching the heights he took them to.

PETER REID

SUNDERLAND MANAGER
29 MARCH 1995 TO 7 OCTOBER 2002
MEETS GRAEME ANDERSON

'I think you need stability at a football club, that's the key,' says the ex-Sunderland manager as we discuss why a club of such size, support and tradition has underperformed so much in the living memory of most. 'If you're going to reach your potential, if you're going to have the best chance of long-term success, I'd say you need a settled, focused club at board level, and you need to find yourself a good manager and stick with him. If you look at all the top clubs, they all have that stability in one form or another. Now, you can quote Chelsea at me [14 managers in the last ten years], but they've got the money to buy in the best managers and best players, so they're different. Watford would be a better shout against what I'm saying [13 managers in 10 years], but they obviously have stability and effectiveness within the club and boardroom. Now, I know there's no guarantees, of course. I'm not saying it works every time – you could even point me in the direction of Ellis Short, who owned Sunderland for a decade and didn't make it happen long-term – but I'd point at too many different managers and maybe not enough focus on where the money was going.

'Getting back to what I was saying, I think if you ignore the exceptional cases, then nine times out of ten, if you've got a club where the owner, the board and the manager are focused on what they want to achieve and are all pulling together, then you've always got a chance.'

As usual when Reid gets deep into discussing football, he is animated, enthusiastic, words flowing out of him as he considers a footballing conundrum. This is what it used to be like in the Charlie Hurley training ground 20 years ago when I'd go down for the *Sunderland Echo*'s morning press conference and walk into the middle of a full-scale and usually noisy debate: 'Now he *was* a player,' (Sacko); 'Not very quick though,' (Heath); 'Didn't need to be!' (Sacko); 'Never rated him,' '(Reid); '*WHAT?!?*'; 'I never rated him – a bit lightweight for me,'; '*LIGHTWEIGHT!?!*' . . .

And so it would go on, often in language which I'll tone down for this chapter, with others sometimes dragged into the debate (Pop Robson; Ricky Sbragia) before it was time to head out for training. Passion for football hung in the air and dripped off the walls in the old training ground in that era – be it playing it, talking about it or planning it. And that enthusiasm and fascination for it remains undimmed in Reid today.

On this occasion we'd been talking about the takeover of Sunderland AFC by new owner Stewart Donald and the challenge of steering the Black Cats out of the third tier of English football. Stability and unity were the keys from Reid's perspective – qualities that had been in short supply when relegation to the old Third Division was memorably avoided in Reid's first seven games in charge. After that unlikely survival at the death of the 1994–95 season, Reid and Sunderland embarked on a rollercoaster run of largely ups, sometimes downs, which finally hit the buffers, for the manager at least, barely seven games into the 2002–03 Premier League campaign.

Sunderland had struggled as a side for over a year before the axe fell, but when it did, it fell at a surprising time, the Black Cats having negotiated a difficult start with a set of winnable fixtures ahead and not even in the bottom three at the time.

'It was disappointing the way it ended and I'm not going to say that it doesn't hurt you to be sacked,' admits Reid. 'But I came to terms with that a long time ago and I prefer to think of the good times.

'There were a hell of a lot of them.

'It was a big chunk of my life, and for a lot of it it was a great time and an amazing experience – and I think we can look back with a bit of pride on what was achieved. I came in when Sunderland were seven games away from going into the Third Division and I kept them from going down. I left when they were fourth bottom in the Premier League, with plenty of time to stay up. So from that point of view, I think it was a good run. For long spells everyone was working together and a whole load of people contributed to the successes we had – which were plenty.'

He asks when the last time was that Sunderland finished higher than the two seventh places managed in the top flight between 1999 and 2001. Not since 1955 comes the answer – when they finished fourth, during manger Bill Murray's 18-year reign. 'Well, maybe that says something about my point about stability,' he replies.

We are talking in the bar of the Gosforth Park hotel in Newcastle – enemy territory you might think for the longest-serving Sunderland manager of the past half-century and more. It proves to be anything but though. Reid, like Sir Bobby Robson – two men who were in opposite dugouts for several titanic Tyne–Wear derbies at the turn of the century – is a figure whose appeal has largely crossed the north-east divide over the years. As the open, airy bar fills up over the course of a warm afternoon, the distinctive Liverpudlian attracts smiles and nods, and the occasional double-take, but no one bothers him. Intermittently, an autograph is asked for.

'I never had a problem with Newcastle supporters,' he shrugs, with a smile. 'I used to get loads of stick and all that "Monkey's Heed" stuff. I still do. But, to be fair to them, they're great to me, they love to give me stick but they respect the fact I can take it with good humour. They're passionate about their football, just like Sunderland fans are, and that's what makes the derbies such great occasions.'

We're meeting at the hotel because Reid is taking part in a charity fundraising night there for Grainger Park FC Juniors – a favour he's doing for former England teammate Steve Hodge, who has connections with the club. The night will bring together three of Sir Bobby's 1986 World Cup squad – Reid, Hodge and Peter Shilton – in the hotel's packed function room. Only, unfortunately, Reid had forgotten about the charity night, which is why instead of flying from Dubai to Manchester and heading to London the next day as planned, he has flown in and diverted himself via the north-east. It is a hell of a schedule to put himself through, but the thought of backing out of the event never crossed his mind: 'Well, I couldn't leave them having to put up with Shilts, could I?' he laughs. 'He's the most boring man in football!'

Having flown in from the Middle East that morning and driven up to Newcastle, Reid will take part in the function and then, around midnight with the event winding down, drive through the night to London for his next-day appointment. It's an impressive show of stamina and determination from a man who turned 62 on 20 June 2018.

But then, those were attributes Reid had in abundance throughout his playing and managerial career – nowhere more so than at Sunderland, where his approach to the gaffer's job was pretty much 24/7. When he first arrived at the club, with just a handful of games left to stop the club being relegated, that's the way it had to be.

'Taking the job, a bit like leaving it, happened pretty quickly,' says Reid. 'I'd met one of the Sunderland directors, Graham Wood, in Sheffield after a friend, the journalist Paul Hetherington, got in touch with me to see if I'd be interested in taking on the club. Graham was representing John Featherstone because, if you remember, Bob Murray was not technically in charge any more having stood down as chairman, even though in reality he was pulling the strings behind the scenes and was obviously the power behind things. I took the job and just threw myself into it. I only had a couple of days to my first game, so it was all about making a quick impact, any impact.'

That first matchday, not without irony, was 1 April 1995: Sunderland v Dave Bassett's promotion-chasing Sheffield United. Only fools, or Sunderland fans, had been rushing into Roker Park in the difficult months leading up to the game. The Rokermen had been sleepwalking towards the drop since before Christmas, with the pace accelerated by a run of three points taken from 21, which led to the resignation of Mick Buxton. But it was not just six defeats in seven which hurt the faithful, it was the nature of the losses, with the team as dull and dour and lacking in charisma as its newly departed, flat-capped boss.

Reid though, refreshed by an 18-month break from management and full of enthusiasm, saw hope: 'I came in and I just remember having a look at the squad in that first training session and thinking, "Not bad." I didn't know where I was going to get a goal from, but I thought, "Not bad" – in terms of first looking at it.

'I knew it was a difficult gig. That was obvious through looking at the results previously and the fixtures we had. They were horrendous from the start: Sheffield United looked good for promotion, they were bombing on; Derby County were bombing on; West Brom were solid; Bolton were bombing on. I think we had three of the top six in those seven games, and no form at all.'

Reid lost no time looking at ways he might make a difference in the time given to him. He held press conferences issuing rallying cries to fans, insisting they had their part to play, urging them to keep the team going, pleading that they give everything from the terraces. But his primary focus was on his players.

'I spoke to the staff who remained after Mick left – Trevor Hartley, the chief coach; Ian Ross, the reserve-team coach – and that helped give me insights,' he says. 'I also had a good chat with John Cooke, the kit man, who was still a young lad then and who I'd known from our playing days. He said something like there had been no shortage of training on the training ground – working hard, running their backsides off. Mick Buxton was under extreme pressure, so I don't blame him for doing that, but I thought, "There's seven games left, they're already fit, I'm going to go short and sharp." I thought everything's going to be small-sided games, everything's going to be fun, everything's going to be bright and breezy. Sod doom and gloom.'

But if Reid was consciously looking to change Sunderland, Sunderland accidentally changed him from his very first game at the club. It was the game he ceased to be a tracksuit manager. Not a soul noticed – perhaps unsurprisingly given the enormity of that first match against the high-flying Blades and the memorable way it was decided by a last-minute goal which the Fulwell End seemed to suck into the net.

But Reid explains: 'Before the game I got asked to say something to the supporters in the Roker Suite. That was what was expected of you in those days and I thought, "Yeah,

I'm the new manager, I'll do that." John Featherstone was still chairman at the time, Cathy Kerr head of corporate, and they asked me to go through. I went in and afterwards I got word that Bob Murray wanted to see me. That was actually the first time I'd met him. I always remember, I had my blazer on because I'd been in the Roker Suite and Bob offered me a glass of wine and I said no, because I needed to get changed. But Bob persuaded me and we stayed and we talked and then all of a sudden I thought, "What time is it?" And I looked at my watch and, bloody hell, it was quarter to three! So, *bumph*, drink down, ran downstairs, gave a talk to the players, didn't have time to change, so went out to the dugout as I was, and we've only gone and won the game!

'So afterwards, you know how it is, I thought, "Right, we've won . . . I'm going to keep wearing this blazer and tie! And that's why, from then on, I always wore a collar and tie for a game. Amazing, really, how things happen. You look back at every photograph of me at a game in the dugout before that and I'm wearing a tracksuit, because that's what I was most comfortable with – that changed on day one at Sunderland.'

As Reid stood in the dugout, I was standing on the Fulwell End – my last season as a news reporter before moving into sport full time. I vividly remember Reid coming out in that checky jacket and the great roar from the crowd as he acknowledged the fans, fists clenched. It was similar to the black and white checky jacket his great friend and former England teammate Bryan Robson had worn when unveiled as Middlesbrough manager a year previously and left me wondering if this was the new football-manager fashion.

'Brown and white,' he firmly points out. 'It was brown and white. Black and white at Roker Park? Come on, Graeme, even I'm not that thick!'

Sartorial switches aside, it was largely the same old limited Sunderland performance on the day but the crowd, all 17,259 of them, were bursting with noise and clamour, and there was a real spirit of determination from players facing opposition which would have swept them aside on previous form.

'I always remember the atmosphere in the crowd was fantastic for that first game,' Reid says. 'I'd played in front of 50,000 there in a league game for Bolton in 1976 so I knew all about the Roker Roar, and that first game was all the diehard fans giving their all. I got the players set up – I told them they all knew their game, the way we were going to play. I just said, "When they get it, be in their faces; and when we get it, try to play."'

His players performed above themselves, but that only meant the two sides cancelled each other out. The game was headed for a draw – a point not really good enough – when the new manager made a late substitution.

'It was a nothing game, and I knew Craig Russell had pace, and I thought I had to at least try it, so I got him stripped and asked him to get me a goal with 20 minutes to go. He went on and he was really on his game, and I was just hoping for someone to put it into the left-hand channel for him. Then it happened: a great ball to him, and he chipped a shot just under the crossbar, and we were off.'

What he doesn't mention is that Russell had to wait until the 90th minute and Roker hearts were sinking, just as the striker moved to lift that ball over Sheffield keeper Alan Kelly. I can remember many special Sunderland moments in games under Reid's long tenure but that was the first of them, observed from the terrace rather than the press box, when time seems to slow, and the crowd is silent, the eye unable to calculate whether the ball is dropping over or under the bar.

And then it was in the net.

Time restarted, huge roar, crowd go mad, laughter, joy, final whistle and ecstatic supporters pouring out of the ground daring to dream.

Reid was no fool, though – it had been a desperately close-run thing.

He kept on tinkering in the games ahead, kept on keeping the mood light but the message decisive.

'You don't have time to do much in such a short space of time, so I just wanted to be positive and clear from the start, offer leadership and be strong,' he says. 'When I first got there, our skipper Gary Bennett was injured but playing through it and then, after my third game, he said he was struggling but would have a late fitness test and try to make it. And I said, "No you're not. You're out until you're fit again, and there's the teamsheet there!" That wasn't anything against Benno. I just wanted to show I was in charge, being decisive, not making a decision at the last minute. That, and the fact I'd seen Richard Ord in training, really liked the look of the kid, and wanted to see how a central defensive partnership with Andy Melville would work! But little things like that decision to leave the skipper out sends a message to the players that you're in charge and you're not messing around.

'I remember in my second game – a win over Jim Smith's Derby County, who had also been going well – I acted firmly with a couple of players. Our big striker Brett Angell ran off the pitch during the game and I followed him into the dressing room to see what the matter was, and he explained his contact lens had come out.

'*Contact lens out?!*

'I chased him back out of the tunnel and I kept on driving it home to the players in those games that they had to battle every inch of the way, no excuses. Brett couldn't run and he had no physicality – he was a smashing lad but he was no use to us. The same game, I substituted Steve Agnew – I thought he'd ducked out of a tackle, so I hauled him off. He was a good player, Aggers, and a good pro, but I was sending out a message that if I even thought you were ducking out of a challenge, you'd be off. That was just another way of trying to get the players thinking positive. I was looking for effect, effect, effect.'

By the time what was to become the long-term central defensive partnership of Ord and Melville came together in a match against Bolton Wanderers, Sunderland had beaten Derby with a Kevin Ball goal and taken a point from Luton Town, thanks to a strike from former Hatter, Phil Gray. The Bolton game ended in defeat but in the very next match, a relegation six-pointer against Swindon Town, Martin Smith smashed home a volley in front of the Roker End to seal a vital win which finally made survival likely.

'Smithy scored a lot of the goals at the back end of that season,' says Reid. 'He had a great left peg.'

Safety was officially secured in the next match, a 1-1 draw at Burnley in which the away fans turned up in their droves, delaying kick-off, and the season ended with a 2-2 draw against West Brom in front of an ebullient Roker Park crowd. Skilful winger Martin Smith, the most promising young player in the squad, scored in all of the last three games.

But Reid says, 'The Swindon goal – that was the one. That was the one where we knew we weren't going down; that was the one that got me the job; and, if I'm ever asked what was the most important goal scored in my time at the club, that's always the one I point to. Without that goal and that win, we might not have stayed up. And if we hadn't stayed up, I doubt I would have had a job at the club the following season.

'On top of that, the stadium wouldn't have been built. Bob wouldn't have floated the club, he wouldn't have returned to take charge – everything would have been different.'

Murray might argue that he would eventually have built the new ground at some stage. But what is undeniable is that relegation would certainly have delayed it and might have reduced the scale of the build. That last-day Albion draw underlined what Reid knew already: the team needed strengthening. The challenge was to find a transfer budget, and that led to Reid's very own Kevin Keegan 'it's not like it said in the brochure' moment, when he threatened to walk if money promised wasn't forthcoming.

He had managed to get his former Everton teammate Paul Bracewell from Newcastle United for a bargain £50,000 – 'what a signing that was for us' – while relegated Burnley's promising young striker John Mullin had been picked up for £125,000. But Reid he knew he needed an experienced, capable goalscorer if the club was to progress. A summer of frustration trying to get money from the board reached breaking point during a middling start to the new season, which brought 12 points from the first ten games. Reid told the board he'd had enough.

'I'd signed a contract that would give me £1 million to spend on players if I kept Sunderland up, but then I couldn't get the money,' he says. 'It dragged on for a long time, and then in a board meeting I remember throwing the keys to my company car across the table and saying, "I'm off." I think it was John Fickling who tried to calm the situation down, asking me to wait a minute. He said I couldn't just leave like that but I said I could, "I'm off – I'll leave the car, get the train home, and that will be that." He got on the phone to Bob Murray, and in the end I was able to get the money to go out and get the striker I wanted. But I was serious about walking away because I felt at the time we really needed the dough if we were going to do anything. The squad was showing it was good enough now to stop up, but we need strengthening if we were to have a hope of going up.'

If Reid was prepared to be ruthless in the boardroom, it was the same in the backroom too, where huge changes took place to the staff within a few months of his job being converted from stand-in to permanent manager. Only youth-team coach (and future manager) Ricky Sbragia was to survive the cull. Hartley and Ross would have expected to go, but the axe fell on many, including all-time club greats George Herd and Jimmy Montgomery in youth development, a decision Reid admits was not an easy one to make.

'Jimmy Montgomery was a club legend, perhaps *the* club legend, and he might never forgive me for letting him go,' he admits. 'It was a big thing. But managers have to make difficult decisions, and I wanted a completely clean slate to work from. Like a lot of managers, you have your own ideas, your own vision and that's going to mean new staff, new players. I made loads of decisions that weren't popular, and I made them from the start. I made one when I allowed Benno to leave early in my first season in charge. There's nothing vindictive about it, it's just that you make decisions and that's what managers do.

'And sometimes you get it wrong.

'I'm not saying you get it right all the time, because you can't. But I just felt if I was going to turn Sunderland around I had to continually keep facing up to the tough decisions that had to be made. As a result I was able to make Brace my assistant, Bobby Saxton my first-team coach and put Pop Robson in charge of the reserves. They were great to have on board and none more so than Sacko, who is a brilliant coach and who had a huge impact. Sometimes people say that if you're going to be a good coach you can't be emotional, you've got to show you're in control. I don't necessarily see it that way. I don't mind sometimes if the players see that emotion – and they'd see it with Sacko. The *Premier Passions* clip of him effing and blinding did him a disservice because there were many, many times we saw the positive side of that emotion. He was razor-sharp in his analysis, he had a great way of explaining simply to the players what they should be doing, and he was a force of nature when it came to just saying whatever was on his mind. It was hard for players to be too down when Sacko was around, and it's often underestimated how important it is at a club to have people who keep spirits up when things are tough.

'I always remember being interviewed once. Very serious interview, very important – I can't remember when it was, but I remember we'd lost two really key games in the space of a few games – and the interviewer said to me, diplomatically "It's been a bad week for you, Peter." And Sacko, who was making tea in the next room, stuck his head around the corner while the cameras were rolling and said, "It's been a bad week? *A BAD WEEK?!* If I had a gun I'd effing shoot myself!"

'He was just being Sacko, thinking out loud, not thinking about the filming, and I just fell about laughing. I couldn't control that about him, but I wouldn't have wanted to. That was the way he felt, that was the way he was, but partially as a result of that he was very, very good with the players. They loved him, but, as well as being easy going, he'd learned under Brian Clough, and he was very big on high standards, discipline and professionalism.'

Saxton's love of the game was infectious, his vast knowledge of football crucial.

'I did have a good staff through the years though,' Reid adds. 'Pop Robson [and] Ricky Sbragia were great for us, and so were many others.'

With things more in place on and off the field, Sunderland settled into the season bedding in the new signings, evolving a style of play and hoping to make the most of the arrival of their new striker, Republic of Ireland international and former Newcastle United goalscorer David Kelly – £900,000 of Bob Murray and John Fickling's money heading to Wolves to secure him. The former manager sighs as he recollects how that particular signing worked out.

'I'd made all this noise about needing to get a goalscorer in, and when they gave me the money I'd spent it on David Kelly,' he says. 'I thought it was going to be an ideal signing – he'd scored goals wherever he'd been, he knew the area, having played at Newcastle, he knew the Championship too – and, on top of that, he was a clever player as well as a finisher.

'But it never really worked out for him.

'He arrived a dozen games into the season, he scored a couple of goals, and then he got an ankle injury away on international duty just after Christmas and was out for the rest of the season.'

For most of the campaign, therefore, Sunderland relied on the presence up front of Phil Gray (later replaced by loan signing Paul Stewart) and the pace of Craig Russell. That was supplemented by the positive intent of the likes of Steve Agnew and Martin Smith across the middle of the park, but Reid accepted that such a team was never going to score a hatful of goals.

'I didn't have a goalscorer going into the season, and I wanted goals,' Reid recalls. 'We were hanging on, we were doing great, we couldn't get a goal but we were dogged, well organised. Phil Gray would get goals occasionally, but he just couldn't get away from people, so I went and got Kelly, only to be back to square one. Paul Stewart came in on loan from Liverpool at the back end of the season and gave us some physical presence up front, but we knew long before that stage that we were going to have to grind out results week in, week out, especially with Kelly sidelined for so much of the season.'

By now, though, the mood in the camp was very different from what it had been a few months previously. One of the first changes Reid had made was the installation of a drinks cabinet in the manager's office.

The nearby Italian restaurant, Romano's in Cleadon, not more than a few goal-kicks from the Charlie Hurley training ground, became legendary as a meeting place for the manager and his staff. It was used early for a famous team-bonding drinks session with Reid and his squad which cost nearly double the £500 Bob Murray had provided for the afternoon – money the manager pointed out proved to be well spent. The new era was to be open and sociable.

'I like a drink and I like good company, and I didn't mind if my players enjoyed a drink, within reason,' he shrugs. 'That side of the game has changed over the years for players, but I was always conscious back then that players weren't machines, that they needed to let their hair down from time to time and that, done right, it could be great for team-bonding. Everyone knew I enjoyed a drink and good crack on, but I was always off it in pre-season – I made a point of that. Pre-season is a time for players to be serious about getting fit, and I always wanted to show I was taking it just as seriously at them.

'Mind you, no-one spoke to me much in those training camps because they knew the manager was off it and wouldn't be in a great mood!

'I was a stickler for that, though, when they were away, pre-season. I liked them seeing me not drinking – it was a psychological thing. It had to be clear there was a time and a place, that fitness and football came first, and I always had a good idea if players were in danger of overdoing it. Even if I hadn't have done, the fans would have let me know anyway – they're the first to tell you if they've seen a player out on the town or doing what they shouldn't be! We tried to treat the players like adults, though, and I thought they responded to that.'

New assistant manager Paul Bracewell also commanded respect, if not love, from his teammates – a serious presence on and off the pitch, he helped guarantee focus. He was the fulcrum on which so many of Sunderland's performances were to pivot that season, with his phenomenal ball retention.

'Brace was different class,' says Reid of the former midfield partner he won silverware with at Everton. 'It was great for us that Kevin Keegan let Brace go. I don't know if he did it because he doubted Brace could do it at the highest level, or was worried about his injury record, or what. Either way it was great for Sunderland to have a player of his ability and experience who could hold onto the ball and who had such a presence.'

With Bracewell forming a vice-like partnership with skipper Kevin Ball in the centre of the park, Sunderland had one of the most defensive midfield pairings in the game – fantastic for the defence, even if it was rarely an aid in attack.

'Bally was as good a captain as a manager could get. An absolutely fantastic pro,' says Reid. 'And, as someone who had been a defender his whole career, he also deserved a lot of credit for approaching the midfield role in the way he did, because I know that at first he doubted he could do it. We raised it with him because we wanted him in the team, but I know he wasn't convinced at first, because his game was all about tackling and not about playmaking. The main thing we did was not to ask him to do anything that wasn't natural to his game. We just said, "Close people down, stop their runs, win the ball and pass it simple" – that's all. And he did a brilliant job for us, along with Brace, in shielding a back four that was already strong.

'Goalscoring remained an issue – the top scorer that season was Russ with 14 goals, 13 in the league. But that's another decision I made that people weren't sure of – was he ready for a proper run in the side, with him being so young? I got Russ in the team, though, and he benefited from having a good understanding with Martin Smith from their youth-team days. I brought the boy Bridges in for his debut too – Michael Bridges, just a 17-year-old kid – and now and then the kid Sam Aiston, who had great pace. He sometimes didn't know what he was doing with it, Sam, but he gave us an outlet, and these were big decisions for us as a management team over the course of that first full season, because you've got to think twice about bringing kids into the side. I knew they were raw but, on balance, I knew they could also give us something extra going forward.'

With a settled squad and a settled way of playing, Sunderland began a slow rise up the table. But it wasn't until December, and three consecutive wins, that they emerged as genuine promotion contenders. The game that really started fans thinking was a 6-0 win at Roker Park over a Millwall side which had Alex Rae in midfield and Mick McCarthy in the dugout.

'Mick was in charge that game? Yeah, of course he was, I'd forgotten. He'd have been absolutely fuming with that result,' smiles Reid. 'I remember the match, they were up near the top with us at the time but ended up going on a slide after that, but, yeah, it was great to be part of a game where we found goalscoring easy and not have to battle it out, for a change.'

There were not many games in which Sunderland scored many goals in that first half of the season, but they put eight past Millwall over the course of a campaign which saw the Londoners go from promotion contenders to a relegation finish.

Sunderland, meanwhile, headed in the opposite direction.

The decisive moment as far as Reid was concerned came in January when 19-year-old goalkeeper Shay Given arrived on loan and launched his talent on an unsuspecting world.

'I made the decision after an FA Cup game against Manchester United, which I thought we were going to win,' remembers Reid. 'We'd given them a hell of a game at Old Trafford, got a draw and brought them back to Roker Park – and were looking good for another draw late on when they got a free-kick for what was never a foul. David Beckham put a ball in from the right and I'm going, "Keeper, keeper, keeper!" but the keeper, Alec Chamberlain, doesn't come, Eric Cantona nods it in close to the far post, and I just thought, "That's it, sod it, I'm getting a keeper." A number of things had been building up and that moment just completely made my mind up.'

A round of phone calls over the next few days ended with Reid speaking to Blackburn Rovers' coach Derek Fazackerley about a young reserve-team keeper he'd been hearing about. Given had earned rave reviews for a recent loan spell at Swindon Town, and Robins' boss Steve McMahon confirmed the youngster was an outstanding prospect. 'Are you going to play him?' Fazackerley asked, knowing many clubs used the loan system purely to strength the squad and left loanees on the bench. 'Yeah, I'll play him.' Reid replied. 'He'll be in at the weekend.'

Looking back, he remembers, 'Everyone thought I'd gone mad bringing this young kid in, and it could easily have gone wrong. My keeper, Alec Chamberlain, actually didn't have a bad record, and he maintained it at the back end of that season. But sometimes you just get a gut instinct and I just thought, "Sod it, I'm getting a keeper, and I remember Shay came in, Leicester City away, and I remember people saying, "Eh? Are you sure?" The whole decision on Given could have gone belly up when you think about it, but he kept a clean sheet, we ground out a draw, and he never looked back. I've got to say, he was absolutely unbelievable in his time with us: his agility and his reflexes, his bravery and his reading of the game at such a young age.'

Given played 17 games, keeping 11 clean sheets, during which time the Rokermen moved from eighth in January back to the top of the table in March, where they were to remain for the rest of the season. He also became a huge favourite with fans as the feel-good factor came back to Roker Park. This was the spell during which the song 'Cheer Up, Peter Reid' was released, as the upturn on Wearside started to make waves nationally. The song reached number 41 in the charts and I let Reid know that I later heard *Top of the Pops* was monitoring its progress with a view to putting it on the show if it broke into the top 40. Had that happened the song would have surged up the charts much higher.

'I never knew that,' says the ex-Sunderland manager, shaking his head. 'But I can tell you something, it did its job anyway – it's still with me today! If I'm on the plane to, say, Majorca and there's a few lads there, it'll start up. I don't mind, but sometimes it goes on and off till we land! You'd think it would fade away, but it doesn't seem to. I get it a lot from the black and whites as well – although they change the words! It was strange for me when I first heard it, because I'd always thought of myself as a happy fella – I didn't need cheering up. But I was made to realise it was because I was always so intense during matches, and all the fans could think about was how we were flying and winning games, and I'm there being so serious.'

The song, a footballing version of the Monkees' 'Daydream Believer', was so iconic and became so associated with Reid that it was used as the title of his recent autobiography.

But he makes no apologies for his intensity.

'When things are going right in football that's often the time when it goes wrong,' he says. 'You've really got to guard against complacency and over-confidence, even if you only suspect it's creeping in. I remember absolutely hammering the players in a game against Grimsby Town during that unbeaten run with Shay – and that was a game we ended up winning 4-0! I'd thought I'd seen signs of us easing up before half-time when we were 1-0 up, and I had a real go at all of them, even Bally, and it got heated in the dressing room before being sorted out after the game.

'But the manager has to have the players at it and, while losing games is the biggest problem in football, when you're winning games it doesn't mean problems aren't round the corner if you're not watching.'

Reid's almighty bollocking of his players, which still lives long in the memory of those who endured it, came in the middle of a nine-game winning streak which cheered everyone in Sunderland up. It was the club's best run in a century, and the 18-game unbeaten run it was part of set a new club record which saw promotion won with three games to spare. The 26 clean sheets shattered the previous record of 21, set in the 1974–75 season, while only ten goals were conceded at home, the least in a 46-game season. Stats like these helped Reid to the League Managers' Association Manager of the Year award – his peers celebrating his achievement in getting a club on the verge of relegation a year earlier promoted as champions with only a modest outlay.

But Sunderland were far from being the league's leading goalscorers that season – despite putting those eight past Millwall. Promotion was down to a superb defence, wonderful team-spirit and sheer, bloody-minded tenacity.

'They were a real team,' says Reid. 'They had a team spirit which reminded me of the best sides in my own playing days at Everton, with everyone working to help each other. We didn't have standout stars, but everyone worked so bloody hard to make something special happen, and it happened.

'Andy Melville was a brilliant player for us, and Richard Ord was too – a great central defensive partnership – but everywhere you looked through that squad you'd find players putting themselves on the line for each other. It was real commitment, and it was great to see.'

Once again, though, Reid wasn't fooling himself when it came to looking at the next season – Sunderland's first in the Premier League. Once again the problem was cash, but also, in some respects, sheer bad luck. There was a clear reason, though, why funds were limited this time around – Bob Murray and John Fickling were driving on with the creation of the Stadium of Light, a spaceship of a football ground in comparison to tired Roker Park. The new stadium would be a shining beacon for football by the Wear, a home to last the next 100 years, and the catalyst to the sleeping giant's reawakening. But it would take money to build, and that would impact on the transfer budget. Rejuvenated by a revitalised and buoyant Sunderland AFC, and comparing Reid to Sunderland's version of Bill Shankly, Bob Murray had stepped out of the shadows and resumed the chairmanship. And in December 1996 Sunderland became one of the first clubs to float on the London Stock Exchange, raising £12 million worth of new money for the club – but all of it ring-fenced to go to the building of the new ground, not to reinforce the newly promoted squad.

'We knew the deal,' shrugs Reid. 'I had hardly any money because they were looking to build a stadium. We had to try and box it – the board would look to find me a budget, and our job was to try to keep the club up until the new stadium was ready the next season and we could look to kick on. It was a challenge, but I took it on – you couldn't not do after the season we'd just had.

'I had the bones of a squad – players who I thought could handle it in the Premier League – but I needed to strengthen up front and, most of all, I needed a goalkeeper, with Shay having gone back to Blackburn. I decided to spend pretty much all I had on three players who I thought would give us a chance: I needed an excellent keeper, and I needed someone up front who could hold the ball up and bring others in. Tony Coton and Niall Quinn – who I knew well from my time at Man City, where both had been magnificent – were the players I went for and was over the moon to get. They had loads of top-flight experience and were big characters in the dressing room, and the price I got both for was great value for money. The third signing I went for was Alex Rae. I spent almost £1 million on him because I needed an attacking goalscoring midfielder, and I had to gamble he could do it in the Premier League.'

Sunderland's start to their new season was solid, beginning with an opening day goalless draw against a Leicester City side at Roker Park which had future Sunderland manager Simon Grayson in its back four. After a couple of games Sunderland were a heady third place (!) and as the season progressed they managed to stay mainly in mid-table to lower mid-table – and that was despite Reid losing his two key signings early in the campaign. Sunderland were 10th when injury to Quinn in September at Coventry ruled him out of all but a handful of games at the end of the campaign. They were 13th when Coton's career was ended by a double break of the leg at Southampton the following month.

'That's what killed us over the course of the season,' says Reid. 'You can never really know, of course, but I believe if those two had stayed fit we would have stayed up – hey, I think if Tony Coton had stayed fit we would have stayed up! He was just starting to get back to his very best when he was injured, and we had to use back-up keeper Lionel Pérez after that.'

Despite the loss of such key players so early, Sunderland's defensive strengths and team spirit saw them grind out enough decent results to lie 11th for the return game against Coventry City at Highfield Road on New Year's Day 1997.

'I think that game just summed up what we were up against,' Reid said.

Michael Bridges gave Sunderland an early lead, Dion Dublin pegged them back, Steve Agnew restored the lead then Coventry levelled again before Dublin was sent off in the 40th minute.

'We should have won that game but we just didn't have the strength we needed to do it. We were up against ten men but we couldn't create or finish or get the ball over the line. We didn't have the bodies over the Christmas programme to change it around, and against Coventry City it just caught up with us. In the second-half Sacko turned around to look at the bench, thinking how we could change the game, and I just said, "Forget it." We had four kids on the bench.'

None of that quartet started a Premier League game in their whole careers, underlining the lack of strength in depth at the club. And yet it looked as though Sunderland would have enough to somehow fall over the line and survive. When they beat Man United 2-1 at Roker Park in a great victory in March, with John Mullin and Michael Gray getting the goals, they were 15th in the league.

'Before getting back on the United team bus after our win, Fergie popped his head around the corner and said to me, "You'll be all right, you'll stay up," recalls Reid. 'He's not a bad judge. There's not many he gets wrong when it comes to how seasons are going to pan out, but pressure came on us after that. We couldn't buy a win and it all came down to our inability to score a goal. We'd lost Quinny early, and even when he came back he was nowhere near right. Paul Stewart was never really a goalscorer. He could hold it up but we couldn't get anyone off him. With him a hold-up man and no one around him able to get goals either, we were just clinging on in games, being strong defensively, always looking to grind things out. The players knew that and they gave everything, but it was hard and we knew that if we conceded it was going to be bloody difficult.'

This was the season in which fly-on-the-wall football documentary *Premier Passions* shone a light on life at the raw end of football, with all its pressure and profanity. The nation were to gawp at the industrial language of Reid and Saxton during games, while what was meant to show Bob Murray's attention to detail – famously focusing on the quality of the taps at the new Stadium of Light – perhaps unfairly looked like arranging the deckchairs on the *Titanic* when viewed through the lens of the club's relegation.

'*Premier Passions* was genuine,' Reid says. 'It's not acting, but sometimes it didn't convey the full picture. At first it was strange having the cameras around, but after a while you tend to forget they're there. Bob was keen to do it for the publicity it would bring the club. I was less keen, but I could see where he was coming from. On a couple of occasions, though – the game we played against Arsenal stands out – you could feel a bit hard done by the impression it created. I'm laying into Michael Bridges and Craig Russell, our two young strikers, at half-time, telling them to get hold of it and to hold the ball up. I'm not holding back and it looks bad on TV, but they were up against Tony Adams and Martin Keown that day, and that was a conscious decision on my part to push them. I knew they were young'uns but I had to get something out of them. It was either go on the front foot with them, or say, "Well done, lads, you're doing well. I know Adams and Keown are good players, you just play your best." And I thought, "Nah, I have to get something out of them. I can't give them an excuse, I can't give them an easy way out." And it worked – we did get something out of it. In fact, we worked so hard, tried so much, that we ended up winning that game – Adams scored an own goal: 1-0. It was a great win for us, but as the season went on you could feel more and more how much we were down to the bare bones. You know, to get to 40 points that season, with the squad we had – superb. It was superb.

'I'm looking down the list of games here in the record book and the number of games we lost by the odd goal, it's a joke – we just couldn't get a goal.'

Sunderland scrapped so hard that they didn't drop into the relegation zone until mid-April – the first time all season they had been in the bottom three. A week later they were out of it thanks to a headed winner by 19-year-old Darren Williams against his home-town club Middlesbrough.

Then a defeat to Graeme Souness's Southampton – a six-pointer in which Reid was criticised for playing one up front in a home game – was followed by a stirring 3-0 win over Everton in the last competitive match ever played at Roker Park. That left a final game away to a Wimbledon side which looked for most of the match as though the players were already thinking of their summer holidays. But by that time, with just three wins in 15, Sunderland were spent mentally and they failed to rise to the occasion – a 1-0 defeat to the Dons condemning them to an immediate return to the Championship.

'I will freely admit I might have made a mistake in that game against Southampton when I played 4–5–1 at home against a side that were struggling just as much as we were,' Reid reflects. 'But we were low on confidence and I thought that would make us solid. We didn't really have much in the way of options up front anyway, and I thought that was the right way to go. We were going to grind something out. That was the plan. Maybe it wasn't the right plan – but I will say one thing, though, in my defence: my effing goalie!

'Egil Østenstad scored the only goal of the game and the result really hurt us – really hurt the supporters too, knocked their confidence in me. But if you look at that goal, you look at the shot, it is going straight at my goalie – straight at him! – middle of the effing goal!'

Then there was the game against Nottingham Forest . . . Warming to his theme, Reid adds, 'It was the same when we played Forest a few games earlier: Bally has got us a goal and then a few minutes from the end their full-back, Des Lyttle, who has never scored a goal in his life, puts one straight through the centre of the goal.'

In such seasons everything turns on fine lines, on narrow margins, and it is the pivotal moments that only emerge afterwards that often continue to haunt.

'First and foremost, I think it turned on the injuries,' says Reid of a season which also saw key defender Martin Scott lost to an ankle problem in early November. 'I'm not going to complain about the money because we accepted that and we went into it with our eyes open. I think if Quinny had stayed fit, we would have scored more goals that season, no doubt about it. If Tony Coton had stayed fit we would have conceded fewer goals that season, no doubt about that either. So if either of those injuries hadn't happened, I think we'd have stayed up. But we had our moments in games as well, I'm not denying that. I remember the 1-1 derby at Newcastle United – Mickey

Gray scored first-half, Alan Shearer late in the second – where we rode our luck but missed the easiest chance of the game.'

He's referring to an opportunity that fell the way of former Newcastle United favourite David Kelly in the second half. A goalmouth scramble saw the ball drop to the Sunderland attacker but he somehow managed to stab it wide from close range with the goal at his mercy. Easier to score it seemed. Pivotal moments.

Sunderland suffered only a couple of pastings that season: a 5-0 defeat at Old Trafford, with the famous Eric Cantona goal; a 6-2 defeat at Stamford Bridge in which the Rokermen fell apart after a cynical foul by Dennis Wise on Paul Bracewell largely negated Sunderland's key player for the remainder of the game, and the Blues added two late goals. 'Generally, the matches were really close all the way through the season,' Reid agrees. 'Jeez! David Kelly misses an absolute sitter in that game against Newcastle, I can still see it now – I was thinking, "Just bury it." And he shoots wide. He just couldn't get one for me. He must have gone his longest spell for us without scoring.'

He did. Kelly didn't score at all that season.

'I know he played on the right wing quite a few times, but you would expect more goals – and that chance at Newcastle was the sort he'd made his reputation on burying,' Reid continues. 'That's football, though. If you're in a position like we were at the time, as a coaching team and as players, you're working so hard to get openings in front of goal, and you know you've got to take the best ones.'

Even in that final game of the season, safety was within Sunderland's grasp, their fate in their own hands.

Win and they stay up.

The tentative and tepid performance that day though against a disinterested Dons side showed how much their game had gone.

Afterwards, a sad-eyed Darren Williams, goalscoring hero after his header at Boro just a few weeks earlier, revealed that when Paul Stewart had stretched to head Sunderland's best chance of the game high over the crossbar, he had been poised directly behind him. 'I saw Craig Russell's cross coming in and I thought it was perfect for me,' said Williams. 'I was just on the way up to head it when Stewy got in front of me.'

Reid, though, remembers the veteran Chris Waddle, a late signing for Sunderland that season, a boyhood fan of the club who could have written his name in folklore: 'Waddle had one of the sweetest left foots in football, and twice the ball dropped to him on the edge of the area. It was perfect goalscoring territory for him, and we were in the dugout going, "Go on, go on!" But he passed it both times instead of going for goal. They were two chances you wouldn't believe, absolutely made for him, but that's where we'd got to.'

Afterwards, Reid put on a brave face in the morgue-like press conference. At the conclusion of it, he said, 'It's not the end of the world.' Then, with his words greeted by stony silence, he added, 'It just feels like it.'

And yet, oddly, Reid describes that season as probably the most enjoyable of his whole time at Sunderland – better than the previous promotion, better than the 105-point record-breaking promotion or the two seventh-place finishes that were to follow. And that probably says a lot about him as a person.

'The season we went up, and tried to stay up, it was a horrible, scrappy season,' he acknowledges. 'We had to fight for everything. But you know what? I loved it! I loved pretty much every second of it in terms of the fact that I loved a scrap, I loved a battle, and that was a battle! It was tooth-and-nail. It was hard work and, by rights, with the resources we had, we had no right to get as close as we did. If you ask me what our biggest achievement was in my time at the club, it's hard to look past those 40 points, given what we had. We were so close to pulling it off. I think it was more of an achievement than either of the promotions or the two seasons where we were in the top few teams in the country. The players gave everything, you couldn't have asked for anything more than they gave me. And the way we planned at that time, it was a fantastic experience – everything was tactical and thought out. We used to work out game-plans: when to get the players wide, when to bring them in narrow, where to stop the crosses, how to frustrate. Nothing was left to chance. We knew our options were limited and we tried to squeeze every last drop out of the players physically and, as coaches, everything out of ourselves tactically. We had two seasons like that: the first full season when we won promotion, and the second when we came within a whisker of avoiding relegation. The amount of planning was phenomenal, and the challenges in getting the most out of every player, every situation, every game . . . I loved it.'

In the immediate aftermath of relegation the opening of the new ground might have felt like an anticlimax – the first-class facilities opening for second-tier football. It was a new era for the home of the club, but back to square one for Reid and Murray as the new season began in the Championship. The ignominy was felt by the chairman, and it was felt by the manager.

Even so, the new ground could not have been given a finer start than a 3-1 win over Manchester City with, significantly, Niall Quinn and new summer signing Kevin Phillips getting on the same scoresheet for the first time.

But either side of that game were defeats, and with the team struggling for form and fitness and becalmed mid-table, the fans' patience broke after an abject 4-0 away defeat to an unfancied Reading side in October.

Reid had seen a problem weeks earlier, though: 'August 30th, that date always stays with me – the night Princess Diana died. We lost 1-0 to Norwich City at home, Quinny came off with the knee problem – booed off, spat at, everything – and I worried then that that might be a season-defining moment. Quinny's knee had never been right, even when he came back at the end of the previous season.'

In early October, the night of that Reading defeat, the mood was menacing and the scenes ugly as red and white fans surrounded the team bus haranguing and barracking players they had been celebrating a year earlier. I was there and it was a sad and upsetting sight. Questions were now openly being asked about whether Reid had taken the team far enough and should be replaced, but the manager himself wasn't worried about losing his job.

'I was more worried about Quinny and his state of mind,' he says. 'I knew we hadn't been playing well, and I knew the Reading performance and result was unacceptable, but it was October and we were mid-table. It was a horrible night, but I had no indication from the chairman there was a problem. No, I was more worried about Quinny than anything else. We had some great characters in the side, but the problem was that a lot of those characters were playing through injury or loss of form, and no one was more injured than Quinny, whose knee problem was so severe he couldn't run. He hadn't been doing himself any favours in the games he'd been playing through – the fans weren't seeing the best of him and were getting on his back – and I could tell he was really down. I got wind that he was thinking of packing in the game altogether, that he was sounding out life after football and looking into what he might do back in Ireland and I thought, "No, not having it." We got him in to see top surgeon, Mr Bollan in Yorkshire, and he sorted the problem with an operation that was a complete success. It was incredible. He missed a few months with the op, but when he came back it was like the Quinny of old – it was great. Before that happened, though, I had changed everything after the Reading game. Over the next few weeks I brought in fit, young players at the back who were itching to play, and left out the experienced players who were either not fit or out of form.'

Into defence came the likes of Mickey Gray, Darren Williams, Darren Holloway, and summer signings Chris Makin and Jody Craddock, with their energy and freshness lifting the side.

'You get players in and you get them organised, that's half the battle,' says Reid. 'You get them playing to the best of their ability – Williams, Craddock, Holloway – and you look to make them the best they can be.'

Fully fit now for the first time in well over a year, Quinn was back by mid-November for a 4-1 win over Portsmouth on the south coast in which he scored and Martin Smith, who enjoyed an excellent game, got injured. Players like Smith and Michael Bridges had been holding the fort in Quinn's absence, aided by classy midfielder Lee Clark, which meant the team had climbed the league table. Now the team was really beginning to gain momentum – new signing Nicky Summerbee scoring on his debut in that Portsmouth game – as the elements of what was Peter Reid's best squad started to come together.

Summerbee's career had been going nowhere. He had become a bit-part player at Man City before moving to Sunderland, with homegrown striker Craig Russell heading in the opposite direction and the Black Cats also being paid £900,00 transfer fee for their forward. Reid felt at the time it was a good deal, just not how good a deal!

'I made good signings and bad signings – every manager does – and I'm no different,' he says. 'But I've got no doubt that the good outweighed the bad over the years I was at Sunderland, no doubt at all. What I will say, though, is that every now and then I was fortunate sometimes when I sold people, and I acknowledge that. Russ going to Man City, with Nicky Summerbee coming the other way, and Sunderland getting nearly £1 million out of it, was one of them. When you look at Russ's subsequent career, when I think he'd admit not much happened, that was a fantastic deal for us. And Summerbee surprised me – I thought we were getting a good player and he would fit into our team well. But I tell you what, he was so intelligent as an attacking winger – he kept the ball, he worked up and down and, most of all, he produced quality crosses you couldn't believe – he was up there with Beckham for his ability to whip a ball in. And the two of them on the right flank – Makin and Summerbee – when they were playing well and fit and at their best, they were bob-on, absolutely bob-on, great to watch.'

With Summerbee and Allan Johnston now on either wing, Phillips flourished with the return of Quinn to the side. Their prolific partnership would go on to produce 50 goals between them that season, 15 for the resurgent Irishman, but it wouldn't be enough to go up automatically. Sunderland played some wonderful, free-flowing, goal-laden football – including a 4-1 revenge win over Reading in February, and a 2-1 away win at Swindon capped by a Phillips wonder-goal, a beautiful chest and volley on the swivel – but they had started their run too late. They had the misfortune of trying to chase down

Nottingham Forest and Middlesbrough, who were enjoying similarly successful runs. Briefly, Sunderland made it into the top two, but in a nail-biting finish dropped to third.

The Black Cats still had every hope of going up via the playoffs – they were the form side of the division – and they overcame Sheffield United, the team which had formed the opposition in Reid's first game for the club, in a titanic night match at the Stadium of Light to clinch their place in the final at Wembley.

But everyone knows the tale of that epic playoff final which finished 4-4 after extra time and 7-6 to Charlton Athletic in a penalty shootout. Each time Sunderland looked as though they had got over the line, they would be pegged back.

'It was tough,' says Reid, with understatement. 'I won't relive the day, but my abiding memory was just how hot it was, incredibly hot. I remember the heat and I remember that we played well. I dragged off Darren Holloway at half-time – I think the heat and the occasion got to him.'

Alan Curbishley took his right-back off too, Danny Mills.

'I put Chris Makin on and he did brilliant for us, but my goalkeeper let me down again – rush of blood late on. Then the penalties. Mickey Gray misses the last one and the season is over. I wouldn't care but we trained on the Stadium of Light pitch, practised and practised the penalties, and Mickey was brilliant at them. It's different in a Wembley playoff final though.'

Casting our minds back to the enormity of a day, which was as epic as it was agonising for Sunderland fans, and which always gives pause for thought, we reach a natural break in the interview.

'Another two coffees please, ta, love,' says Reid of the Gosforth Hotel waitress, as we recharge our glasses. That sun-kissed, heartbreaking day, forever seared on Wearside consciousness, seems a long time ago now – as indeed it is: more than two decades ago. Similarly, Reid's departure from Sunderland is a long way in the past – a lot of water has flowed under the Wear Bridge since then, and much has happened to the former manager in the meantime. After leaving Sunderland, Reid ended up firefighting at various clubs – Leeds United, Coventry City and Plymouth Argyle – all basket-case clubs in deep trouble on and off the pitch at the time. He also had brief, bizarre and enjoyable stints managing the Thailand national team and India, but in recent years, as well as regular media work, he has carved out a reputation as a football consultant, putting his knowledge at the disposal of other managers. He was invaluable as a sounding board for Tony Pulis when Stoke City were in the Premier League. And he is currently enjoying the same role at Wigan Athletic, who were promoted to the Championship in the summer of 2018, ironically swapping places with a Sunderland AFC heading in the opposite direction.

'It was a good season at Wigan, you can't argue with that – promotion – and I enjoy the work,' he says. 'The manager Paul Cook got me in there. He's just signed a four-year deal and I'm very happy to be involved and have an input. I have the gig at Wigan, and I do a bit of media work, and that's great, but I really enjoy the Wigan side of it – good lads, and I don't miss much in the way of games at all, it tends to be only because of media commitments.'

We have been chatting and flicking through some of the reference books lying on the table that divides us – chiefly the definitive *Sunderland, the Complete Record*, edited by Rob Mason, but Reid's mind is still flickering around that Wembley day which many regard as the greatest contest ever seen beneath the twin towers.

'My main penalty-takers, Kevin Phillips and Lee Clark, were off the pitch, otherwise it might not have gone all the way down to Mickey's turn,' he said. 'Clarky did brilliantly for me that season, got pissed up at Wembley afterwards, but I didn't mind that – you couldn't blame anyone for that, pretty much everyone had a lot to drink.

'Besides, he'd played with a hernia for months so that he could help the side, and I thought he deserved a lot of respect for that – he'd be in tears with the pain sometimes after games, but he wanted to play on for us. He didn't have pace, but he was clever – knew when to pass it, knew when to receive it, and he timed his runs beautifully. Some lads can do it naturally – find space – and Clarky was one of them. He was superb during the time he was with us, but then Bally was terrific alongside him too, because Bally used to look after him on the pitch when the opposition were looking to keep Clarky quiet. As for the final itself, we were naïve in defence and it cost us.

'Penalty shootouts are a lottery, and it was a shame it had to be Mickey most of all, as a young local lad, to miss the last one especially as he had been putting them away for fun in the run-up to the game.

'We played some great football that season and, like the previous season, in a different way, we came so close to success. We went on great runs, but I look back and one of the games which really sticks out is the game we played against QPR at home when we were 2-0 up in pouring rain and Mike Sheron scored twice in the last quarter of an hour. To come away with the score 2-2 in mid-April when we were on a charge, I was devastated. We were second at the time and those two extra points would have kicked us on with just a few games remaining. It's always those games you think about in the final analysis.'

Despite the QPR disappointment, Sunderland fans still had one of their most memorable nights ahead of them at the Stadium of Light – the second leg of the playoff semi-final against Sheffield United – when more than 40,000 fans whipped up an unforgettable atmosphere, so intense it felt like a wall of noise.

'It was a night game and we won 2-0 to take us to Wembley,' remembers Reid. 'That was a night. I think the new stadium really came into its own that night because the atmosphere stood comparison with anything. I've never felt an atmosphere like that Sheffield United game – well, I have, because I played at Roker Park many years ago when I was a kid and they were going for promotion; that was similar. You could literally hear the air crackling and fizzing. Unbelievable. The place was on fire and it was amazing – that's why you want to part of a club like Sunderland.'

Asked to give a preference for either Roker Park or the Stadium of Light, Reid says he can't.

'They were both fantastic grounds, even though they were completely different,' he muses. 'Roker Park was just a special place, a proper football ground with all that history and tradition, and the Roker Roar was famous. I felt it as a young player at Bolton when there were more than 50,000 crammed in there. It was an amazing experience, 1976, Sunderland were going for promotion, Tony Towers scored. The memory of that day stayed with me, and when Paul Hetherington first sounded me out on whether I'd be interested in taking over at Sunderland, that was what came to mind: that's what I could be taking over. From being a young lad, it made a big impact. And my first game back as a young player, after a long time out with serious injury in 1980, was an FA Cup game at Roker Park, which we won. So I've had a connection of sorts with the club for many years, and a lot of things tied up with Roker Park.

'I remember the Bolton team stayed in the George Washington Hotel, and I thought I was just going up for the experience, to get back into the swing of things after such a long time out. But the Bolton manager Ian Greaves played me, and we won the game – and that was a big moment for me. Ian Greaves was a big, big influence on me, as was Howard Kendall at Everton later in my career, and a lot of the things I took into management were influenced by them. The thing I learned from both of them was that they were strong characters, and that you have to be a strong character to succeed in football – especially at big clubs with passionate fans. It's not easy to manage a club where there's 40,000 managers. Greavsie, Howard – they knew the game really well and they were great man-managers, and I think those things stood me in good stead at Sunderland.

'I loved games at Roker Park and I loved the fans and the way they were so passionate about football and so down to earth. I remember I'd only been there a couple of games in charge when I met one of the old fellas from the executive boxes – nice bloke, I found out later. He sized me up and down and said, "So you're the new manager, then?" And I said, "Yeah." And he said, "Well, they'll have your name written in chalk on the door!" I thought that was a brilliant line. It took me a second to get what he meant, but I loved that and burst out laughing.

'I loved how honest the supporters were, and the humour; how much they cared for the club – and that was a feeling and a closeness Roker Park never lost. The same goes with the old Charlie Hurley training ground – the gym, the head tennis out on the training pitch, lads grafting, salt of the earth times. I loved all that.

'When it eventually came I felt the change over to the new ground went really well, even though it was a very big stadium, a very modern one, a different dynamic. I mean, the Stadium of Light used to rock for the big games, the derbies, the top teams coming, and you can't knock that. I think the passion transferred over to the Stadium of Light – that walk out of the tunnel, with the music blaring on matchday. You could tell, that night against Sheffield United especially – but there were plenty of other games where there were good times and the new stadium was rocking and it was fantastic. It comes into its own in night games, or in big fixtures, and that's why it's a ground that needs to be in the Premier League, really. It's where it belongs.'

The new stadium was denied that privilege by the playoff final of 1998. And if there was one thing Reid learned from that Wembley defeat it could be summed up in five words – five words he was no stranger to: 'I need a new goalkeeper.'

Pérez could be a superb shot-stopper, and the crowd loved his flamboyance, but the perception was the technical side of his game was lacking – what was needed was a keeper of genuine all-round ability.

The new keeper would not be Shay Given – that ship had sailed the previous summer when the Irishman joined Wearside rivals Newcastle United in a £1.5 million deal, despite a genuine pursuit by the Black Cats to lure him back. That particular race was always likely to be an uneven one: the Magpies were flying high in the Premier League, Sunderland were in the process of being relegated, and the new man in charge at St James' Park was Given's childhood hero Kenny Dalglish.

'I was desperate to get Shay when I knew he was going to be moving from Blackburn,' admits Reid. 'We were going to pay the dough too, to be fair to the chairman. He was going to pay the money for him because I said to Bob, "He wins you games, the kid, keeping clean sheets, inspiring the team, demoralising the opposition." And Bob was a massive fan of Shay's too and would have gone to get him, even though it meant spending big. But it wasn't to be.'

Sunderland did eventually find the top-class stopper they were hoping for though and, just like Given at Roker Park, 22-year-old Thomas Sørensen arrived at the Stadium of Light pretty much a complete unknown. Tony Coton, by now on the coaching staff, had scouted the great Dane at Odense and helped snatch him from under the not inconsiderable nose of Peter Schmeichel, the legendary Man United number one who was in the process of recommending the young keeper to Sir Alex Ferguson at the time.

'Sørensen was a great find and went on to become my first-choice keeper for the rest of my time at the club,' says Reid. 'He was only young but he had everything: he was 6 foot 4 inches tall, had a real presence, was brave, capable of making fantastic saves; but he commanded his box too and communicated well with the defence, which was so important to us and something we'd been lacking.'

The manager knew he didn't have to spend big that summer in terms of improving his attacking options because they were already exceptional. Instead he bolstered his back four still further, with the signing of man-mountain central defender Paul Butler, a no-nonsense defender very much in the mould of Sam Allardyce as a footballer – a physically imposing barn door of a player who took no prisoners on the pitch. In an era when ball-playing centre-halves were in vogue, Butler was a throwback to a more basic defensive style.

'We had played some wonderful flowing football from the back the previous season with the young lads, but I felt we were trying to play too much football at times,' Reid explains. 'Players like Darren Williams and Darren Holloway had played regularly in midfield when they were younger and their instincts, like Mickey, like Jody, were always to look to be comfortable on the ball and pass it. That was great further up the field and it wasn't a problem in defence most of the time. But sometimes you just needed a player whose first instinct was to put his foot through the ball, and that was Paul Butler. Butts was really strong in the tackle, was more than happy just to put it into row Z, and, with so many ball-players in the side, we needed that element to us too.'

The new signings clicked from the very start of the season and, with a far more solid defence, Sunderland made light of their playoff heartache, setting the pace from the start of the 1998–99 Championship campaign. After a closed-season spent impatiently waiting to put their playoff agonies behind them, a motivated side hit the ground running. Looking back now, the statistics are staggering: the Black Cats won six of their first seven games of the season, drawing the other one. In fact, the campaign began with a 24-game unbeaten run, defeat not being tasted until 21 November in a narrow 3-2 home defeat to Barnsley. They were to lose only two more of their 46 league games in the remainder of the campaign.

The opening burst of fixtures featured a spell which saw 20 goals scored in the space of five home games, and included the 7-0 defeat of Oxford United. That mid-September game had just about everything you could hope for from a Sunderland supporter's perspective: a gloriously sunny day, a huge crowd and a team performance that simply overwhelmed the visitors. Blossoming talent Michael Bridges put Sunderland ahead in the third minute of the game and Michael Gray doubled the score three minutes later. Bridges was to notch twice in that game, as was strike partner Danny Dichio and livewire midfielder Alex Rae. But that sparkling day was to mask a private agony for a player still battling his inner demons.

A couple of months later Alex Rae was admitted to the renowned Priory clinic suffering from alcohol and drug problems, which he later admitted had led him to contemplate suicide. From the boardroom to the backroom, the club rallied around the talented but troubled Scot, who had lived on the edge for most of his career but still managed to establish himself as a firm crowd favourite for his aggressive and energetic style, his range of passing and his eye for goal. Popular among his teammates too, who were sympathetic to his situation, Rae spent a month in rehab as rumours circulated across Wearside of just how serious the situation had been.

'Alex had his problems long before he arrived at Roker Park, but he managed them as best he could and was still capable of great performances,' says Reid. 'Even though he wasn't looking after his body, he was still quality. I remember him knocking balls and passing and moving and it was wonderful to watch, but then in certain games he blew up after an hour. I remember dragging him off in one game after an hour – Huddersfield, I think – because he wasn't right. He was a fantastic footballer, but footballers are human and they have problems that you have to deal with within the club. You know that saying: "football is more important than life or death"? Well, it isn't.'

So it was heart-warming a month later when Rae returned as a late substitute in the 1-0 home win over Stockport County, cheered by the massive crowd as he warmed up and returned to the fray in the 85th minute of the match.

'Alex was a fantastic player but he'd had drink and other problems pretty much all the way through his career, and they'd finally come to a head,' says Reid. 'The problems he had, gradually got worse and, eventually, when it did all come out, we were genuinely worried about where he might be heading as an individual. The club was great at that time, I thought, and I know how grateful Alex was for the support he got.

'But it was how we were as a squad, and as a club at the time, and the fanbase was a part of that too, as we saw in the way they responded to him on his return. The way Alex has turned his life around since that time has been incredible, and I think he is an inspiration to so many people when it comes to dealing with being an alcoholic. He was always a character, always a great lad to have in the dressing room – and no one doubted his talent or his ability to turn a match – but the Alex Rae I know now, and have met long after we both left Sunderland, is a magnificent human being.'

An interesting feature of that Oxford United hammering, though, was the absence from the starting line-up of Sunderland's first-choice strikers Niall Quinn and Kevin Phillips. Both were to suffer injuries that ruled them out for significant spells of the season, Phillips especially, who missed four months with a broken toe sustained in a League Cup game against Chester City. From mid-September to early January, Sunderland were without one of the hottest finishers in football – something which still has Reid shaking his head.

'I remember it well – I messed up,' says Reid, still sounding a little rattled 20 years on. 'I shouldn't really have let him play in that Chester City game. I didn't want him to. It was a nothing game, really, a game he didn't need to be involved in, but he was desperate to score goals and desperate to play. He'd broken Cloughie's goalscoring record the previous season and he was on fire at the start of this one and just didn't want to miss a game. He obviously knew the Cup tie facing lower league opposition was a great chance to get more goals and, against my better judgement, I let him play. Sod's Law, he gets a knock, and our top goalscorer was out for months with what was a very tricky foot injury.'

Phillips had scored eight goals in ten games before limping off in the second half of an easy win over Chester with an injury which could easily have derailed Sunderland's season. But the strength in depth at the club, which had been steadily building since relegation, was to come to their rescue. Phillips was replaced in the Chester game by Bridges, who would go on to score within minutes of being introduced to the Cup tie. The young striker would contribute 12 goals that season, the same number as Quinn's stand-in Danny Dichio, while Quinn himself notched 21 and Phillips 25. Sunderland even had a fifth striker in reserve in Martin Smith, who could be pushed up front. This was the key to Sunderland losing just three times in the league programme and the key to the team achieving an English league record at the time of 105 points on the back of 91 goals scored.

'Phillips did his metatarsal in that Chester game and Quinny got injured as well shortly afterwards – my two main men out,' says Reid. 'But the two lads who came in up front were brilliant, and so was everyone else who contributed to produce some fantastic football – and it was great football.'

The strength in depth extended throughout the team: Melville, Butler and Craddock competed for the two central defensive positions; Scott and Gray at left-back; Makin and Williams, right-back; Johnston, Smith and Gray on the left wing; and, in central midfield, Rae, Ball, Clark, Paul Thirlwell and later, Gavin McCann, who signed midway through the season. In areas where the squad strength was a little limited, Sunderland enjoyed the happy circumstance of goalkeeper Thomas Sørensen playing all but one game that season, while on the right wing Nicky Summerbee missed only a handful of games, in which Smith, Rae and McCann all adequately deputised. It says a lot that when Phillips was injured against Chester, Sunderland were third in the table, and when he returned in January, they were top.

The Black Cats finished the season in the sort of form they had started, completing the campaign with 11 wins and two draws in the last 13 games. For Sunderland fans it was the closet they came to experiencing what it must have been like to be a supporter of Man United or Liverpool at the height of their success. Supporters turned up not so much wondering if their team would win but by how many, and whether or not Phillips would score that day. Reid's side – having played some wonderful free-flowing, attack-minded football in the second half of the previous season – were largely irresistible across the whole course of this one. The aggregate home attendance of that campaign has never been bettered since. The last time it was exceeded was the 1954–55 season, when Sunderland finished fourth in the top flight.

'As a manager during that season, my biggest problem was picking the team and trying to keep players happy,' says Reid. 'We had so much talent in the side, because the new signings really came off, young players were coming through and others were coming back to form and fitness. Everything came together, but at the same time we also worked hard on building up partnerships and understandings across the pitch. Mickey and Johnno loved the overlaps on the left, so we went with that, but Makin and Summerbee preferred it so that Makin just did the defending and Summerbee the attacking, so we went with that too. Also the players really bought into the need to develop those partnerships. They bought into it because they could see the value of it on matchday and also because everyone wanted to be in the squad.'

Sunderland's squad strength overflowed and poured into the reserve side, which coasted the league that season – unsurprisingly, with Dichio and Bridges often up front while Smith, Rae, McCann and Thirlwell were regulars in midfield at Durham's New Ferens Park.

'I used to enjoy watching the reserves. They played some brilliant football and were ready to step up at any time. The backroom reckoned if that reserve team had played in the Championship that season they'd have had a good chance of promotion too! I don't think I'd disagree. We were just in a different position altogether from where we'd been a couple of years previously in terms of goal options. I just used to say to them, "Go and play" – that was pretty much it: "Go and play" – because those partnerships that we worked on and encouraged were all coming good. They knew what they had to do in games and they knew if they did it right we were almost certain to win.'

More records tumbled that season and Kevin Phillips, now universally known as SuperKev, had marked himself out as something special. With 60 goals in two seasons he was well on his way to establishing himself as a Sunderland legend. But oak trees grow from acorns, and the seed of the unheralded move for the lower-league forward had been planted in Reid's mind several years earlier.

'I scouted him and I can I tell you the first time he came across the radar,' Reid says. 'We played Watford at home, it finished 1-1 – Martin Scott scored for us – and I saw their striker and thought, "Bloody hell. He's not bad, him!" He didn't score, but you could see he was a player. After the game I had a drink with the Watford management and I remember the manager Glenn Roeder didn't seem to rate him but the assistant manager, Kenny Sansom, my old England teammate, raved about Kev. So we kept tabs on him, because we thought he was one we might get further down the line.

'As I said, I made some great signings as a manager and I made some rubbish ones too, but around that time we got a hell of a lot right – Thomas Sørensen, Lee Clark, Jody Craddock . . . And then Kevin Phillips was among the very best. When you think he cost just over half a million and scored well over 100 goals for the club – every type of goal too, from reflex tap-ins to shots from outside the box, he was just a natural finisher.'

That season ended with Sunderland setting the following records in the Championship: most points in a season (105); fewest losses in a season (3); and most wins in a season (31). It banished the blues of both the Premier League relegation and the playoff final, and with the club on a high again everything seemed set fair for the Premier League.

Such a transformation had not happened by accident. It was a triumph for the planning, imagination and intelligence shown by Reid and Saxton and the backroom staff as they developed and moulded a squad in which the sum exceeded the parts: 'We worked hard on trying to get partnerships that really gelled well and systems that really suited the players we had. If you remember, Bally was playing centre-half originally and then we moved him into central midfield to see if he could do a job for us there. He could, and with having someone of his style in midfield it meant we could really play attacking midfielders around him. And we just kept on tinkering like that all the time to see what might work and what wouldn't.' I remember that policy from an abject pre-season friendly performance and defeat after which I delicately asked whether the manager had learned anything from the game.

'Yeah,' he replied with a grin. 'Jody Craddock's no left-back!'

At the time I did not pay that much attention, the centre-half being played out of position seemed to be purely down to limited selection options. But the coaching staff were always exploring options – like switching Johnston from the right wing to the left wing.

'I think Mickey Gray we experimented with most of all,' muses Reid. 'If you remember in those first couple of seasons we had him left-back, left wing, right wing, all over the place. Some worked, some didn't, but we were learning on the job, really, and so was he – eventually he was able to play equally as comfortably either in defence or midfield, which was useful to us when we had to shuffle things around. But as a left-back with his overlapping runs he was absolutely outstanding.

'Getting to know the players and how they fit in is key to what any good club is about. A well-designed team doesn't just happen by accident – you might get a lucky break or two but, overall, it's all about experimenting and putting in the mental work.'

This time when Sunderland came up, no one was talking about the club's relegation prospects. The only two talking points were, firstly, could Kevin Phillips do it at the highest level? Yes, was the verdict of most before a ball was even kicked – apart from Sky pundit Rodney Marsh who memorably reckoned the Sunderland striker would be lucky to score six all season! The second talking point was: could Niall Quinn, with his lack of pace, avoid being a liability in the top flight? Yes again. I remember Lee Clark laughing and telling me, 'People who say that about Quinn's pace have completely missed the point. Quinny has *never* had any pace – that's not what he's about. He'll be great in the Premier League – he's a defender's nightmare.'

There was also the enticing prospect of unleashing some of the jewels of the promotion push on an unsuspecting top flight – Sunderland's devastating left-wing combination most of all. I remember Sunderland coach Adrian Heath at the training ground, chatting excitedly about the prospect of Michael Gray and Allan Johnston tearing Premier League defences apart. 'They're unstoppable,' he said. 'Mickey's overlaps and Johnno's ability to cut inside or find Mickey with a pass – that will work at any level. It doesn't matter if you're a Premier League full-back or not – you'll not know which one to go with. If you go with Mickey, Johnno cuts inside; if you go with Johnno, he'll find Mickey with a pass and the cross is coming in anyway.'

Two decades later Reid agrees: 'Johnno was magnificent for us,' he enthuses. 'A great signing for not much money. He contributed in the Premier League in the relegation season when we had Waddle on the left and him on the right. But he really came into his own when we moved him from the right to the left wing. He didn't have pace but he could see a pass and he could chip a ball, and when you've got someone with that ability, to pick a pass, and others giving you options – Quinny going on the diag, Phillips coming short, Mickey going past you, runners from midfield – it's brilliant.'

Sadly, that scorching partnership was never to be tested at the highest level – Johnston, along with Michael Bridges and Lee Clark, were all transfer-listed on the same day and all three left the club that summer. At a stroke Sunderland lost three of their most exciting and creative talents. Wearside was stunned and for days afterwards not quite able to digest the news. I remember that close-season day in June very well, because I broke the story. Hungover and working from home, I rang Reid at the training ground to see if there were any scraps to be had for the *Sunderland Echo*. In close season, with football largely in hibernation mode, you rang more in hope than expectation. As a journalist, you never knew which Peter Reid you were going to get when you got him on the phone, but you knew the call was likely to be brief. He was never really one for small talk.

'Morning, Peter. Anything for me today?'

'Yeah. Michael Bridges, Lee Clark and Allan Johnston all on the transfer list. Today. Put that in your bloody newspaper.'

And then he hung up.

I took my life in my hands and rang him back.

'Definitely, Peter?'

'Definitely!'

And then he was gone again.

I was dumbfounded. Couldn't quite believe what I'd just heard. Didn't know whether to print or not. Wasn't sure if I'd woken up yet. But print the *Sunderland Echo* did and Wearside had its story of the summer, which divided supporters – should they stay or should they go?

Clark had blotted his copybook by wearing a t-shirt in front of Newcastle fans on the day of the FA Cup final between Newcastle United and Manchester United that May with the caption 'Sad Mackem Bastards' on it. He was to later say that he only had it on for a matter of seconds. But this was the new world of social media, a Newcastle supporter photographed him, and the moment was frozen in time on the internet for the whole world to see. Speculation over what would happen next, with Sunderland fans enraged when the story broke, had gone on for days. Clark was one of the few players of proven Premier League experience in the promoted squad, but his antics had hugely angered the faithful.

Meanwhile, Bridges and Johnston had both been stalling on new contracts, with Johnston's camp suggesting he run the last year of his contract down with Sunderland and become a free agent the following summer. The club had pushed hard to get Bridges to sign a long-term contract. The striker was sponsored by the chairman's wife, Sue, and was regarded as the next future homegrown hero at the club – the crown jewels, as far as Bob Murray was concerned. But Bridges knew his options were limited with Phillips and Quinn clear first choices and now, almost 21 years old, he was aware that he should perhaps be looking to be more than super-sub or stand-in. This was an era, remember, when Robbie Fowler established himself in Liverpool's first team at just 18 years old; Michael Owen at 17 – Bridges, at 21, was in an uncomfortable position.

But the indecision on all three's futures was not to be tolerated for long. Everything had been up in the air before that phone call, although the situation relating to Bridges and Johnston's contract were not issues that had been particular talking points publicly. Most assumed they would eventually get sorted. Clark's position was clearly an awkward one, and most supporters were open to all options, but prodigy Bridges and Magic Johnston were two of the most loved and treasured favourites of the fans. The call was huge.

'*Wow!*' chuckles Reid, with an intake of breath as he casts his mind back to that day. 'Some of the decisions I used to make, you look back at them and you think, "*Wow!*" That was one of my biggest calls, but I had no doubts then that it was the right one and, to be honest, no doubt either now. With Clarky and the Sad Mackem Bastard t-shirt, things just weren't right. They weren't right. There are certain things you can't do at a club, and he'd done one of them. If he'd come on bended knee and said, "Sorry, I've made a mistake, I want to stay" and been genuine about it, we might have looked at standing by him, because he was such a good player for us. But it would have been incredibly difficult, and what was really annoying with was how easily avoidable the whole mess should have been. I wouldn't care, but when the club had agreed to let him go to the Cup final he'd been specifically told before he went to make sure he didn't get caught wearing colours . . . Well, I suppose he didn't wear colours!

'But I also knew there were other things at play with Clarky too. I knew that playing against Newcastle the next season in a Sunderland shirt was on his mind, and how he would cope with that, as a proud Geordie. He had been great playing for us in the Championship when the whole Newcastle thing wasn't an issue – Mickey Gray was his best mate and you couldn't get more Mackem than Mickey. That side of things was great, he was very popular among the squad. But he knew after what he had done with the t-shirt, he would struggle. He thought he should go, and I felt it was right for him to go too. It was a pity because he had been such a good player for us in those two seasons in the Championship.

'As for Bridgey and Johnno, they had deals on the table with us and they backed out of them. Things were changing and I felt I couldn't trust them. I knew Glasgow Rangers had gotten into Johnno – Glasgow were absolutely flying at the time and had just won the treble – and I knew Leeds and Spurs, who were flying in the Premier League, were circling Bridgey. I wanted them to sign new contracts and we worked hard at it, but it wasn't happening. There were agents around them and that wasn't right, and then came that point where I felt I just had to make up my mind. That was the day I decided.'

Financially the departures were not bad news for Sunderland: Johnston, who had been bought for a modest fee, may have left on a free, but the club made £500,000 profit on Clark, who joined Kevin Keegan's Fulham, and youth product Bridges was for some years the club's record sale at £5.5 million after his move to Leeds United. Morale in the squad and the fanbase took a hit, though – and for one of the trio, in particular, the move was an own goal in terms of his career.

'Johnno went to Rangers and barely kicked a ball that season,' Reid nods. 'He would have been a key player for us but he barely got a game for them. He spent most of the time in the reserves and moved on at the end of the season. How will he look back on that now? I suppose that's one you have to go and ask him. I mean, he's a manager now, so he'll probably understand that you have to be strong in terms of needing your players all focused and on board – but, bloody hell, you look back, and that day, that decision, that was bloody massive, that.'

In danger of being derailed by events – even if he had, ultimately, precipitated them himself – Reid's work in the transfer market now had to be outstanding. It turned out that it was, as Steve Bould and Stefan Schwarz proved the standout buys that helped Sunderland hit the ground running on their return to the Premier League.

'As well as the three players leaving, Martin Smith and Martin Scott went that summer too, and I also lost Andy Melville,' points out Reid. 'I didn't sign Melville, but he was a great servant for us, a really high quality defender in both the Championship and the Premier League. I offered him a year deal getting renewed every six months if he kept doing it for me. I thought it would incentivise him because he'd really shaped up and had been such a fantastic player for us – often underrated, I felt. I offered him terms that I thought would keep him on the straight and narrow because I knew he had had this reputation of enjoying a drink with Phil Gray. But Fulham offered him a two-year term and a good deal, and I can't blame the kid for taking it. He was a miss but we managed to get Steve Bould in from Arsenal on a two-year deal for just £400,000, and he was unbelievable for us. He was arguably my best bit of business. We only got six months out of him before he got injured but he was absolutely bloody brilliant, absolute class at the back. Magnificent. The way he controlled and ordered everyone in defence was amazing – my players were learning so much from him. He commanded total respect and, after Arsenal, he was really enjoying the new challenge when he picked up the foot injury which ended his career. It was a terrible shame.

'I also brought in a replacement for Johnno. I needed to, and I had to spend big in terms of Sunderland. But after patiently trying to persuade him to join us for weeks, we managed to bring in Stefan Schwarz, who was fantastic. And there's another one I was unlucky with – him getting injured playing away for Sweden.

'Now, he was a different type of player altogether from Johnno. Where Johnno was magic and skilful and all that flair, Schwarz was intelligent, read the game and played the simple pass all the time, usually to Mickey Gray. He'd come inside and read the game unbelievably well, and he really made us solid. He had a presence and a calmness to him. It meant we had to play narrower, because he wasn't a winger like Johnno was, but Mickey Gray could go past him and give us that width, and Stefan could give us a solidness and a stability.'

With the new signings adding defensive strength, the Quinn and Phillips goalscoring partnership hitting new heights, and with the Stadium of Light average attendance by now regularly over 40,000, the club looked finally to be on their way to regaining former glories. It was a sleeping giant no more, and that return to the Premier League proved it.

Sunderland had a spell of winning 11 of 16 games in the early stage of the season, scalps including Spurs, Villa, a 5-0 win over Derby County and a spectacular 4-1 defeat of Chelsea in December still talked about by fans to this day. The Chelsea game has entered folklore for a first-half performance which saw Sunderland give a footballing master-class to a team which had become one of the leading lights of the top flight. Few could believe their eyes, the way Sunderland shone that day, especially considering the Blues had steamrollered the Black Cats 4-0 at Stamford Bridge in the opening game of the season. Just over an hour after the final whistle blew on that defeat in the capital, Bobby Saxton took the players out on the pitch and gave a talk in which he told them to draw a line under the loss and move on. The players did exactly that, and when Chelsea came to the Stadium of Light with the Black Cats riding high in the league, Sunderland were ready for them.

Underlining the power of their partnership, Quinn and Phillips scored two goals each before half-time, Quinn's first coming after 48 seconds, with the Blues' World Cup winning centre-half Marcel Desailly given a particularly torrid time alongside fellow central defender Jon Harley. Both were replaced at the break.

At half-time I always remember walking across the concourse from the press box, which in those days was situated just behind the opposition dugout, towards the press room and past fans who were laughing openly in disbelief at Sunderland's total domination. No one could believe the confidence and the mastery they were witnessing from Sunderland. It was epic, historic, unheard of, Phillips capping it off with a wonderful solo goal from range which could have come straight out of a *Roy of the Rovers* annual.

Second half, Chelsea did a containing job: Gus Poyet, who was to become Sunderland manager many years later, and who, as a Chelsea player, had a habit of doing well against the Wearsiders, got a consolation goal late on.

'Great game, a great day,' recalls Reid. 'Quinn and Phillips were on fire and the whole team were brilliant, but can you tell me who our central midfielders were that game?'

I can. Youth product Paul Thirlwell, and veteran French midfielder Éric Roy.

'Correct!' says Reid. 'People tend to forget all about them, but Thirlwell was a very intelligent player who was great at seeing the game and helping us keep our shape. Whenever we went forward and the move broke down and the opposition came at us, who would you find covering at the back, having dropped in? It was Thirlwell, if he was playing – just like Schwarz always did. Schwarz was great at covering for Mickey if Mickey had gone on one of his runs, and just as good moving into midfield if we were being stretched across the middle.'

And the elegant and cultured Roy, a £200,000 signing from Marseille?

'Lovely player, good temperament, good feet, passed the ball well, tall. I just wish I could have got him earlier in his career. He was 32 when he joined us.'

Age is only a number to some players. Bould and Quinn never lost their effectiveness – only injuries did for them. Bould retired at 37, Quinn at 36. But others, in the view of Reid, do find themselves compromised after a certain age. The coaching staff felt that way about Roy, who certainly contributed to Sunderland as a squad member but made only 27 starts in his 18 months at the club. And age was also a factor in one of Reid's most enigmatic signings that summer, former Germany captain Thomas Helmer.

The 68-times capped Helmer represented a great coup in the close season after promotion was won, signing on a free for the Black Cats and rejecting (as did Schwarz) an offer from Liverpool in the process. Many thought Helmer, not Bould, would be the rock upon which the Sunderland defence would be built. Reid too says he had high hopes for the German, only to find Father Time had caught up with the 34-year-old.

'Thomas Helmer was a fantastic player,' says Reid. 'But his legs had gone and that became clear to us soon after he joined. I might have gone with him in a five, as a holding midfield player, but I always wanted a decent back four and he couldn't get in there, he'd have got found out there. It got to the stage where I was toying with the idea of playing him as a defensive midfield player because he really was an outstanding footballer – his touch, his awareness, honest to God, wonderful. But his legs were gone – I felt so unlucky with him.'

Helmer played in only two games for Sunderland that season, both in August, before leaving the following month on loan to Hertha Berlin, where he appeared to make a nonsense of the Black Cats' judgement by playing in a Champions League victory over Chelsea. But Hertha lost the return, Helmer was soon back on Wearside and, later in the season, Sunderland bought out his contract with the defender opting to retire immediately afterwards.

'Age catches up with some players faster than others,' says Reid. 'When players get into their thirties there's always the sense they could be living on borrowed time. Éric Roy was 32, Helmer 34 – quality players who you hope to get a season or two out of if you're looking to step up a level. Players like Quinny and Bouldy are very much the exception, not the rule.'

With the emphatic win over Chelsea Sunderland had sent out a message that their form was not an early season blip. Still riding high in December they had even had the chance to go top of the Premier League in October on a visit to West Ham. Despite having Bould sent off early in the game, Phillips scored half a dozen minutes later and Thomas Sørensen was outstanding in the Sunderland goal, keeping the Hammers at bay. But second-half substitute Danny Dichio missed a great, late chance to make it 2-0 and then conceded possession minutes later, which allowed another Sunderland manager in the making, Paolo Di Canio, to set up an 89th minute Trevor Sinclair equaliser. Reid still bristles at the sending off.

'The officials messed up in the way they sent Bouldy off,' he sniffs. 'They had no idea what had happened and went with the crowd reaction. We tried to box it but couldn't quite see it through.'

A couple of months earlier Sunderland fans had enjoyed what was to be the high point of the season for many of them – the memorable 2-1 defeat of Newcastle United at St James' Park in torrential rain. Widely expected to lose going into the game (Newcastle were still remembered as The Entertainers from the early part of the nineties; Sunderland were just up from the Championship and their derby record was poor), the Black Cats stunned their rivals with their first league win in the celebrated fixture for 19 years. Kieron Dyer's early goal was cancelled out in the 64th by Quinn and a stunning turn and shot from Phillips ten minutes later saw the United net bulge again. At this stage Sunderland looked in as much danger of the game being abandoned for rain as they did from a Newcastle equaliser. The water came down in stair rods and under the exposed Milburn Stand, which was in the process of extension, sports reporters' laptops filled up, overflowed and shut down, one by one, inside the makeshift press box. There was trouble on the touchline too as, seeing the way the game was going, Newcastle's forthright chief executive Freddie Fletcher appeared next to the dugouts urging referee Graham Poll to call the game off in the last ten minutes.

Reid recalls, 'We were doing brilliantly in difficult conditions, and it was a case of just seeing the game out when Freddie suddenly pops up and we're all thinking, "What's *he* doing?" He was told in no uncertain terms by us where to go!'

Fortunately, Poll realised that the storm caused by calling the game off at this late stage would be even worse than the one everyone was enduring on the pitch, and the match ended with puddles on the turf and wild celebrations in the Sunderland dressing room.

These were high points in a run which left the club third in the league on Boxing Day but, in both this campaign and the one that followed, the early season momentum could not be sustained beyond the turn of the year. There were reasons for this in the 1999–2000 campaign: if injuries to Coton and Quinn had been a key to the previous Premier League relegation, then there is an argument for pointing at the same culprit as Sunderland slowed in the opening months of the new millennium. Having lost important players pre-season, the Black Cats finished the campaign without either or their of most effective summer signings – Bould and Schwarz – but it was the loss of the commanding defender that was to be most keenly felt. Bould suffered a freak toe injury in the last quarter of an hour of a defeat to Leeds United when he launched himself into a no-prisoners challenge on Darren Huckerby. Sunderland were already in a sticky run at the time, with the squad tiring, recent signing left-winger Kevin Kilbane struggling to gel with his new teammates, and Quinn sidelined – but Bould's absence from the end of January, followed by Schwarz in March (with a severed tendon), was hardly helpful as efforts were made to arrest the tailspin.

'My only regret with Bouldy is that we couldn't have had him for a little bit longer,' sighs Reid. 'He was like Quinny – age didn't affect him. And he used all that experience to bring the very best out of the young legs around him. I felt I was dead lucky to get him, and then dead unlucky to lose him. I only had six months of him, but he was magnificent. I loved Bouldy. I gave him a two-year-deal – which some people might have thought a bit mad – but I actually wanted to give him a three-year deal. He would have been worth every penny, and the fact he had to retire when he did was one of my biggest disappointments. When you've seen a top player – I was a coach at Everton when we tried to sign him from Stoke City in 1988, and he went to Arsenal as a young kid – and when you get that player in eventually, it's a great feeling. And when you see that top player, and you work with him, and you think, "Hey, he's better than I first thought, even at 34" – that's better still as a manager.

'At the time, getting a good player from abroad or getting a player in their thirties was a way of potentially getting your transfer budget to go that little bit further, because the prices for British talent were so high then. Obviously, that strategy could come with risks – players tend to be more susceptible to injuries the older they get. But I felt I was unlucky with Bould in the way he got the injury – and Schwarz was another one I was unlucky with.

'Schwarz goes away on international duty in March – a meaningless friendly – and comes back with a serious injury which keeps him out until December! He gave up international football after that but, physically, the damage was done.'

Sunderland failed to win a game between mid-December and a week shy of April before eventually staging something of a revival – five wins in their last nine games – to earn a seventh-place finish in the Premier League. That finish was their highest in the top flight since the mid-1950s but it still felt tinged by disappointment given the swashbuckling nature of what had gone before in the first half of the campaign. That belated return to form saw Quinn and Phillips scoring eight of Sunderland's last 11 goals, which underlined how important the strike duo had become to their side's hopes of getting something out of games. It also underlined how vulnerable they might be to losing either striker for any period of time.

The 2000–01 campaign was to be almost an action replay of the previous one: third at Christmas, seventh at season's end, once more just missing out on European qualification. But this time it was achieved with a squad that was steadily evolving away from that which had carried Sunderland so far in previous years. Having lost Melville, Clark, Bridges, Johnston and Smith at the start of the 1999–2000 season, inspirational skipper Kevin Ball would be gone in December and Bould before the end of the campaign.

Ball's departure was precipitated by the fact that at 35 he was no longer going to be playing Premier League football regularly but remained as keen as ever to be a footballer who played every week. Leaving his beloved Sunderland allowed him to do that. He was to go on to play almost 100 more games – for Fulham and Burnley – before retiring at the age of 37. Though by the end he might not have been the presence on the pitch he had once been for the Black Cats, he was always hugely influential off it, where his insistence that players adhered to the highest levels of standards and discipline was legendary. It was inevitable that his departure would see a lessening of the relentless focus he demanded of all around him. In the summer, after that first seventh-place finish, Sunderland plunged into the transfer market to make a string of signings that were to have varying impacts on the club's fortunes: midfielders Don Hutchison and Julio Arca; centre-halves Stan Varga and Emerson Thome; and goalkeeper Jürgen Macho.

Crucially, though, the club struggled to find reinforcements up front who could put serious pressure on the places of the two main strikers – although fleet-footed young French forward David Bellion looked, for a short time, as though he might offer hope.

'We had some good players through the door that summer,' says Reid. 'Arca was a brilliant player and it was no surprise he became a fans' favourite. And I wouldn't be too harsh on Bellion: he cost very little and the club made a decent profit on him, selling him to Man United for £2 million. But, yeah, it was hard to find reinforcements up front who could improve us. Phillips had won the Golden Shoe, Quinn was one of the best target men in Europe, let alone England, so it was hard to find the money to bring in forwards who could challenge them – those sorts of players don't grow on trees. And it was also difficult to find a top-quality striker willing to come in and be prepared to be third choice.'

In both the 1999–00 and 2000–01 campaigns Sunderland were among the top two or three teams in the league at the halfway mark, before subsiding to seventh at the end of the season. In 2001, as with the preceding season, injuries played a part: Sørensen and Summerbee suffered knocks; Schwarz did not return until December and was not as effective then as he had been previously. There were form and fitness issues: the ageing Quinn managed only two goals after Christmas; winger Kevin Kilbane was still struggling to find his feet in the side. And there were departures too: the Manchester trio of Nicky Summerbee, Chris Makin and Paul Butler all leaving within months of each other, with rumours of factionalism arising in the camp.

Maybe this was an area where the iron-hand of Kevin Ball was missed. Maybe the rumours of cliques developing were just rumours, but there was no doubt the winds of change were blowing through the squad and not always for the best.

'There were outside influences sometimes in transfers, and that's always the case,' Reid says. 'With Alex Rae, for example, he was still playing well for us. I just felt he needed a change.

Martin Smith we wanted to keep, but he decided to leave. Same with Melville, and so on.'

Other signings simply just didn't come off. Danish goalscoring midfielder Carsten Fredgaard, for example, who had arrived the previous summer, hailed for his speed and being touted as a key signing, made only two substitute appearances. Pint-sized South American striker Milton Núñez was utterly unsuited for the physical power of the Premier League, where it was almost no exaggeration to suggest someone like Arsenal's Tony Adams could literally have had him in his pocket! John Oster had the skill of a Magic Johnston but neither his consistency nor visibility on the pitch. Arca's Argentina under 20 teammate Nicolás Medina and big young defender Baki Mercimek, who similarly had zero impact, arrived in the summer of 2001. Mercimek was free but Medina cost £3.5 million – a lot of money to Sunderland at the time.

On top of that, in terms of young players coming through, Michael Reddy and Michael Proctor were prospects but no Michael Bridges; reserve-team defender George McCartney and midfielder Thomas Butler looked as though they could be stars of the future, but not now. Almost imperceptibly, the circle was turning on the downward slide for Sunderland.

'Carsten Fredgaard, was a top drawer, young Danish player, but he couldn't handle England and English football,' says Reid. 'He was just like Nicolás Medina, when I bought him over from Argentina – an exciting young prospect abroad, who found English football completely different. There were a few times over those seasons when I was trying to get players in, but the players you want, you can't get in, they're too expensive – which at the time, British players who I would have loved to have had in – tended to be. And in those circumstances you take the risk of a punt abroad in the hope you might find a gem, a bargain buy compared to what you might spend on a proven British player.'

Despite all this, Sunderland ended January of the 2000–01 campaign still in second place in the Premier League. The season had started with a stunning single-goal home win over Arsenal with giant Slovakian centre-half Stan Varga having one of the best debuts of any Sunderland player in the history of the club. It was a big blow when he suffered a serious leg problem in just the second game of the campaign, at Manchester City, which he never truly came back from as the same player. A sluggish August and early September were followed by a seven-game unbeaten run in the league, which included four wins, and Sunderland were suddenly upwardly mobile. More mini-runs followed. Four successive league wins across November and December included the second 2-1 win over Newcastle United at St James' Park – goals from Hutchison and Quinn and a Sørensen save of Alan Shearer's penalty. A six-game league unbeaten run across December and January featured four wins, but once again Sunderland began to blow up in the home straight, winning only three of their last 15 games of the season. In both seasons, Quinn admitted finding the going tough after Christmas as a long campaign took a strain on his body – and given he was so pivotal to the way Sunderland played, that was always going to have an effect on results. The loss of that supremely functional right flank with the departures of Makin and Summerbee also had an effect. And across the wings, without Johnston too (who, along with Summerbee, provided the perfect supply line, according to Phillips and Quinn) the crosses began to dry up. They could not be replaced by Kilbane, or even the skilful Arca. And when central midfielders deputised out wide – Schwarz was deployed on the left, Hutchison on the right – the effect was that Sunderland played narrower in midfield, and still failed to get the crosses in that Quinn and Phillips thrived on.

Phillips, who in his first season in the Premier League had become the only Englishman to win the Golden Boot, managed a creditable 18 goals in all competitions in the 2000–

01 campaign; Quinn, eight. But the shortfall was partly made up by Don Hutchison, Sunderland's player of the season – yet he was to stay only one season at the club.

Versatile Hutchison could play all the way across the midfield positions and even played up front on occasions. That ability was invaluable, given that Reid had somewhat surprisingly sold Alex Rae to Wolves for £1 million in September – although Gavin McCann becoming a regular in the side mitigated the Scot's loss.

'Alex did brilliantly at Wolves when he left us,' admits Reid. 'But I was actually pleased about that because I just felt that at Sunderland he'd got to the stage where he needed a different challenge, a fresh start. He had his problems and the move just seemed the best for him at the time. You have to make decisions that involve the football club and the player's personal life and you just hope to get it right. We've kept in touch over the years, like I have done with quite a few of the players, and I have to say that the way he has turned his life around is inspirational. At the moment Alex left things were looking good for us, but it's hard to account for how quickly things change.'

One of those changes was Hutchison's unexpected departure. Reid would dearly have loved to have kept the Geordie at the club long-term but found himself unable to break the club's pay structure when the midfielder came looking for a substantial pay rise at the end of his sole Sunderland campaign.

'A year into Hutch's contract he wanted a new one,' sighs Reid. 'He said, "I've played a year and I've been your best player." "Well," I said, "I don't pay you to play bad!" He says, "I've been offered £24,000 a week at two other clubs." I went to the chairman, and the chairman wasn't having it, and I had to agree with him. If Hutch had got what he wanted, we would have had a queue of first-team players outside my door demanding their contracts be looked at – that's the way football works. We made the right decision from a purely practical point of view, but I was sorry to see him go. Hutch was quite loud in the dressing room, and there's no doubt he was a miss. He came in and did a great job playing on that right-hand side mainly, when we had to go narrow across the middle. He was intelligent, no pace, but a clever footballer, and he got me goals, which was really important. It's a shame I only had him for a year. If money hadn't been an issue, I would have given it to him – but you hear managers say that a lot when they are only interested in the short-term success of the squad. At the end of the day, you can't argue with the owners because they have to find the money. In terms of Hutchison, he'd done very well out of the move to Sunderland in the first place, and we couldn't break our wage structure – so that was it, he was on his way. I got £5 million for him when he moved to West Ham, which was good money – twice what we'd paid to bring him to Sunderland. But it was hard to replace him. And that tended to be an ongoing problem for us: players that had come in and done well were hard to replace with similar quality.'

When it came down to it, in both seasons Sunderland fell away from the top, a successful January transfer window might have breathed fresh life into their charge. But on both occasions, the funds weren't there. One of the reasons for that was the investment, in the first season back in the top flight, in extending the North Stand. That meant the Stadium of Light capacity increasing from 42,000 from 48,000 in the summer of 1999, sucking up £6 million of potential transfer funds. Reid opposed the move to extend the stadium on the basis that the ground was pretty much full every week, creating a great atmosphere and a demand for tickets, and that the money was more needed for urgent team strengthening. This could have been interpreted as the manager taking a short-term view. Bob Murray was thinking longer-term – an extra 6,000 fans would bring in extra revenue potentially for ever. The Sunderland chairman was also thinking about chasing down local rivals Newcastle and their 52,000-capacity ground: Sunderland's Stadium of Light could go from 48,000 to 55,000, and to 63,000 in future years.

'At the board meeting we had which discussed the extension, I did comment that I wanted it minuted in the boardroom minutes that we didn't have to go up to 48,000. We could have kept the stadium at 42,000 and spent the £6 million on players, but Bob was obsessed with Newcastle. He always was. He always wanted to get the stadium up to, and, if possible, beyond Newcastle's capacity. I used to say to him, "You can't affect what they do. The only way you can affect what they do is when you play against them, otherwise you can't." But I knew it was a passion of his.

'But when we finished seventh in the league twice we should have got international footballers in. Looking back, that's when we really should have gone for it. Expectations were being ramped up all the time in some quarters, and it was becoming a problem for us.'

Those rising expectations were brought home to Reid when the crowd began to express their unhappiness in a home game against Everton in March 2000 that Sunderland weren't winning – a sentiment that was reinforced to the manager in several games subsequently when a section of fans at the Stadium of Light made clear their dissatisfaction that smaller teams were not being rolled over.

'No club has a divine right to win games, especially in the Premier League, but because we had done so well the view seemed to be growing that some clubs should be just swept aside. It was a concern I raised with the chairman. We won that Everton match, but the fans were clearly expecting us to be challenging at the very top of the table and, for that, we needed a lot of investment. I told Bob we needed to kick on and bring in international level footballers, but Bob's response was, "If we finish fourth from bottom every season, I'm happy." Maybe he was trying to take the pressure off – letting me know that as long as were in the Premier League he wouldn't have a problem. After being part of a yo-yo club for so long maybe he just wanted us to be a solid member of the top flight. But looking back, I think I should have been more demanding. When we needed to push on at that stage, I felt the chairman was content to stand still in terms of when to put the money in. We had got up there with the highest teams in the land, but to stay in that top five or six is the hardest bit of all, and that needs money to bring in top players. I did get some money to spend and, in the last couple of seasons, I could have spent it better, but the moment to spend big was when we right up there, not when we began to struggle. I felt it was too late when he let me buy Flo, Stewart, Wright, Piper in my last season – by then we were fire-fighting.' If he was sometimes frustrated in the transfer market at Sunderland, it was never serious enough for him to really consider his position once Sunderland had reached the top flight. He could have swapped the Black Cats for former Premier League champions Blackburn Rovers in 1999. Jack Walker's newly relegated Rovers tried to persuade Reid to forsake Sunderland and take over the north-west club. But staying at Sunderland, having taken the club as far as he had and moulded it so much in the image he wanted, always meant he was unlikely to walk away from Wearside. Having established Black Cats as a Premier League force, Reid was now in the process of trying to build his third Sunderland team – the first one having earned promotion and narrowly missed out on survival, the second one having stormed to promotion and produced two top-half finishes in succession. Sunderland desperately needed to transition because it was clear now that Niall Quinn couldn't go on for ever, and he had been so central to how Sunderland played. The likes of Ball, Melville and Ord had moved on long ago, but now so had Summerbee, Makin, Rae and Hutchison. Not having big funds to play with compared to many of the top Premier League rivals they were now chasing meant Sunderland needed to get full value for money out of transfer windows pretty much every time in order to progress. All managers are only one or two good transfer windows from success, and, equally, one or two bad windows away from failure. Schwarz and Bould were big hits that first season back but Fredgaard and Helmer emphatically were not. The following season Mercimek and the £3.5 million Medina were failures, while Arca and Hutchison were successes.

Failures and departures meant Sunderland were under pressure to get it right in the transfer market going into the 2001–02 campaign – the pre-season expectation for the club now was to qualify for Europe, having missed out by a whisker in the previous two seasons. With a tough brief to fulfill, Reid tried to make the most of his funds in that summer's transfer window. He bought midfielder Jason McAteer for £1 million, centre-half Joachim Björklund for £1.5 million, and Swiss right-back Bernt Haas for £750,000 – and paid a minimal fee for pacey young striker David Bellion. But his main investment was £3.6 million in Bordeaux frontman Lilian Laslandes to provide a challenge and a support for Phillips and Quinn. This time there were no success stories among the signings – in a season where relegation was only avoided in the last game of the campaign.

Key-signing Laslandes was brought in to take the pressure off Quinn, who needed increasingly to be physically managed through games, but the Frenchman was hopeless from the start – and it turned out he was as unhappy off the pitch as he was on it, and did not last long at the club. The others had only a limited impact on displays, and it was left to the old stalwarts to do the heavy lifting. Laslandes' last game was a forgettable display against Blackburn Rovers in which, tellingly, his replacement, weary substitute Niall Quinn, notched the winner.

'In fairness, it was difficult to get players across the last few seasons and there were one or two that we agreed deals for and they did not come,' says Reid. 'There were times when I used to look at some of the players Bolton were getting in at the time and wished we could have done the same. I tried to get Ruud van Nistelrooy in before he went to Ajax, but I couldn't do that. I tried to get Zlatan Ibrahimović on a couple of occasions. We needed someone to come in and take the pressure off Quinny, and I looked at a lot at possibilities but we couldn't get them for one reason or another. Laslandes was the one that we could get, and that I thought might do it for us. I watched him several times and I thought, "I've got one here!" But I messed up. I didn't do my homework, I didn't realise he had problems off the field, and those had an effect on him. On top of that he just couldn't buy into it at Sunderland – that was a key signing that didn't work.'

Laslandes played poorly, failing to score a single goal in the league in 12 forgettable appearances. He also contributed little in the way of build-up play either before a drink-driving charge helped speed an eventual loan move to Cologne. History has enshrined the 2001–02 campaign mentally as a season-long slog, a miserable 'after-the-Lord Mayor's-show' in which Quinn finally began to break down, Phillips struggled for goals and the team flat-lined. But a look at the record books shows that's not entirely the case.

Despite the ineffectiveness of Laslandes in the opening games of the season, Phillips was on typical top goalscoring form – six goals in the first ten games – and partially as a result of that Sunderland spent the opening six weeks in the top half of the table. True, Phillips' season was not as prolific as his previous ones, but he still managed 13 goals overall and his goals brought points. He scored the only goal of the game in the season opener, against Ipswich, and the only goal of the game in the final match of the season, against Derby County – and those points were taken from two of the three teams which ended up below fourth-bottom Sunderland proved crucial. You'll also find Sunderland seventh in the table at the end of September and ninth on Boxing Day – so it wasn't as bad a campaign as it felt before the traditional turn of the year slide.

What had changed, though, as well as the pressure of expectation, was the undeniable fact that Sunderland had lost the flair, the finesse and the fluency with which they had formerly played. The slide and the struggle began in mid-September – one win in nine games, before victories over Everton and Blackburn Rovers either side of Christmas briefly took Sunderland up to ninth.

From the New Year, though, the form and the football were pretty much atrocious, and it was awful to see several top-quality players struggling so badly. Sunderland squeezed to a fourth-bottom finish after a long and depressing spell of rancour and recrimination during which just three of their last 19 games were won. Some of the football they played that season was awful, the lack of partnerships in the team glaring – as a side, they had gone backwards. On the back of that, or possibly allied to that, things were turning against Reid himself. Despite his helplessness when it came to spending big in the transfer market, Reid was increasingly perceived as all-powerful at the club. By the time he was sacked in 2002, only Mickey Gray remained from the day Reid first arrived. In many ways this was now the club that Reid had built – Sunderland's success was his success, so its failings were his failings. Reid had made a virtue out of his decisiveness, his ruthlessness, even – if he thought it was for the good of Sunderland. He believed, like Brian Clough and Sir Alex Ferguson did, that until sacked the manager has to be the most powerful man at the club – that there can only be one boss. From virtually the first day Reid was making decisions that would make him unpopular in one quarter or another and, eventually, some of those decisions left him isolated. Inside the club, which had grown in scale and function over the years, there were those who did not owe him any sense of allegiance. The club had changed from the Roker Park days, and that in itself presented a long-term challenge. Empire builders, who thought of what they might do for themselves rather than what they might do for Sunderland AFC, were a spin-off of the huge amounts of money which began to flow into the club on its return to the Premier League. This process was to continue for many years after Reid left.

When future managers talked about a darkness at the heart of the club, it was this bureaucratic structure they were referring to, where sometimes the tail could wag the dog; where there was always someone on the make in the corridors of power, and often not in the best interests of Sunderland.

More than that, the club had offended powerful influencers of public opinion under Reid. Local fanzines had had their run-ins with the club, as had local radio talk-in hosts and, as Sunderland struggled, they had no reason to save or support the manager. This too was also the era where, for the first time, the rise of social media made it that much easier to foster a toxic atmosphere. Depending on which side of the media you were listening to, increasingly you were either in a pro-Reid or anti-Reid camp at this stage. The result was that, at the closing stages of a disappointing season, there were isolated occasions where fans openly fought each other on the terraces, as those who backed Reid and those who wanted him sacked came to blows. Reid was fully aware of the dangers building around him, but powerless to do much about it as the pendulum swung.

'The relationship started really well but, as things go on, the club's circumstance changed,' he reflects. 'And I think you have to be very careful as clubs grow. When you get different sectors developing – commercial, marketing, press offices, elements around the board, one department after another or different structures being put in place at the top – there's the danger you see the growth of different interests and often competing interests that aren't always healthy for a football club. Sometimes it goes on – I could see it happening. Once the financial side of the business really started to come in, it became too big for one person to handle; too big for Bob, too big for me. But I think I should have been party to some discussions, like, for example, players getting goalscoring contracts – that's the best example of how things can get away from you – and that was before we even got back into the Premier League.

'I remember watching a game once. We're on the attack and I'm waiting for the ball to come in for Quinny or Phillips, who are perfectly placed, and one of my players lashes a shot wide instead of passing it. I had him at the break. "What the hell were you thinking of? Quinny and Phillips were waiting to tap it in?" And he says, "I've got a goals target in my contract." And I said, "*A what?!?*" Turns out that in his new contract he had been set a target for goals, at which point he would get bonuses. Someone probably thought that was a good idea at the time, but it cost the team a goal. I went mad about that.'

Although Reid cites Laslandes as the big disappointment of that 2001–02 season, in a curious way you could argue the case for it being USA international skipper Claudio Reyna, who arrived in the January transfer window hoping to help prevent that second-half-of-the-season slump. Reyna, a £4 million buy, was a class act whenever he played, and might have made all the difference to that Sunderland side had he been able to have a consistent run in it. Instead, he appeared to be as brittle as balsa wood, and injuries restricted him to just ten appearances all season. Captain America was a high-quality footballer, able to dictate play, distribute the ball masterfully and create dangerous attacks. His absence for large chunks of his time at Sunderland was keenly felt.

'Claudio Reyna,' says Reid, shaking his head. 'He was another one – he never played. We couldn't get him on the pitch! I loved him as a player but I couldn't get games out of him – and I hit a patch like that: Matt Piper, Stephen Wright, Stan Varga. But, personally, Laslandes was possibly the biggest disappointment for me of all my signings.'

The 2001–02 season proved a long slog and supporters became increasingly unhappy that the second-half-of-the-season slump could not be arrested. Perpetual gloom seemed to be settling over the Stadium of Light. Captain Michael Gray and midfielder McAteer came under fire from sections of fans simply for mounting a public defence of their manager. Kilbane still hadn't been able to win fans over, though his manager was satisfied with the wide man's performances.

'I think Kevin Kilbane did work out as a move, but I think the fans wouldn't have him because he looked ungainly,' he says. 'He went on to have a great top-flight career for many years and, despite all the pressure on him at Sunderland, he never hid, he was always there to receive the ball. He was strong and had a great left foot, but he just wasn't a fit for Sunderland – he was effective, but the supporters wouldn't have him. It was hard for him, and I felt for him.'

By this stage there were times when Reid left his dugout to organise the team which sparked boos from the crowd. He was stuck in a cleft stick – go to the touchline to organise his side but be booed and have his players distracted; or stay in the dugout and be accused of hiding. Rumours circulated of transfer misdealings, training ground bust-ups and affairs. Fans shouted, 'Where's the money gone' at him from the terraces.

Reid shrugs, 'Yes, we used to hear the rumours – some of them were just ridiculous or laughable – but there's nothing you can do about that. You have to try to get your football to do the talking for you. I knew that some of the stuff that was going on out there was naughty, was wrong, and wasn't making our lives any easier. There were agendas. But what I never forgot at Sunderland is that it is the fans' football club, and I understand that finishing four from bottom in the Premier League and then not having a great start to the next season puts the pressure on.'

By now Reid's enemies sensed blood in the water. Despite having signed a contract in 2001 to keep him at the club until 2005 – Reid earning rich words of praise from Bob Murray when the deal was done – the season that followed had thrown everything up in the air. Disappointed but not defeated by a demoralising campaign, Reid knew he had to spark a major resurgence in the 2002–03 campaign if he wanted to be part of the new Academy of Light which was in the process of being completed.

That it had gone beyond football, that there were those who wanted him out of the club at all costs, was underlined by a ropey pre-season when Kilbane flicked the V-sign at supporters who were barracking him and Reid had beer thrown in his face by an individual who does not deserve the title of supporter. It was a horrible and humiliating moment in the dressing room for Reid, before the mood was lightened by kitman John Cooke who strolled in casually and said, 'Hey gaffer, I thought you were off the drink in pre-season!'

Reid was more focused on his next signing, who he was determined this time would be the one to make all the difference. He decided to put all his money in one basket and go for guaranteed class he could rely on: Irish goalscoring maestro Robbie Keane.

Keane would cost top dollar, and that meant early summer signings were modest – goalkeeper Thomas Myhre, veteran defender Phil Babb – with money being reserved for the Leeds and Republic of Ireland international striker. The summer-long pursuit of Keane – under the radar for fear of alerting rivals – stretched across the whole close season and stalled Sunderland's other transfer dealings. In press briefings to the *Echo* while on pre-season tour in France, Reid would give near daily updates, just waiting for the green light from Elland Road. But for one different reason after another – a succession of holidays, paperwork, work commitments – the prospective signing dragged on and on and on, and eventually when the move was ready to be made, Spurs came in and nabbed Keane.

'I tried really hard to get Robbie Keane that summer and for a long, long time we thought it was going to happen,' says Reid ruefully. 'I worked hard on that one – me, and Quinny too – but we just couldn't get the deal done, and when Spurs came in to get him, there was nothing we could do about it.'

Chairman Bob Murray had at last found a budget to back Reid to the hilt and with the money earmarked for Keane now burning a hole in his pocket, Reid splashed £10 million on acquiring former Chelsea striker Tore André Flo from Glasgow Rangers and Marcus Stewart from Ipswich. A further £3.5 million was spent on England under-21 winger Matt Piper, and £3 million on promising young Liverpool right-back Stephen Wright. The signings arrived late in the window and briefly calmed the anxieties of supporters – a front four of Phillips, Quinn, Flo and Stewart looked, after all, decent on paper.

But the reality was that both Flo and Stewart failed to hit the ground running, Quinn was now coming into what would have to be his last season, and Phillips was increasingly feeling the pressure of shouldering the burden and responsibility of goalscoring. None of the new signings could spark a revival:

Wright and Piper were injury-prone from the start, Flo was a flop, Stewart was only to come good in the wake of Sunderland's relegation that season. And just nine games into the new season, with results not having picked up from the previous campaign, Reid was sacked.

Sunderland had been on the slide for months by then, but the timing of the sacking was still odd, given the Black Cats had just negotiated the trickiest of starts to the new campaign. Reid had previously suggested to the board that if they wanted him to go, he would go, but they had always made it clear they wanted him to stay.

Looking back on that difficult start, Blackburn Rovers, who were to finish sixth that season, were the first opponents, and included in the early run were Leeds United, Everton, Man United and derbies against Middlesbrough and Newcastle. They were followed by a 1-0 win over Aston Villa and a thumping 7-0 League Cup win over Cambridge United, before a 3-1 defeat to Arsenal at Highbury. When Bob Murray called Peter Reid after the Gunners defeat and arranged to meet him in Manchester, Sunderland lay fourth bottom with an inviting set of fixtures finally ahead of them – having weathered the hardest of starts, Sunderland now had to play three of their fellow bottom four: West Ham, Bolton and Charlton.

Reid never got the chance to see if he could turn the ship around again. It turned out fourth-bottom in the table wasn't good enough for Bob Murray, after all.

It is now believed the decision was taken to sack Reid in the wake of the September loss to Newcastle United but the axe was delayed because the club did not want to give the impression a derby defeat had done for Reid. Even so, it's reasonable to think an upturn in results and the easier fixtures ahead might have forced a rethink by the board.

'After nine games they got rid of me, so I didn't really have much chance to mould a new team,' frowns Reid. 'Stephen Wright had got injured at right-back and Matty Piper, the wide man, he got injured too, and people say they were bad buys. They might have been, but if the chairman and the board had thought so, they should have sacked me in the summer. Having spent the money I was disappointed not to have more time to work with the players, especially with those games coming up.' Reid's departure left a vacuum that he recommended the board fill with the imposing presence of Mick McCarthy. Instead, there was the curious appointment of Howard Wilkinson – albeit the last Englishman to steer a football club to the English championship (Leeds United in 1992) – but whose last job in management had been in 1996.

Peter Reid met Bob Murray and vice chairman John Fickling in the Marriott Hotel in Manchester, the pair showing him the respect to at least sack him face to face.

In terms of the surprise appointment the story was that Murray had rung Wilkinson, head of the League Managers' Association at the time, to ask for advice on who best to appoint, having parted ways with his manager.

Out of the blue, Wilkinson had suggested himself, and the chairman was intrigued at the idea. Rumours circulated however that Wilkinson may have been lined up some time in advance – and if that was the case, it would have perhaps explained the speed of the appointment and the readiness to relieve Reid of his duties ahead of a set of winnable fixtures.

Whatever the truth was, there was no doubt that Wilkinson's six-month tenure was a disaster. Despite the most inviting of starts, Sunderland dropped into the relegation zone in the new manager's first game in charge and were soon to become becalmed there. The club had been rock bottom for weeks when Wilkinson was removed in mid-March, having won just two of 20 league games, and McCarthy belatedly installed. By that stage, though, McCarthy could do little with a squad bursting apart at the seams. One of Wilkinson's first actions had been to roll up the head-tennis court so beloved of Reid and Quinn and, within a few weeks, Quinn himself had gone – the Irishman seeing no need, after Reid's departure, to put himself through agonies to squeeze a few more games out of his creaking frame. Quinn had become a bit-part figure on the playing field by then but his departure, like that of Ball previously, was keenly felt.

It was sad to see the remnants of that great Sunderland side – Phillips, Gray, Craddock, Sørensen – struggling to produce good results as the likes of Flo and co failed to fill the boots of those that had gone before.

Sunderland were relegated at the end of the campaign with a then record all-time low points total of just 19. For Reid, the humiliating relegation was not something he took any satisfaction from: 'You've got to remember how much the club had meant to me. I'd been involved in the Stadium of Light being built and I'd been looking forward to really getting to work at the Academy of Light, but that wasn't to be. On top of that these were my players – players I'd signed – and you feel a connection and a responsibility to your players, even when you're gone. I knew the squad of players was better than that, and I wanted them to stay up, I wanted Sunderland to stay up.'

Reid reckons that sacking him was not a fatal error by Sunderland, but appointing Wilkinson was.

'I think Mick would have done OK for Sunderland if they had appointed him straight after me,' he says. 'I said as much when I was in the middle of being sacked. I said, "If you're getting rid of me, bring Mick in." But I suspect the Howard Wilkinson deal may already have been done by then. I think the players I had at the time would have responded to Mick's style, which was not a million miles away from mine. If they'd chosen

Mick, they probably would have stayed up – Quinny loved Mick and would probably have got a few more games out of himself that season, rather than packing in pretty much immediately. And as for me that season? Would I have kept them up? We'll never know. But I can guarantee you one thing: I would have got more than 19 effing points! We had nine games and eight points after a tough start when they sacked me, and at the end of the season, 29 games later, we had just nine points more. So you tell me . . .!' Bob sacked me a couple of months after I spent the money, and I could not see the sense in that.'

Having had plenty of time to consider it, Reid is in little doubt that the club got the timing wrong.

'When they sacked me I'd only had a few weeks and it was very early days in the new season too. I only had a few games with Flo and Stewart, and we never had a chance to really work with them. I understand things didn't work out well at Sunderland in those final stages, but maybe they would have if I'd stayed and been able to work with the players I brought in. As it was, I think I only had about three training sessions in the new Academy before I was gone.'

The sacking wounded Reid, even though he tried to be philosophical about it.

'Getting sacked is not a nice thing but I'd had the sack at Man City when they'd done particularly well,' he points out. 'You have say to yourself that some of the greatest managers in the world – from Cloughie and Sir Alex Ferguson downwards – have been sacked, so it goes with the territory, but it still hurts to be sacked.'

Reid's relationship with the chairman might have survived his removal but it fell away in the weeks and months that followed.

'I don't speak to Bob these days,' Reid admits. 'I think what happened with that . . . I think it's fair to say that coming out from the club – and that might have been from the chairman, or the people who were working for him – there was an effort to rewrite history. And I thought that was poor. It felt to me that what seemed to be coming out afterwards was that everything that went wrong was down to me, and that everything that went right had nothing to do with me. That's the impression I got from this distance. When I first left, the club did me right in terms of acknowledging what I'd done for it with the statement they made. But then the message seemed to change, and it became very critical and I thought that was unnecessary and wrong. Bob and I had a good working relationship. I wouldn't say we were really close, but we had good times together. He was an interesting character to work for – a very strong chairman, and I had a great seven and a half years there. I prefer to look back on the fact that during my time there we got the stadium and academy built, and they are world class – they were the great things he gave the club.'

Reid says his biggest disappointment during his time at the club was not how it ended, but that he couldn't give the fans their first Cup win since 1973. The Black Cats went close in the 105-point season before losing the League Cup semi-final to Premier League Leicester City, led by future Sunderland manager Martin O'Neill in 1999.

'I would have loved to have won a major trophy for Sunderland fans,' Reid says, echoing a comment he made to me within days of his 2002 sacking. 'We went close in the League Cup that year, we had a brilliant run up to that semi-final, and we genuinely thought we would get through. It still annoys me.'

Looking back, Reid remembers the big decisions he made and which he says the current owners of the club and their manager will have to make as well as they try to steer the club out of the doldrums.

'They'll already be making the big decisions you have to make,' he says. 'They've just got to try to make sure they get most of them right. I mean, that decision I made with the three transfer-listed players was typical of some of the big calls I had to make. Some of the decisions I made, that you've mentioned, they're massive decisions and. They scare me now. But you have to do what you think is right at the time and I'm still in touch with many of the players.

'You make decisions that upset many players but I think what happens is they know the decisions you make are ones you think are right for the football club, and that's what you have to do as a manager. And, by the way, I might have got some of them wrong, but if you are a good manager, invariably you get most right.

'I look at my transfer record and I dropped some huge bollocks, especially when it came to the overseas market. But I tell you what: I can point to Sørensen, Makin, Johnno, Schwarz, Butler, Craddock . . . Butler and, of course, the likes of Quinn and Phillips and others – I bet the club wish they had them now. It takes a lot to get a club going in the right direction, and if you're not careful it can easily go in the wrong direction. Looking back on last season, when the club was getting relegated to League One, you could tell things were wrong when some good people were losing their jobs.

'Having an impressive stadium is great, but people make football clubs. It's a shame what has happened, but hopefully the new ownership can get it back to what it was and what it deserves to be.'

Long-term, the former manager knows that Sunderland, like the 'Cheer Up, Peter Reid' song, will always be with him.

'I think you have an affinity with a place after seven and a half years,' he concludes. 'The fans, every time I come back, they've been brilliant, which is nice. And Everton and Sunderland are still the first two results I look for.

'Bob, when he floated the club on the Stock Exchange, found the money to build the new stadium in the way he wanted. When push comes to shove he might have let me down a bit on that front, but when you think of the stadium and the academy that was built, you can't knock it. I was involved in my own small way for getting us there, but you have to give Bob enormous credit for what he achieved and for making it happen.

'When I look back on it now, I always go back to where we started: fourth from bottom in the Second Division and every chance of going down, to leaving the club fourth from bottom in the Premier and every chance of staying up.

'I started at Roker Park and the Charlie Hurley Centre and by the time I left, the club had a magnificent new ground and new academy, delivered during a period which made big spending difficult.

'I can live with that.'

At that point, we break off. More than two and a half hours have flown by, and Reid needs to be ready for the evening's fundraising show. As we leave the now-packed bar and make our way to the function room, the shy smiles, acknowledgements and double-takes of staff as he passes through corridors and rooms remind me that he remains a household name and face almost two decades after he left the north-east.

A man of substance.

It doesn't guarantee respect, though – among the auction items stacked behind the top table is a framed England player wearing the 1986 World Cup strip and sporting a monkey's heed.

'Brilliant!' roars Reid with laughter. 'I bet you that raises more money than anything else on the night. I love that'

EPILOGUE

Since Reid's departure and Sunderland's subsequent relegation the same season, the Black Cats have never reached the heights the Scouser took them to. Heart-warming promotions were to follow under Mick McCarthy and later Roy Keane, but neither could bring the same degree of success in the top flight.

Steve Bruce briefly managed to steer the club to a tenth-place finish on the last day of the 2010–11 season.

But even though the club managed a ten-year stay in the top flight under the ownership of Ellis Short, the recurring story tended to be of Great Escapes from relegation before Sunderland finally crashed out of the top flight under David Moyes in 2017.

After Bruce's departure, Martin O'Neill, Paolo Di Canio, Dick Advocaat and Sam Allardyce all produced unlikely survivals. But probably the greatest of the Great Escapes came in the 2013–14 campaign under Gus Poyet, which is the subject of our next chapter.

5

With his appointment as Sunderland's head coach in October 2013, Gus Poyet stopped being the slayer of north-east dreams and started to become their creator. Like several other top-class attacking midfielders down the years – Tim Cahill and Frank Lampard spring to mind – Poyet always seemed to score against Sunderland: five goals in seven games against the Black Cats for Chelsea and Spurs.

On the positive side, the Uruguayan international was even more lethal against the Magpies. Once described by Sir Bobby Robson as the 'scourge of Newcastle' he scored four goals against them in three games, which included knocking them out of the FA Cup at the semi-final stage in the 1999–2000 campaign.

As manager of Brighton & Hove Albion he went on to knock Newcastle out of the FA Cup twice more in consecutive seasons immediately before joining Sunderland. And in his very first home game in charge of the Black Cats, he brought the Magpies crashing down to earth yet again. Victories in the derby were one dream delivered to the Sunderland faithful, and before his departure just 17 months later he was to deliver the club two more: an appearance in a Wembley Cup final, and the greatest of a series of Great Escapes the Red and Whites made from Premier League relegation.

GUSTAVO POYET

SUNDERLAND MANAGER
8 OCTOBER 2013 TO 16 MARCH 2015
MEETS LANCE HARDY

It remains arguably the greatest of the 130 goals Kevin Phillips scored for Sunderland, as well as possibly the finest strike ever seen at the Stadium of Light. On a December afternoon at the end of the last century, Phillips unleashed a fabulous dipping volley from 30 yards out to put Sunderland in control against a supreme Chelsea side, featuring international star names such as Marcel Desailly, Gustavo Poyet and Gianfranco Zola, in the Premiership. By half-time the scoreline was 4-0. It finished 4-1. This was the pinnacle of the Peter Reid era: Sunderland would go on to finish seventh in the top division that season (the club's highest final league position since 1954-55); Phillips would go on to win the European Golden Shoe award with 30 top-flight goals; and his opening goal celebration against Chelsea that day would feature in the opening titles of *Match of the Day* on BBC One the following season.

But on that special day for Sunderland there was a totally different type of atmosphere in the away dressing room, especially during the interval. Marcel Desailly was substituted at half-time (as too was the other Chelsea central defender, Jon Harley) as visiting manager Gianluca Vialli searched for an answer to the unstoppable force of the home attack. Meanwhile, one of Desailly's esteemed teammates sat and pondered.

'It was the worst half-time for me, no doubt,' Gus Poyet recalls, 18 and a half years later. 'Sunderland were outstanding that day. Niall Quinn and Kevin Phillips got two goals each. It was 4-0 at half-time and game over.'

Poyet scored a late consolation goal for Chelsea that day, but it was his recollection of that amazing first-half Sunderland performance and the noise generated by the 41,377 Sunderland fans inside the Stadium of Light that afternoon that, many years later in the autumn of 2013, was to play such a massive part in his decision to move to the north-east and take over the Black Cats.

'I remembered my experience with Chelsea at Sunderland,' Gus reflects. 'It was there in my mind. I said to [assistant] Mauricio Taricco, "Listen, I was involved in a game at Sunderland and you can't imagine what it is like when the fans are behind their team." I told him how Sunderland destroyed us that day and how the entire stadium was rocking in their support for the team. It was incredible. You think to yourself, "I can be on that side now! Wow! Fantastic!" So, yes, that day helped me a lot in making my decision to go to Sunderland, no doubt.'

The two of us are chatting over a coffee on a grey May day in Chelsea Harbour. The previous week Poyet had reached the qualifying-round stages of the 2018–19 Europa League with his new club, FC Girondins de Bordeaux, after they had won 4-0 at Metz on the last day of the season to finish sixth in Ligue 1. The previous month Sunderland had been relegated to League One after losing 2-1 at home to Burton Albion, despite being ahead with just three minutes left to play.

Typical of the nature of this man, the first comment Poyet makes when we sit down to begin our interview is about his former club. 'It is awful what has happened at Sunderland,' Gus says. 'I just hope this is the bottom and now the club can rebuild. The one thing Sunderland needs as a city is to have a proper, successful football club.'

As a player Poyet is best-known for the success he achieved at Stamford Bridge, just down the road from where we are sitting, between 1997 and 2001. He played in the last FA Cup final to be held at the old Wembley Stadium in 2000 (Chelsea beat Aston Villa 1-0) after he scored both goals in the 2-1 semi-final win over Newcastle United. He also won the UEFA Cup Winners' Cup and UEFA Super Cup with the Blues. The Uruguayan previously played for Grenoble, River Plate Montevideo and Real Zaragoza before coming to England. He won the 1995 Copa America on home soil with Uruguay, which was secured after a 5-3 win on penalties following a 1-1 draw against World Cup holders Brazil at the Estadio Centenario in Montevideo. He finished his playing career at Tottenham Hotspur in 2004 at the age of 36.

As head coach, Poyet led Sunderland to the Capital One Cup final at the new Wembley Stadium in 2014. This is the only major Cup final the club has reached in the last 25 years and counting . . . He also oversaw the greatest escape from relegation in Premier League history in the same season. Some have called it a miracle. Since leaving Sunderland, Poyet has managed in Greece, Spain, China and France.

His managerial career began at Brighton and Hove Albion in 2009 after assistant manager roles alongside Dennis Wise at Swindon Town and Leeds United, and a period as a coach under Juande Ramos at Spurs. After leading Brighton to the League One title in 2009–10 and the Championship playoffs in 2012–13 Poyet was temporarily out of work and available from the beginning of the 2013–14 season. He appeared as a pundit on *Match of the Day* but was also keeping a close eye on the bottom of the Premier League and the top of the Championship just in case any early season managerial opportunities arose.

'I had an idea about the possible options,' Gus recalls. 'My idea was maybe a team that is not doing well in the Premier League may change their manager, and there becomes an opportunity – or maybe a big team in the Championship which had started badly and needed a change because they were losing too many points. So I was looking at all that carefully. There were a couple of things there. And then there was Sunderland.

'Sunderland was incredible because it was so scary. It was actually really scary. I don't know how many people told me that I was crazy. "Why are you going to take the risk of going to Sunderland?" they asked me. Football changes so quickly and nobody now remembers that the club had won just one point from seven games. But you cannot wait for the perfect job. It is never going to come!

'When I started at Brighton my idea was to show what I wanted to do in terms of playing and character; what I was bringing to the team and how I was treating the players in a certain way. I thought that what we did at Brighton was possible to do at any team – but it's not. I thought I could start by making decisions and putting new things into place at Sunderland, but after ten days I knew that it wasn't possible to go into that level of football and play the style that I wanted and immediately have that understanding.

'It was tough,' Gus adds. 'When you want to impose a new style of play it will always be tough because you want to do something [new], but at the same time you need to win on Saturday. If you don't win there may be no tomorrow for you. So you need to adapt, but when you adapt you are not trying to achieve what may be the best for you.'

The tough task that Poyet mentions was underlined in his first match in charge of Sunderland - a 4-0 defeat by Swansea

City at the Liberty Stadium. Two of the Swansea goals were own goals.

'Incredibly, I think that game helped me a lot,' Gus reflects. 'I didn't know it at that time because at that time I was mad – I had just lost my first match in the Premier League as a manager 4-0 – but it helped me a lot because I think it helped the players to understand that this was not really only about the manager. It was deeper than that. That was important because it would be very easy to change the manager again and again and again. That result changed the thinking of everybody at the club, including the players.'

A large number of those players had arrived at Sunderland in the previous summer during Paolo Di Canio's brief reign at the club. Emanuele Giaccherini, a £6.5 million buy from Juventus, was the standout signing. But more than £13 million was also spent on bringing Jozy Altidore (AZ Alkmaar), David Moberg Karlsson (IFK Gothenburg), Charis Mavrias (Panathinaikos), El-Hadji Ba (Le Havre) and Vito Mannone (Arsenal) to the club. Cabral, Modibo Diakité, Andrea Dossena and Valentin Roberge also joined on free transfers, while Fabio Borini, Ondřej Čelůstka and Ki Sung-yueng came on one-season loans from Liverpool, Trabzonspor and Swansea City respectively. Duncan Watmore, an undisclosed signing from non-league Altrincham, also arrived at that time. He is the only one of those 14 summer signings who remains at the Stadium of Light.

Sunderland had shown a lack of leadership and team spirit on the pitch during the early part of the season, but that all changed in Poyet's second match in charge, the north-east derby against Newcastle United, in front of a crowd of 46,313 at the Stadium of Light. The Lads stormed into a fourth-minute lead with a Steven Fletcher header, but they were pegged back to 1-1 around the hour mark. The turning point in a pulsating derby came after Poyet's double-substitution of Borini and Ki for Adam Johnson and Lee Cattermole with 20 minutes to go.

The Black Cats had been on the defensive when, with just six minutes left, Borini hit an absolute screamer from outside the box. The goal produced what was to become the trademark 'knife between the teeth' celebration from the Italian as well as what was to become an equally popular trademark celebration from Poyet, clenching his fists by his side on the touchline. Sunderland won 2-1. It was some way to mark your first home match in charge.

'That is me,' Gus smiles. 'I think one thing that helps me a lot when I am working for a club – as a player, as a coach, as a manager – is that I become naturally very supportive of the club. From the moment I get there: that is my club! The rest, I don't care about. Everything that happens at the club, I will take it; whether it is for right, or for wrong, or for good, or for bad. That's me. So when I am there and it's a derby, well, I am sorry, everybody, but in derbies there is only one result that matters and that is winning!

'That win against Newcastle was very important,' Gus adds. 'Given the position we were in, losing 4-0 against Swansea the previous week, a derby, everything. It was just a perfect way to start at the Stadium of Light.'

The following week, at Hull City, Sunderland were reduced to nine men by half-time after both Lee Cattermole and Andrea Dossena were sent off in first-half injury time. Goalkeeper Kieren Westwood had also been replaced just minutes beforehand after he sustained a neck injury while conceding an own goal from Carlos Cuellar. Those few minutes were to prove crucial and Hull held on to win the match 1-0. Regardless, Sunderland's second-half performance pleased Poyet and offered further evidence to him that his players were moving forward together in the right direction.

'That game was very significant,' Gus explains. 'I made two changes at half-time after the sendings-off [Wes Brown for Jozy Altidore and Adam Johnson for Fabio Borini] and I played a system that I like to play if ever I am down to nine and I need to win – or at least score. I told the players, "We are going to have one chance." And we had one chance. It was by Adam Johnson. If we had scored, it would have been the perfect tactical decision in a football game. Unfortunately we didn't score, but we could have done, and we could have won a point. So the players knew what they had done in that second half and they could feel that what I said works.

'You have to convince a player with actions,' Gus adds. 'If it is just talk and it doesn't happen it is no good. So that second-half performance at Hull was key. We played nine versus eleven for 45 minutes and we didn't concede. That helped me convince them regarding other things afterwards, and we then started to see improvements in the following games.'

Fate can also play a big part in football. Kieren Westwood's injury and Lee Cattermole's suspension meant that Vito Mannone (who came on to make his Sunderland debut at the KC Stadium) and Ki Sung-yueng now came into the side. Both of them would become almost ever-presents for the rest of the season.

Progress to the Capital One Cup quarter-finals was also adding to a new-found positive momentum. Four goals in the last 12 minutes from Jozy Altidore, substitute Connor Wickham (2) and Adam Johnson had overturned a 2-0 deficit against League One side Milton Keynes Dons under Paolo Di Canio back in August; caretaker manager Kevin Ball oversaw a 2-0 win over another League One outfit Peterborough United in September; and four days after that courageous nine-man second-half display at Hull fellow Premier League side Southampton were beaten 2-1 at the Stadium of Light, courtesy of goals from Phil Bardsley and Sebastian Larsson.

When Bardsley followed that up with the only goal of the game – a cool right-footed finish from the left-hand side of the penalty box courtesy of a right-back who was currently playing in the left-back position – against Premier League leaders Manchester City at home four days later it certainly suggested that an important corner had been turned. But then there came a ditch and something of a glitch . . . Two points from the next five Premier League games – both achieved through goalless draws (against Aston Villa and West Ham United) away from home – left Sunderland at the bottom of the table again by mid-December.

'After two or three months I would be looking at the Premier League table on Sky Sports TV and sometimes, depending on the format of the picture, Sunderland were not even on the page because it looked like we were below the television screen,' Gus remembers with a smile. 'It was tough to keep looking at that table! It hurts, and even though I was not there at the beginning of the season it was not like I was now going to say it was because the team didn't do this or didn't do that before me. I am not that type of manager. That has gone. I take the responsibility.'

The Capital One Cup quarter-final tie at home to Chelsea could not affect Sunderland's position on the Sky Sports screen, but it could take them one step nearer to their first appearance at the new Wembley Stadium.

'I played a good team against Chelsea in that match, but I didn't go into the game thinking we were going to reach the League Cup final,' Gus admits. 'I was trying to be responsible, but at the same time I was trying to be careful because the league position was a bad situation for us.'

On a memorable night, a late equaliser from Fabio Borini cancelled out an unfortunate own goal by Lee Cattermole at the start of the second half before a glorious strike from Ki Sung-yueng after 118 minutes lit up the Stadium of Light and achieved a 2-1 victory that secured Sunderland a place in the last four of the competition. Both Borini and Ki had started the match on the bench.

Another goalless draw at home to Norwich City – Wes Brown was sent off in injury time – followed in the Premier League. Sunderland remained bottom of the table at Christmas.

Boxing Day provided the next turning point in what was already becoming a rollercoaster season when Sunderland visited Goodison Park, a ground where they had lost their previous six Premier League matches, to take on an Everton side competing for a Champions League place. Sunderland had to go into the game with an untried central defensive partnership of Modibo Diakité and Valentin Roberge that day due to injury and suspension that had robbed Poyet of his regular former Manchester United pairing at the back. Meanwhile, up front, The Lads had not scored in four of their previous six league matches. Sunderland supporters would have happily snatched at a draw pre kick-off. But on 23 minutes a poor back pass from Leon Osman led to Everton goalkeeper Tim Howard racing from his line and fouling Ki in the penalty box. After Howard was sent off the South Korea international calmly stroked home the penalty past stand-in Joel Robles to give Sunderland an unexpected lead.

A backs-to-the-wall defensive display by the visitors ensued, particularly from Vito Mannone, now firmly established as the number-one choice goalkeeper, who made impressive saves to deny Phil Jagielka, Bryan Oviedo and Ross Barkley. Diakité and Roberge did their bit too as Sunderland achieved their first away win since April.

'That was one of the worst games that we played but we won,' Gus says. 'It was eleven versus ten. But we couldn't pass the ball, and it was that kind of nervous team performance where we were thinking we cannot afford to lose this game rather than let's go and score more goals against them. I had to ask Diakité and Roberge to play. They hadn't played for me in their career and now they had to play two games in three days [Cardiff City v Sunderland was scheduled for two days later]. Everton was a tremendous result. Getting those three points was another key moment for us. We talk about the derby, we talk about certain other things, but this was very important for us because we had two difficult away games – Everton and Cardiff – and we had a lot of problems at the back. But somehow, without playing fantastic football, we won at Everton and we drew in the last minute at Cardiff to win four points away from home over Christmas.'

Sunderland had been 2-0 down with just seven minutes left at Cardiff before Steven Fletcher got a goal back. Then, in the fifth minute of injury time, Jack Colback scored a dramatic equaliser. The Lads were still bottom of the table but, crucially, they were now just two points away from the safety zone.

There followed a lot of activity off the pitch at the Stadium of Light in the first few weeks of 2014. Director of Football Roberto De Fanti – a man who will be forever associated with the Paolo Di Canio summer spending spree – was sacked halfway through a January transfer window which brought in the stylish Spanish left-back Marcos Alonso on loan from Fiorentina, as well as three Argentinian players – Óscar Ustari, Santiago Vergini and Ignacio Scocco – on loan, on a free, and for £3 million (from Almería in Spain, Estudiantes in Argentina and Brazilian side Internacional respectively), plus a £2.5 million signing from Brighton, Liam Bridcutt.

'Marcos Alonso is a very good player,' Gus nods. 'Look at where he is now!' Since leaving Sunderland Alonso has won the Premier League and the FA Cup with current club Chelsea and was also named in the Professional Footballers Association Team of the Year for 2017–18. Alonso made his Sunderland debut in early January in the Capital One Cup semi-final first leg against Manchester United at the Stadium of Light, allowing Phil Bardsley to move to his more natural position of right-back in place of the Czech Republic defender Ondřej Čelůstka.

Ryan Giggs deflected a Bardsley cross into his own goal on the stroke of half-time to give The Lads the lead but Nemanja Vidić equalised early in the second half before a Fabio Borini penalty – awarded after Tom Cleverley had fouled Adam Johnson – followed by yet another 'knife between the teeth' celebration from the Italian wrapped up a 2-1 win. It was Sunderland's first victory over United in any competition since Kevin Phillips won another League Cup match against them with a 100th minute penalty at the Stadium of Light back in the autumn of 2000.

'I was sure that a good Cup run would help us and when we beat Chelsea in the quarter-finals we then realised, "Now we have got a great chance of getting to the League Cup final." 'So we prepared for the Manchester United games in a totally different way. We worked on set-pieces in training and after we won the first leg at home, we went to Manchester with an option.'

It was to be an incredibly tense night at Old Trafford. A header from former Sunderland loan player Jonny Evans levelled the tie on 37 minutes and no further goals meant extra time. After 119 minutes United were on the verge of going through to the final on the away-goals rule when David de Gea fumbled Phil Bardsley's shot over the line. Sunderland were now heading to Wembley. But only for a matter of seconds! Moments later, Javier Hernández scored to make it 2-1 to United on the night and 3-3 on aggregate. A penalty shootout was needed to settle it. Incredibly, only three of the ten players scored their spot kicks as Sunderland went through to the final 2-1 on penalties: Darren Fletcher netted for United and Marcos Alonso and Ki Sung-yueng did so for Sunderland. Goalkeeper Vito Mannone was again the Black Cats hero, backed by a 9,000 strong-support in a crowd of 71,019.

'We talk about emotions and how they change during a game,' Gus says. 'Explain those last minutes at Manchester? I can remember when we missed the first two penalties [from Craig Gardner and Steven Fletcher], I went over to our fitness coach, Antonio Pintus, and I said to him, "We have got no chance! We cannot miss the first two penalties and win." But, incredibly, it happened.'

Pintus has worked at Real Madrid since 2016 and as a result has celebrated the last two of the Spanish giants' Champions League final victories. But it is unlikely he will ever witness a penalty shootout like the one that took place before his eyes at Old Trafford again.

'I think it is probably the worst penalty shootout ever in history in England, no?' Gus asks. 'We won 2-1 after five penalties each!'

It was a moment to savour! As the visiting supporters sang, *'Que será será, whatever will be will be, we're going to Wembley'* in the away end, up in the directors' box Sunderland chairman Ellis Short could be seen excitedly hugging 1973 FA Cup-winning hero Jim Montgomery.

'That night was a great night for the club and the players,' Gus says. 'When you win a match like that and you celebrate like that it brings along something extra.'

January turned out to be a very good month for Sunderland. In addition to reaching the Capital One Cup final Fulham were beaten 4-1 away and Southampton were pegged back from 2-0 to 2-2 at home in the Premier League. Furthermore, League One side Carlisle United and non-league Kidderminster Harriers were beaten 3-1 and 1-0 respectively in the FA Cup, and so another Cup run was building . . .

But it was on the first day of February that it felt as though everything had finally clicked into place. Sunderland went to St James' Park and absolutely destroyed Newcastle United 3-0 away from home again with another penalty from Fabio Borini and further goals from Adam Johnson and Jack Colback.

'I think that we went there with the knowledge that we were already in a better situation,' Gus recalls. 'We were feeling confident after the 4-1 win at Fulham, and now things were happening constantly. We were coming together, we were solid. We also had that special mentality to play against Newcastle. Paolo Di Canio won there 3-0 the year before, we had beaten them at home with that great goal by Fabio Borini, and so we were now thinking, "We are going to beat them again."

'One of my best times at Sunderland happened to me that day,' Gus adds. 'We beat them. Outstanding. There was an unbelievable celebration in the dressing room, obviously, and then I go into the press room and then I go back out and the stadium is empty – except for the Sunderland fans. I was on my own and it was spectacular. I was the only one in front of the whole group of supporters and I wanted to run into the corner to join them, but unfortunately it was closed. I only had 30 seconds with them and I was whistling to them and celebrating with them. It was incredible.'

Seven days later a home Premier League match against Hull City was to be a big disappointment when goals from Shane Long and Nikica Jelavic gave Steve Bruce's side a 2-0 win. Wes Brown had been sent off again after just four minutes for a foul on Long. By the end of February Sunderland were back in relegation trouble following a 4-1 defeat at Arsenal.

Poyet now offers a sobering and sombre observation from that time: 'I was convinced that the Cup run was to be good for us, but it was the opposite. We are all human beings and so when we reached the final everyone was now thinking about the final, even if they tried not to. It's natural, for both the players and the fans, but they were not talking about anything else, only the final, yet we were still in trouble in the Premier League.'

The big day at Wembley finally arrived on Sunday 2 March 2014. It was Sunderland's first major Cup final appearance since the 1992 FA Cup final defeat to Liverpool. Manuel Pellegrini's Manchester City were the opposition.

Before the match, Sunderland's heroic 1973 FA Cup winners were paraded in front of the fans, along with the 1976 Manchester City League Cup winners. Dennis Tueart and Dave Watson, both of whom played in both matches, swapped over from one side to the other. It set the scene for a much-anticipated Cup final between two of English football's greatest club sides – but there was no doubt who were the favourites to lift the trophy.

Sunderland lined up as follows: Vito Mannone; Phil Bardsley, Wes Brown, John O'Shea, Marcos Alonso; Sebastian Larsson, Lee Cattermole; Adam Johnson, Ki Sung-yueng, Jack Colback; Fabio Borini.

This was the Manchester City team: Costel Pantilimon; Pablo Zabaleta, Vincent Kompany, Martín Demichelis, Aleksandar Kolarov; Samir Nasri, Yaya Touré, Fernandinho, David Silva; Edin Džeko, Sergio Agüero.

The attendance was 84,697.

'I had to make very strong, critical decisions for the final,' Gus explains. 'I left Jozy Altidore out of the squad, which was extremely difficult. I needed to play certain positions and I needed to put certain players on the bench. There was a reason for it, and unfortunately somebody paid for that decision. I put Fabio Borini up front as the main striker for the first time. He was playing on the left so by moving him up front I had to find another midfielder too. We knew that a high midfield would close the space and then we would have the option of Fabio going one on one. Early in the match, we have a long ball, it is one against one, and Fabio scores! Fantastic. Now, the players believe. As I have mentioned to you before, the most important thing is to convince the players that what you tell them to do works. The only way to convince them of that is that it works. It is actions and results. If you can do it, you will convince them, and when you can convince a player to do something that you believe is the right thing, and the player does it, and it works, it is amazing.'

Fabio Borini's goal – a brilliant angled drive on his instep – came on 10 minutes, and only a crucial tackle by Vincent Kompany prevented the Italian from having a second chance on goal later in the first half.

For Sunderland fans under the age of 50, this was as good as it gets. Half-time came with a 1-0 lead intact. The Boys of '73 knew that feeling, but it hadn't happened since. The 1985 Milk Cup final and the 1992 FA Cup final were both lost without The Lads finding the net. Could this be our time again?

I remember being so nervous at this prospect that I couldn't speak to my father at half-time as we queued for refreshments on the Wembley concourse. I just couldn't tempt fate . . .

'In the first half we were tactically outstanding,' Gus says. 'At half-time, I tried to convince the players that we were 45 minutes away from achieving something very, very special. If somebody was tired or nervous or whatever we had no time to think about it. We had to really give everything because it was just 45 minutes to go. We were 45 minutes away from winning a Cup against an amazing team – the one that went on to win the Premier League that season.'

Sunderland had been in the lead for 35 minutes at half-time. Ten minutes into the second half that time had increased to 45 minutes. For the Red and White hordes one eye was now on the pitch, the other continually checking the ticking clocks on the giant scoreboards. And then it felt as though we had all been hit by an express train: Yaya Touré and Samir Nasri produced two sublime, stunning goals within 60 seconds of each other to turn the match upside down and inside out. The favourites were in front and despite a late charge by Sunderland – Steven Fletcher had the underdogs' best chance of an equaliser at the end of normal time but was let down by poor control – Jesús Navas completed the scoring and a 3-1 win for City in injury time.

'The Manchester City goals were very high quality,' Gus says. 'It doesn't matter how well you train, if the opposition have that sort of quality they can resolve a game themselves. If you go to a Cup final, you really have to win it. That's my mentality. It is not nice to lose. It was very special for me to play in the last FA Cup final at the old Wembley and win, and it was also very nice, of course, to go to the new Wembley with Sunderland, but, with all respect to the new stadium, I think the old Wembley was better. It was unique. The walk from behind the goal was Wembley at its best. It had something special. It was a shame that it needed to change. But all things change.

'I know that people enjoyed the final,' Gus adds. 'I enjoyed 45 minutes of it! I didn't enjoy the second half. But I know how important it was for the fans. I realise how important it is for the fans to go to Wembley. One person told me that half-time at Wembley was the best time of his life. He had never felt like he did during that half-time! That means a lot – how we can make people feel so happy.'

It was certainly a day to remember. But the next morning we all woke up to the reality of a Premier League survival fight.

However, the next match in Sunderland's season was to be another Cup tie. A Craig Gardner goal had given The Lads a 1-0 FA Cup fifth-round win over Southampton at the Stadium of Light in mid-February and earned the club a place in the quarter-finals of the world's oldest Cup competition for only the fifth time in 40 years. The quarter-final draw took the Black Cats back to Hull. Poyet made six changes to the team that had started at Wembley – Óscar Ustari (who had played in the previous FA Cup rounds against Kidderminster and Southampton) replaced Vito Mannone, his fellow countryman Ignacio Scocco (who had made his Sunderland debut in the Cup tie against the Saints) played up front, and there were also starts for Andrea Dossena, Steven Fletcher, Emanuele Giaccherini and Santiago Vergini. There was a strong feeling of disappointment among the supporters in the away end at the KC Stadium long before kick-off following the announcement of the half-dozen team changes.

That was made much worse by a subsequent 3-0 defeat.

The scoreline was actually still goalless after 67 minutes (Ustari had done very well to save a penalty from Sone Aluko in the first half) when Fabio Borini and Adam Johnson came on for Giaccherini and Scocco in a clear bid by Poyet to win the match. But within ten minutes of the double-substitution the game was over and the travelling supporters started to direct their ire at the team selection.

The result affected the Sunderland fans much more than the Capital One Cup final defeat seven days earlier. They saw it as an opportunity spurned; a potential FA Cup semi-final against Championship side Sheffield United at Wembley Stadium in April was the prize that had slipped away, and victory in that match would have meant an FA Cup final against Arsenal the following month, and with it a place in Europe. However, it is all a case of ifs, buts and maybes . . .

'I swear that I didn't give it away,' Gus says. 'I think it was necessary. I did something similar – not exactly the same, but similar with the team for the League Cup match against Chelsea at home because Fabio Borini didn't start the game and Ki didn't start the game, and they scored the goals for us! There were not many people in the stadium for that quarter-final and maybe the fans don't remember that? So when we are going into another quarter-final at Hull, I did something similar. As I said, I was convinced that the League Cup run would help us to get better, but after we had won the semi-final against Manchester United it killed us. I had a feeling that we were maybe putting more than we should into the Cups, and it was possible that we could completely give away our Premier League place. If we had gone down then it would have been a bad decision to focus on the Cups. So I thought it was very important not to confuse another Cup run and staying up. Luckily, I think I got it right. We lost a bad game and I know how bad the supporters felt about it, but it was a tough decision and I don't regret it at all.'

If the Capital One Cup final defeat had brought the sobriety of a Premier League survival fight into focus, then this FA

Cup quarter-final exit certainly delivered a mighty hangover. A dour and frustrating goalless draw at home to fellow strugglers Crystal Palace – Fabio Borini hit the post in the second half – was quickly followed by a 2-0 defeat at another relegation-threatened side, Norwich City. The first of Sunderland's three games in hand came at Anfield a few days later. Poyet decided to change his formation against title-chasing Liverpool, but his plans were somewhat wrecked by somebody leaking this new-look line-up to the press.

'Most of the time I would tell the players the team on the day before the game for many reasons,' Gus says. 'Sometimes you need to be in a position to plan something, particularly if you change something. At Liverpool I changed to five at the back, and it was in the press in the afternoon! I hated it. I am sure that any other manager, including Brendan Rogers, knew that Sunderland played 4–3–3 all the time, but if we start the game with five at the back [Santiago Vergini came into the defence] then the opposition need to re-accommodate; they need to start sending information to players, and sometimes it is not easy to do that. But if they know all about that before the game it is totally different!'

To add to Poyet's annoyance that night Sunderland competed well and were narrowly beaten 2-1 – the line-up leak may have made a significant difference. In hindsight perhaps the most significant change to the side that night was the reintroduction of the 20-year-old, six foot three inch striker Connor Wickham up front. Signed by Steve Bruce for £8 million from Ipswich Town on a four-year contract in the summer of 2011, the England under-21 international had experienced a frustrating time on Wearside up to this point, with just one Premier League goal in a limited number of appearances over three seasons.

But a successful loan spell at Sheffield Wednesday (eight goals in eleven appearances) had made headlines and, during another loan deal at Leeds United, with Steven Fletcher struggling with injury and Jozy Altidore struggling with form, particularly in front of goal, Wickham was recalled by Sunderland and put straight into the first team.

Poyet remembers the conversation he had with Wickham at that time: 'I told Connor, "I have never said this before in my life, but you are going to have five or six games in a row. It's up to you now. Let's see." I couldn't say that to anyone before or after that at Sunderland – he is the only player I had the chance to say that to,' Gus says. 'Wow! What a run of games he had!'

The following Monday night, Sunderland lost 2-1 again, this time to West Ham United at the Stadium of Light.

Then, seven days later at Tottenham, came the moment – and the word – that will always be associated with Poyet at Sunderland. A first goal in 113 appearances from Lee Cattermole had given Sunderland a shock 17th-minute lead. It was 1-1 at half-time and then Harry Kane gave Spurs the lead just before the hour mark. But three further goals for the home side in the last 12 minutes completed a rout and left Sunderland bottom of the Premier League table, seven points from safety and with Chelsea, Manchester City and Manchester United all still to play away from home. A solemn-faced Poyet walked into the post-match press conference at White Hart Lane and soon afterwards he famously declared, 'I think we need a miracle.' Obviously, the quote made instant headlines. Subsequently, it would go down in football folklore. As always, Poyet had spoken from his heart.

'I look at myself on that clip now and I see how down I was,' Gus reflects. 'It is incredible that you don't realise it at the time. I remember talking to the press, but I didn't realise when

I was there that I looked that down or that it looked that bad. When I said we "need a miracle" I am gone. It is incredible to think about the things we get through in life. At least it showed people that I cared. It was not acting, that's for sure. I am not that good an actor!

'Everything we were doing was not working,' Gus adds. 'We went to Tottenham with a plan, we scored and everything looked all right and then everything went wrong again. We played a more than decent game against Everton in the next match and we concede an own goal [by Wes Brown] and lose 1-0. It was very strange. That saying "typical of a team at the bottom" is true.'

The Premier League table was now becoming a depressing sight. Sunderland had six games left to claw back the seven-point deficit to 17th place and safety. Mathematically, it was still possible, of course. Realistically, given the remaining fixtures and the fact that Sunderland had not won a match in two and a half months, it would indeed be something of a miracle if it was to happen. The two remaining games in hand didn't really seem to make any difference . . .

The first was against Manchester City at the Etihad Stadium. Manuel Pelligrini's side were four points behind top-placed Liverpool with two games in hand themselves. To make the impending task even harder for Poyet and Sunderland there was now a growing injury crisis to contend with. Both Phil Bardsley and Ki Sung-yueng had been injured in the Everton match and were ruled out alongside Steven Fletcher, who had been unavailable for a month.

'We went to Manchester City with a really small group of players,' Gus recalls. 'Without exaggerating – and with all respect to the players that played and were on the bench – I have this team that practically made itself.'

To echo Poyet's point, the Sunderland bench that night included Liam Agnew, El-Hadji Ba, Charis Mavrias and Ignacio Scocco. In total, those four players managed just one starting appearance between them in the Premier League all season.

'I remember asking Santi Vergini that I needed to talk to him. I said, "Santi, I need you to play right-back because of this and this" [both Phil Bardsley and Ondřej Čelůstka were injured]. He said, "No problem, I will play there." He played the last six games there! Phil Bardsley became available again but I had to say to him, "Phil, I can't play you." That is a good example of how it was,' Gus smiles. 'Suddenly, something went click!'

Typical of what would go down as one of the most exciting Sunderland seasons in recent history, the match at the Etihad was to be another true rollercoaster ride. Fernandinho gave City the lead after just two minutes but Sunderland more than held their own and John O'Shea had a chance to equalise with a first-half header which was squandered. It was when Emanuele Giaccherini and Ignacio Scocco came on for Sebastian Larsson and Fabio Borini with just over 20 minutes remaining that the key was provided to unlock the back door of the home side's defence. Subsequently, Connor Wickham gratefully plundered through it with mighty aplomb and a big smile on his face.

On 73 minutes Scocco made the biggest contribution of his brief career at Sunderland when he produced a beautifully paced deft flick to Giaccherini in the left-hand side of the penalty box. The Italian's pin-point cross found Wickham at the far post and the ball was turned into the net from just a few yards out.

Wickham had not scored for Sunderland in the Premier League since October 2011! A long wait of two and a half years was then followed, ridiculously, by another wait of just ten minutes when he ran onto a brilliant through ball from

Giaccherini to unleash a powerful strike that beat Joe Hart at the near post. Interestingly, Steve Bruce had signed Wickham as a player he felt he could develop for the future at the Stadium of Light. Just under three years on, the striker had now finally proven his worth – but in that time Sunderland had moved from Bruce to Martin O'Neill to Paolo Di Canio to Gus Poyet.

To say Sunderland were now in dreamland at the Etihad would have been an understatement. However, heartache followed with just two minutes left on the clock when the excellent Vito Mannone fumbled Samir Nasri's goal-bound attempt over the line in cruel slow motion. An exhilarating match ended 2-2. Around the stadium there seemed to be a feeling of what might have been on both sides.

I was at the Etihad that night as a guest of Dennis Tueart, alongside famous City fan Johnny Marr. We were sitting right above Mannone as he gallantly tried in vain to claw the ball back from over the line in the closing stages of the match. We were all of the opinion afterwards that the result might have cost City the Premier League title as well as cost Sunderland Premier League survival. We would all be wrong. I drove home over the darkened Woodhead Pass in the early hours of the following morning with a feeling of pride and frustration plus an overwhelming sense of 'typical Sunderland'. Little did any of us realise at the time that it was, in fact, a huge turning point.

'I am going to tell you a story which is very good for a book,' Gus says, with a smile. 'When we drew at Manchester City my emotions were mixed because we were so close to winning and it was a big shame because we were leading, which was amazing, and then we conceded that strange goal when the ball went in by 20 centimetres! But we were still bottom, with only one point from the match, and now we need to go to Chelsea, who had never lost at home with José Mourinho at that time.

'At the end of the Manchester City game, Óscar Ustari [Sunderland's reserve goalkeeper that night] came up to me and said that he was a little worried that I would be very upset with the team because we had conceded so late at the end. I wasn't, but obviously he was kind of saying to me, "Don't be hard on the players because they have done incredible." I looked at Óscar and I was thinking to myself, "I am OK." But it was good experienced words from a player who I respected a lot, knowing what the team needed at that time because none of us knew what was going to happen afterwards. It was something very nice from a true professional who came to us, helped us, and waited to play in the Cup matches a little bit. Óscar was always there – he never complained – and it was incredible that even being in that situation he was still thinking about the group and what the group needed at that time, after conceding a goal like that in the last minute at Manchester City. Also, because I was not feeling angry, I noticed his words and I kind of followed his advice.'

Poyet named an unchanged team for the visit to Stamford Bridge. Within 12 minutes Samuel Eto'o had given the Blues the lead. But Connor Wickham equalised on 18 minutes with his third goal in two matches after a well-worked move from a corner. And then, with just eight minutes left, substitute Jozy Altidore won a penalty for the visitors after tumbling down in the penalty box following a clumsy challenge by César Azpilicueta. Sunderland had been handed a lifeline. With nerves of steel, Fabio Borini, on loan from Liverpool, took the penalty against his old club, Chelsea, and placed the ball down the middle past Mark Schwarzer to give The Lads another unlikely lead against another team aiming to win the Premier League title. This time Sunderland held on, giving their survival hopes a massive boost as well as turning the title race upside down for the second time in four days.

'We were losing 1-0 at Chelsea and Mourinho has left two players up front at a corner,' Gus remembers. 'We send Marcos Alonso up and we now stay two versus two, which was a massive risk for us because if we lose the ball and there is a break and we concede it is all over. But if you do what happened and score it is a massive plus. It was a big risk that the team was ready to take and it worked!

'Seb Larsson saw it. He gave it to Marcos Alonso. Marcos had a shot. It was difficult for the goalkeeper and Connor Wickham was on fire at that time and he scored. That changed the game. That changed the half-time team talk. That changed the position that we were in. That gave us something extra. We had drawn at Manchester City and now we were drawing at half-time at Chelsea.

'Connor Wickham was outstanding at that time. He was in the position that he needed to be at the right time every time. He was scoring from anything: headers, chipping, power, rebounds. Every single situation would happen and Connor was there, and when you have a player that makes a difference like he did, the rest is a lot easier for everyone.

'Fabio Borini was fantastic,' Gus adds. 'Fabio was a penalty-taker. The point is you are or you are not a penalty-taker, I do believe that. I was calm because he was a penalty-taker. But he needed to score. He scored. But he didn't want to celebrate. He was a Chelsea player once and now he was a Liverpool player playing for us. He went to celebrate and then he stopped. He kept walking and the Sunderland fans were going crazy and so he started to celebrate and then he stopped himself again. He wanted to run but he couldn't. He was holding the celebration inside. So it was a difficult moment for him. He had the responsibility of the team going down at Stamford Bridge against his ex-team, and also Chelsea and Liverpool both fighting for the Premier League. There were all those emotions going on. It was incredible.

'I think that when we left Stamford Bridge we knew that something had happened there. There was no way we were going to lose against Cardiff City in the next match. No way at all.'

Poyet was proved right. Cardiff were thrashed 4-0 at the Stadium of Light with two more goals from Connor Wickham, another penalty from Fabio Borini and a strike from an ever-improving Emanuele Giaccherini, who had found his richest vein of form for Sunderland at just the right time, as had many of his teammates.

'The team suddenly got something from playing together,' Gus says. 'We had found a group of players that helped each other very well. The team now had to stay the same. I couldn't touch it. It was impossible.'

Sunderland were out of the bottom three for the first time since early February. They then went to Manchester United in search of their first league win at Old Trafford in 46 years – and got it! Sebastian Larsson scored the only goal of the game after half an hour.

'We were very good against Manchester United,' Gus remembers. 'We were solid, we were confident, we were in the game and we had options going forward. We were a completely different team from just four weeks before.'

All this meant that, incredibly, Sunderland could now achieve Premier League survival with a match to spare if they could beat West Bromwich Albion in their last remaining game in hand at the Stadium of Light four days later.

First-half goals from Jack Colback and Fabio Borini ensured that they did. Thirteen points from five games had achieved the much-talked about 'miracle'.

'You can call it a miracle,' Gus smiles. 'I think you have to because it was something that doesn't happen. We were seven points adrift with six games to go and Manchester City, Chelsea and Manchester United to play away from home. But nothing is impossible and we did it! I don't know how many years we can go backwards, but it was probably the best year of Sunderland's history for many, many years, I would say. I guess you would have to go back to Quinny and Phillips to find another season like that one? We had all the ups and downs, getting to the League Cup final, the quality of the games in the middle of the season, beating Newcastle both times (at home and away) – and then at the end there was the miracle. What a season! It was incredible.'

Once the dust had settled on an incredible season, the question quickly turned to how much of an impact Sunderland could make on the Premier League in the 2014–15 season. After successive fights against relegation, mid-table security was the minimum expectation from supporters given the sensational end-of-season flourish – some fans even dared to dream of even better and bigger things.

However, the summer transfer window would soon make an impact of its own.

Lee Congerton had arrived at the Stadium of Light in the new position of Sporting Director in March 2014. The summer transfer window provided the first test of his ability and ambition. Jack Rodwell was to be the big signing, costing £10 million from Manchester City in a five-year deal. Will Buckley was signed from Brighton and Hove Albion for £2.5 million, Patrick van Aanholt joined from Chelsea for £1.5

million, and Jordi Gómez, Billy Jones and Costel Pantilimon all came on free transfers, with Ricardo Álvarez, who had been an unused substitute for Argentina in the World Cup final against Germany in Rio that summer, and Sebastián Coates signing loan deals from Inter Milan and Liverpool respectively.

There was believed to be a conditional obligation in the Álvarez deal that should Sunderland avoid relegation that season, which they later did under Dick Advocaat, he would be signed on a permanent transfer for around £9 million. However, at the end of the season, Sunderland were rumoured to no longer want a player who had a serious knee problem and had made just 11 Premier League appearances for them. Álvarez never played for Sunderland again, but in 2017 the Court of Arbitration for Sport ruled that the Black Cats had to pay Inter Milan the agreed fee. Meanwhile, as a free agent, Álvarez was able to join Sampdoria. He is currently playing for Atlas in Mexico. The whole saga of Sunderland having to pay out such a large fee for a player they reportedly neither wanted nor signed has since been cited as an example of a business strategy that contributed to the club's rapid downfall.

As new players arrived at the Stadium of Light back in the summer of 2015, many players also left. Critically and crucially, the three loan players who had each made such a big difference in the previous season – Marcos Alonso, Fabio Borini, and Ki Sung-yueng – were all lost. Alfred N'Diaye, Ignacio Scocco, and David Moberg Karlsson, none of whom had really featured in the first team, were sold for a cumulative figure of around £6.5 million, but several others, including Phil Bardsley and Jack Colback, who had both regularly featured in the first team, also departed on free transfers.

'It was a bad summer,' Gus reflects.

The departure of the three loan players from the previous season was the bitterest pill of all to swallow. Poyet feels that at least one and possibly two of them could and should have been signed by Sunderland that summer.

'I am sorry, Marcos Alonso was easy,' Gus says. 'We had the money. It should have been easy for us to sign him. Fabio Borini was nearly done for me. In my head it was done, I think. Did we wait a little too much? Maybe. I don't know. Ki was no chance. He was priced at £10 million at that time. So one was impossible, one was a problem with timing, I think, but Alonso was easy to do and we didn't do it. I had signed a new contract and my idea was to bring in specific players for the way I wanted to play. I had a base, and by adding the right players I felt it would make it easier to play the way I wanted to play.

'Obviously, Lee Congerton came in. It was his first job as sport director after something he learned in his past with Frank Arnesen [Congerton worked with Arnesen when the former Danish international was sporting director at Chelsea and Hamburger SV] and he wanted to impose a style of direction, and I didn't like it. I thought it was important to listen to me – I had been there for eight or nine months at that time – but sometimes the manager cannot get what he wants, and I had to accept that. I like it to be clear. They can tell you, "Mr Poyet, you are going to be a coach not a manager. We will give you the player and you coach them. Yes or no?" Yes means "shut up and work", probably. There are different ways and it depends on you. I cannot choose the way I want to be, but I can choose the way I want to live. I don't want to live any life that somebody else wants me to live. It is not arrogance, it is reality. If I think it is not right, it is not right for me. Otherwise, you lose a part of your personality. It is easy to say about every player that has signed for a club that the manager has said "Yes". Obviously – if not you would be playing three against eleven! I needed a left-back. So I am not going to say "No" to a left-back; but the problem of which left-back I am saying 'Yes'.

'Did we sign my first choice that would cost £3 to £5 million? Or the one that cost £1.5 million? Which is better, the one that costs £3 to £5 million or the one that costs £1.5 million? It is a massive difference when you know the player. You know what he is going to give you; you know how he behaves; you know when he plays and when he doesn't play; you know when you tell him things how he reacts to it. So it was easy to get Marcos Alonso and we didn't.

'Recruiting well is having a player in a position who has the characteristics of what the manager wants to put his system into play. If you bring that player in then it is about me, the manager. I am responsible for everything. If we lose, I say, "I am the problem." But you just cannot put luck into recruitment. It is the most important part of football. If you recruit well, you have got half of the job done.

'People say that I didn't have a good relationship with Lee Congerton,' Gus adds. 'But I think I had a great relationship with him. The problem was that he saw football in one way, and I see football in another way. At the end of the day, we all lost: the club, Lee Congerton, me, the players, everybody. If I had resigned in July, who would be the bad person? Me. People would say, "Gus Poyet left the club in July because he doesn't care." But, at the end of the day, I did care, and who paid the price? Me. I was sacked!

'I think it is extremely hard with so many problems and issues without going in and trying to impose a new direction in the club and it didn't work, because if it did work after I left I would say to you now, "You know what? Lee Congerton was right." But Lee wasn't right. Time proved that he was wrong.

'The summer before I arrived, Sunderland bought many players into the club and I needed to change one of those players so that I could bring in a specific type of player for me.

I always told the sport director that one part of the job that is very difficult is to get players away, and this delayed many things.

'I think losing Jack Colback was a genuine mistake. It was a bit late and in the end it was the decision of the player. Before I went to the club Jack would play left-back, but I put him centre-midfield. [Colback made 42 first-team appearances in the 2013–14 season.] I think he thought it was a moment to take advantage of his season. It was his personal decision and I think personally it was wrong. But it was also a club mistake. As a club we waited for far too much to make the offer and, by then, Jack had a bigger and better possibility. OK, we didn't know it was to our rivals, but good for him. You need to make decisions and I always want the players to make decisions themselves, for it is their life.

'By the beginning of the season I had a weaker team, no doubt,' Gus adds. 'I didn't have enough defenders. I base my teams with the organisation starting from the back, and then I try to play football. Playing football is the most important part of the game for me. Without a base, I have a problem. We started the season and I had just one right-back – Billy Jones – and he was injured. So I had to start the first Premier League game of the season with Wes Brown at right-back. I think that is not acceptable for a Premier League club. That is my opinion. It is simple and clear.'

Sunderland drew 2-2 against West Brom in the season opener at the Hawthorns.

'It was actually a win for me,' Gus says with a smile. 'I was the happiest person in the stadium after the game! But, seriously, it was not right.'

The following week, Jack Rodwell scored the first of his five goals in a Sunderland shirt to earn another point in a 1-1 draw at home to Manchester United. Then came a 1-0 defeat at Queens Park Rangers, which was followed by three draws in a row against Tottenham Hotspur, Burnley and Swansea City. By the end of September Sunderland were without a win after six league matches, but were positioned 15th in the table with five points from five draws.

'I thought the team was not bad, but that is not enough. When you are at a club when you have done something incredible in the season before then you need to always be in the top ten or something! But it doesn't happen like that.'

The first Premier League victory came at home to Stoke City at the beginning of October when Steven Fletcher and Connor Wickham linked up well to notch all three goals in a 3-1 win that moved Sunderland up to 11th. But the following week brought a club record-equalling 8-0 defeat at Southampton (previous generations of Sunderland fans had endured the same result at Sheffield Wednesday in 1911, West Ham United in 1968 and Watford in 1982). Ironically, to add a touch of humour to the humiliation of such an annihilation, three of the goals at St Mary's Stadium were scored by Sunderland players, including a quite stunning strike from some distance by Santiago Vergini.

Just one win – a 3-1 success at Crystal Palace in November – from the following eight league matches left Sunderland in the bottom six ahead of the visit to Newcastle United four days before Christmas. An injury-time goal from Adam Johnson secured the fourth win in a row against the Magpies and a personal hat-trick for Poyet against the club's bitter rivals.

'When we won 1-0 at St James' Park with the last-minute goal it was amazing,' Gus remembers, fondly.

But a 3-1 home defeat by Hull City on Boxing Day, a goalless draw at Aston Villa, and then three straight defeats against Manchester City, Liverpool and Tottenham Hotspur left

Sunderland just above the relegation zone in 16th place by mid-January.

There was some good news. Something of a 'miracle' had taken place in the transfer window: a swap deal took out-of-form American striker Jozy Altidore from Sunderland to Major League Soccer side Toronto, and brought Jermain Defoe to the Stadium of Light in exchange.

'I think everybody in Sunderland would agree that it was a spectacular move,' Gus says. 'Jozy had tried everything. I talked to him and he said he had a great opportunity to go back to play in the MLS, and then Jermain, a phenomenal player who I had played with at Tottenham and I knew personally, became available and a deal was done. I was very pleased. It was magnificent.'

Defoe scored his first goal for Sunderland in a 2-0 win over Burnley and followed that up with a goal against Swansea City the following week which earned another point in a 1-1 draw. However, Poyet also came very close to losing midfielder Lee Cattermole to Stoke City during that same transfer window.

'I made a mistake,' Gus accepts. 'You know how it can be when you don't know how much a player actually costs, but you want to put a number in there thinking that the interested club is not going to give us that and then they say, "OK"? That is what happened with Lee Cattermole at that time. I had to call Ellis Short and say, "I have got this problem. I made a mistake. I threw in a number thinking they were not going to pay it and they will" and so on. Ellis said to me, "Do you need him?" And I said, "Yes, I need him." So he stayed. I don't know if Lee is happy with me now, but that it is the truth. It is as simple as that. I had no intention to sell. Ellis sorted it out in two seconds.'

Cattermole remains a player that Poyet admires and, four and a half years on, in the summer of 2018, the 30-year-old was reported to be in talks to resume their working relationship abroad with a potential loan move to Bordeaux.

'I had some of the best conversations I have ever had with a player with Lee Cattermole,' Gus says. 'He was playing in a certain way and, with me, he understood another part of the game. I liked that. I am not saying it is always right what I do – a player needs to adapt to every manager because we all want things differently. But we had a few conversations about what I needed from central midfield and I think he enjoyed that. I think he liked to know that there is another way of playing football, another way of understanding football, another responsibility for the central midfielder. I think he was very happy about it.

'I am an open person,' Gus adds. 'I try to talk to the players, even the ones that don't play, which is always more difficult. Communication depends on characters. At the end of the day, I need a player to do certain things and if he does certain things he has more chance of playing and we have more chance of winning in my style. So when I have a player who has the character of Lee Cattermole, who is accepting, asking, discussing, talking and so on, it is magnificent.'

Sunderland were on the march in the FA Cup again in early 2015 after a 1-0 third-round win over Leeds United and a 3-1 fourth-round replay win at Fulham. However, similar to the previous season, none of these early Cup matches had featured Poyet's first-eleven line-up. Not that anybody was complaining, as Sunderland reached the last 16 of the competition for the second year in succession.

In hindsight, Poyet's time at Sunderland began to quickly unravel after a disappointing 2-0 defeat at home to bottom-of-the-table Queens Park Rangers in mid-February was followed by another disappointing and also frustrating FA Cup exit, featuring another under-strength side, at League One Bradford City five days later.

'Yes, Queens Park Rangers was a turning point for me,' Gus admits. 'I don't think we played badly, but Bobby Zamora had an incredible game for them, and we conceded two goals from not too much.'

The defeat at Bradford was overshadowed by chants from the Sunderland fans, directed at Poyet, over what he believes was a misunderstanding.

'I swear to God that I don't remember saying anything to anybody about the fans, and it came out like I was blaming them. So when I heard the fans at Bradford I thought to myself, "What has happened here?" I didn't understand. If it was some interview or the way that it said that I said something, I don't know. I couldn't understand that they were thinking that I was blaming them for us losing. No chance. In my mind, no chance. Never. So when I went to the press conference afterwards I was very upset.'

Poyet decided to write an open letter to the Sunderland fans in the hope of putting the record straight.

'It is something that I had never done before,' Gus says. 'But I wanted the letter to be from me. My words only. To make it clear.'

Sunderland earned two more points from draws against West Bromwich Albion and Hull City either side of a 2-0 defeat at Manchester United, but the 1-1 draw at the KC Stadium was overshadowed by news of Adam Johnson's arrest the previous day, on suspicion of having sexual activity with an underage girl. The former England international was later convicted and sentenced to six years in prison.

'I have never had a day like that day before the match against Hull,' Gus sighs. 'Never.'

The following match would be Poyet's last with Sunderland. It was a 4-0 defeat by Aston Villa at the Stadium of Light. Many fans walked out at half-time. He was sacked soon afterwards. It was a sad way to end his 17-month spell in charge.

Dick Advocaat was quickly installed as Poyet's replacement the following week and managed to become the fifth man to secure Sunderland's Premier League survival in successive seasons. Sam Allardyce was to become the sixth and the last.

'It was all bang, bang, bang at the end. So it was coming. When it happened against Aston Villa and afterwards, it was awful. Maybe the people who kept coming down behind the bench had an impact? Maybe they were the same people who kept coming behind the bench when Peter Reid got sacked as well?' Gus ponders. 'Peter Reid was outstanding for Sunderland. After what he did with his team, he deserved to stay for another five years. But because he didn't do so well the following year they were asking for his head. You cannot do that. I know everyone loves the club, but you cannot have that pressure. It happened to Peter Reid, it happened to Martin O'Neill, it happened to Paolo Di Canio, it happened to me, it happened to Dick Advocaat and so on. The club needs to change. The past is gone. We cannot play Quinny and Phillips any more, and you cannot find the twin brothers of Quinny and Phillips to play either. They don't exist. But some people keep thinking that is Sunderland. Why? Who told you to play one way or the other? That is a situation that hurt me when people were so stubborn.

'You have to have time to impose your standards, your qualities, and your identity. But I don't think you can go into a Premier League club with a mentality of "I am going to be here for three years minimum" any more because if you think like that you are dreaming. But you need time, and that is something that doesn't exist any more, unless you are Alex Ferguson, Arsène Wenger and maybe Mauricio Pochettino! It is the same in the Championship. How many teams are going to go up from the Championship next year? Three. How many play to go up? 24. So there are 21 teams that fail? It is just not true. The three teams that are going up are from the eight or so teams that have a chance of getting into the top six.

'Who won the Premier League? Manchester City. Who spent the most? Manchester City. Who won the League in France? Paris Saint-Germain. Who spent the most? Paris Saint-Germain. It can happen once every now and again. There was Leicester City, which was unique and the best story in Premier League football ever. But before Leicester it was Chelsea or Manchester City or Manchester United.

'The big difference between England and the rest of the world is the publicity,' Gus adds. 'The Premier League is shown worldwide. When I was at Sunderland, especially at the end of my first season, people were watching our games in China, Hawaii and all sorts of places. Everybody is watching. That is the big difference between the Premier League and France, Spain and the rest. So you become something unique when you are one of the 20 managers in the Premier League. It is an incredible achievement and a privilege. But the pressure at the bottom is such that you need to be very strong mentally. If not it is very, very stressful. It was a shame that the following season didn't work because I think we had the chance to really start building something at Sunderland. What I couldn't achieve in my second year was to control the game like I wanted to control it. That was because I lost a very important player in Ki. We didn't find the player who could do that. We didn't get that player who could bring certain qualities into midfield that controlled the game the way I wanted to control it.

'I will give you an example: there was a game against Manchester City in the season before where Ki was outstanding. He was on a different level. So when you lose that player it is difficult. It comes down to characteristics. How many millions of midfielders are there in the world? Thousands and thousands. Tell me how many players are similar to Ki? Not many of them. He is a player with very specific characteristics and that is what I needed. So we got another player and we played in a different way and we didn't control the game in the way that I wanted.

'There are no magicians in football,' Gus says. 'We are coaches. We do our thing. We believe in our thing and we try to convince the players to do our thing. When we do it right in the summer it is easier for us because we have got half of the job done. If we don't do it right it needs something incredible or unbelievable, but what normally happens is the opposite. I thought we needed something extra, but we didn't do the homework in the summer. That is my biggest regret. I learned a lot. I won't make that mistake again. If I am ever in that situation again I have two options: I do what I need to do, or I go.'

Eleven Sunderland managers in nine and a half years under Ellis Short tells one story, but significant player investment from the former chairman over the first eight of those nine and a half years tells another.

'I had good communications with Ellis Short,' Gus says. 'Every time I needed to call him I was free to call him. Yes, he delegated a lot. He put emphasis on two or three people to manage the club financially, commercially, politically and so on. He appointed me to pick the team. I think it is very easy to blame the manager and then directly the owner without knowing, like I have said before, that there is something wrong inside the club that needs to change; something at its very core – something that I couldn't find. If I knew the problem, I would tell you.

'Martin O'Neill, Paolo Di Canio, Gustavo Poyet, Dick Advocaat, and whoever else can't all be wrong,' Gus adds. 'Maybe one or two of us, but not five or six!'

After leaving Sunderland Poyet managed AEK Athens, Real Betis and Shanghai Shenhua before taking over at Bordeaux in January 2018 with the club positioned 13th in Ligue 1. They finished the season in sixth place after nine wins from 16 matches under Poyet.

'It was incredible for us to reach the Europa League,' Gus says. 'We won six games out of seven and we qualified. Nobody knows how. Everybody was expecting Saint-Étienne or Montpellier [to qualify], but not Bordeaux. We were on the pitch waiting for Nice to finish playing on the final day to see if we got into the Europa League. It was amazing when we did.

'You cannot compare managing in France to managing in England or Spain,' Gus adds. 'Because it is totally different, with bigger, stronger, African players with a lot of power. Three or four teams are better than the rest and they are difficult to play against – Monaco, Marseilles, and Paris Saint-Germain, for example. I would like to see if any of the clubs can get closer to Paris, but it is incredible how every city transforms itself when Paris come to play them.'

Poyet successfully steered Bordeaux to early Europa League qualifying-round wins over FK Ventspils of Latvia and Mariupol of Ukraine at the beginning of the 2018–19 season. But the Bordeaux board's decision to sell Gaëtan Laborde to Montpellier against his advice – and also his knowledge – on the day of the second leg against Mariupol prompted the manager into using the word '*honte*' as he described his feelings about the transfer in a post-match press conference. The English translation of '*honte*' is 'shame', and Poyet used the word to mean 'embarrassing'. While Poyet was reported to be considering his position at Bordeaux as a result, he was also suspended by club president, Stéphane Martin, following his comments. However, presumably in support of their manager, the Bordeaux squad refused to train on the following day. KAA Gent, of Belgium, were later defeated in the Europa League playoff round 2-0 on aggregate to secure les Girondins a place in the group stages of the competition for the fourth time in six years. The following week Ricardo Gomes was appointed Bordeaux manager

It looks likely that Poyet will be one of just five men to have led Sunderland to a major Cup final appearance at Wembley when the 100th anniversary of the opening of the original Empire Stadium in 1923 comes around in a few years time. Therefore it was, and remains, a rare achievement. But Poyet does not list it as his fondest memory from his time at Sunderland. That moment came two months afterwards, at the Stadium of Light, following the penultimate Premier League match of the season.

'I would say that my happiest memory would be West Brom. I remember sitting in the manager's room after we had won that game and really feeling like, "*We've Done It!*" I was asked to do one thing at Sunderland: "Get safe." So when you do what you have been asked to do that is "job done", as we say. That was a great feeling. It was very special,' Gus concludes with a smile.

EPILOGUE

If Poyet's story since leaving Sunderland has been one of never really being able to settle, then the same can be said of his former club. Regardless of how many times Sunderland were steered to safe harbour in one crisis season after another by a whole host of high-profile managers, the club was all at sea almost immediately afterwards.

Martin O'Neill and Paulo Di Canio before Poyet, and Dick Advocaat and Sam Allardyce after him, all led Sunderland to similar versions of the Great Escape in their brief stays on Wearside. In the 2016–17 campaign though, under manager David Moyes and chief executive Martin Bain, the ship finally hit the rocks. Moyes was another high-profile name taking on the challenge of Sunderland AFC and trying to get it right. But the Scot was impressive in neither recruitment nor motivation and Sunderland's decade-long stay in the Premier League came to an end with the club finishing rock bottom with just 24 points, 16 shy of safety.

With owner Ellis Short looking to leave the sinking ship having become tired of pumping in so much money with so little return, Moyes' successor would have to revive a football club divided from top to bottom with the meagerest of transfer budgets. Simon Grayson left a safe seat at Preston to take on the challenge, but no one, including him, realised just how big that challenge would be.

6

Simon Grayson had one of the shortest tenures of any Sunderland manager in the history of the club – barely four months in charge.

Tasked with lancing the boil that was predecessor David Moyes' ill-fated 2016–17 relegation campaign, the Yorkshireman's first challenge was to make the club fit for purpose in the Championship – something he appeared eminently suited for on the basis of his CV. But the problems and issues he faced proved overwhelming on and off the field and, with just one win in 15 league games, he was removed. There remained 30 full games for his successor Chris Coleman to turn things around and avoid the drop, but the fact the former Wales manager failed to do so underlines the depth of the problems the club was dealing with at the time.

Here, Grayson talks about the true scale of the mess he inherited, the hurdles he had to overcome as he looked to steady the ship, and his thoughts on the future of Sunderland AFC on the anniversary of his sacking.

SIMON GRAYSON

SUNDERLAND MANAGER
29 JUNE 2017 TO 3 NOVEMBER 2017
MEETS GRAEME ANDERSON

It seem appropriate that Simon Grayson and I are conducting our interview in the bar of the sprawling art deco Queens Hotel in Leeds. This was the hotel where former Sunderland striker Brian Clough (infinitely more famous to the rest of the world as a colourful and successful football manager), stayed during his short and disastrous spell in charge of Leeds United. From a room somewhere in this hotel Clough would ring Don Revie late at night and reputedly say, 'Don? They're not playing for me, Don . . .'

Clough's 1974 stay at Elland Road lasted 44 days, making Grayson's 128 days on Wearside look positively long-serving in comparison. But whereas Clough's approach to Revie's squad was suicidally antagonistic, Grayson tried every trick in the managerial tool box to conjure performances and results from his players at Sunderland.

'I arrived at the Stadium of Light full of enthusiasm and excited about the challenge of taking on this massive club and trying to get it going again,' he recalls. 'Myself and Snods [Grayson's assistant Glynn Snodin] knew it was all about stabilising the club after what had gone before. But in the games themselves, no matter what we did or what we tried, we couldn't find a winning formula with what we had – and we tried everything.'

A year after his sacking Grayson has moved on, briefly managing League One Bradford City before declining the chance to take the reins on a long-term contract with the Bantams. He has turned down other offers too as he focuses on a break from football and time spent in the comfort of a press box chair, rather than the managerial hot seat. But he says he has no regrets about taking the job that proved to be a poisoned chalice. In the incestuous world of football his path had crossed that of Sunderland many times – he might even have joined as a player at one stage – so he was fully aware of the opportunity the job presented.

Growing up in Bedale, just 50 miles away from Sunderland, his football-mad, head-teacher dad Adrian took him to games at Roker Park, Ayresome Park and, of course, Elland Road during his formative years.

'My dad loves his football and didn't mind driving us to games when I was young so I visited Roker Park a few times and loved the old ground,' he remembers. 'As a young player I used to play in the Northern Intermediate League on a Saturday morning and that would bring me up against Sunderland sides and players like Richard Ord. I think Mickey Gray was a little younger. In fact, it's quite possible I might have joined Sunderland as a player had things turned out a little differently. When I left Leeds as a young lad in 1992 there were rumours that Sunderland were interested in taking me – I think Malcolm Crosby was manager at the time – but nothing came of it and I joined Leicester City instead. That meant that in the games I played on Wearside, it was always as part of the opposition, but I still enjoyed playing there. Roker Park was one of them real, fascinating, historic grounds, with the atmosphere right on top of you.'

SIMON GRAYSON

The 6 foot 2 inch Grayson was at home in defence or midfield, although the vast majority of his professional career was to be played at full-back. He was a pro footballer for 18 years, making his name at Filbert Street where he made 188 appearances between 1992 and 1997, winning the League Cup in 1997 and being voted Leicester's player of the season the same year.

Later that year he moved across the Midlands to another Premier League side, Aston Villa, before going on to play for Blackburn Rovers and ending his playing days at Blackpool. Like every other Sunderland boss in this book Grayson moved into management in his thirties – a precocious age for anyone to take over the running of a professional football club. His first steps were at the Tangerines, where he became manager at the age of 36 in the wake of manager Colin Hendry's sudden sacking at Bloomfield Road. After Blackpool there followed spells at Leeds United, Huddersfield and Preston North End – winning promotion with all of them – before Sunderland came calling in the summer of 2017.

'I knew there was talk going around that Sunderland were interested in me after Derek McInnes turned the job down,' he admits. 'But everything was up in the air because there was German interest in buying the club at the time and, if that had come off, they would have made a German appointment. That didn't happen though, and then Peter Ridsdale at Preston let me know that Sunderland had agreed to pay my compensation clause. I was free to go if I wanted it, and suddenly I was driving up the M6 and across the Pennines. I think when David Moyes had left Sunderland he'd suggested two or three people who he thought were suitable for the job and my name was among them, so I was probably always in the mix. I think that was how it progressed.'

Neither the club nor the new manager wasted time getting the show on the road once Grayson arrived on Wearside.

'I grabbed a bag from Preston's training ground, drove up to Sunderland with my agent and was there by about lunchtime. It didn't take long to sort out the financial terms, and then I spent the rest of the afternoon doing press conferences, having tied down the loose ends. The players had been in that morning and the next day I met the rest of the staff and players, and the day after that we flew out to Austria on pre-season. I quickly had to nip home so that I had enough gear – it was that fast!'

It wasn't just the speed of events that was exhilarating for the new boss.

'My first impressions of the club were that it was unbelievable,' Grayson says. 'I'd been to the academy before, watching my son play, but it isn't until you get inside the academy that you fully appreciate that these are proper, proper facilities. The whole place was superb – I still didn't feel totally familiar with the place by the time I left!

'So it was a great place to prepare and train and, of course, the Stadium of Light – that goes without saying, it's one of the great stadiums. It was good for me that I knew Adrian Lamb, the club's fitness coach, from his days at Preston, so that was a help because as a management team we were plunged into trying to assess the squad really quickly, knowing some players would be leaving. The biggest thing when we looked at the players was how short we were in terms of first-team players – there were only about ten! We had youngsters like Elliot Embleton, Ethan Robson, Josh Maja and Joel Asoro with us but, really, in terms of a senior squad, we didn't have many.'

In the wake of relegation under Moyes there had been an exodus from the first-team squad. The most notable departures were the club's two outstanding performers, striker Jermain

Defoe and goalkeeper Jordan Pickford – a £25 million buy for Everton soon to establish himself as England's number one. Long-serving stalwart Seb Larsson had also left, along with Fabio Borini, the League Cup final goalscoring hero who had just endured a season to forget. With them went a slew of failed first-team players, most brought in by Moyes, who departed unmourned by Sunderland fans – Joleon Lescott, Steven Pienaar, Adnan Januzaj, Jason Denayer, Victor Anichebe and Javi Manquillo.

Two of the biggest flops, though – record signing £13.6 million Didier Ndong and £8 million Papy Djilobodji – remained on the books, as did out of favour Sam Allardyce duo Wahbi Khazri and Jeremain Lens.

'Yeah, we were really, really low on numbers, conscious of the players who might be moving on, and we had to get to work on it really quickly because we simply didn't have the bodies, and the new season wasn't a million miles away,' says Grayson.

The new manager had two obvious issues on his plate beyond a lack of bodies: splits in the camp, and complete uncertainty over who might be sold and who not.

'When I first came in, you had the European boys who wanted to leave, who would be sat on their own,' remembers Grayson. 'Then you'd have the English players, players sat at lunch differently, and it was something I wanted to change around. One of the key strengths I see in myself as a manager is that I try to get the best out of a group of players – my relationship with my players is vital. Even on this transfer deadline day just gone, summer 2018, I had three former players asking my advice on whether they should stay or go – not because I'm their mates, or anything, but because they respect my judgement. I always like to think that it's nice players feel happy to do that. I used those man-management skills as best I could at Sunderland. For example, I've never been one to have a "bomb squad" – players who are bombed out and train on their own. That's because I was treated that way under Graeme Souness at Blackburn and decided I would never do that when I became a manager. I wanted to treat players right, and if players don't play on a Saturday then so be it, they're still in training.

'You are always hoping, though, that somewhere down the line the penny drops with them, and all of a sudden you're getting players coming back into it determined to make their mark. We tried to do whatever we could to get players to interact together, but it probably wasn't until after transfer deadline day when some of the players had left - Khazri, Djilobodji, Lens, and so on – that the likes of Ndong and Lamine Koné started to come into the fold and into the culture. Even then, though, you still know full well, that their hearts might not be in it – that they might not come back in time after an international break, or might not turn up for an interpreter.

'I had known what I was getting into to a certain degree, but what soon emerged as a big factor was having the uncertainty, right up until the end of August, in terms of who would be leaving. That was true especially of the players, who perhaps thought they were better than the league they were in. Would they be staying? Lens was another one who did leave in the end, but all these lads were lads who were on the books and you weren't sure right up until August 31st – by which time the season was well underway – whether they would feature in your plans or not.

'It was quite evident, within a few days of getting there, and talking with agents, that quite a few players didn't want to be at the club. I was quite public about saying I would drive players to new clubs myself if they didn't want to be there. But you have to be careful, because if these players don't end up leaving, you've got a player or players at your club who are on an awful lot of money who you then have to consider playing – more than that, they can have an influence on players around them. It's a balancing act. Somehow you have to keep them on side, to get them to buy into your ideas of what you want to achieve on the pitch, while still knowing full well they don't want to be at the club.'

Another source of irritation was the amount of money being spent on these players and the smallness of the transfer budget in comparison. The wage bill was high for the players who were already there – maybe three or four times higher than the budget for my entire squad at Preston – and we still had to bring in a load of players in order to give ourselves a first-team squad. It's quite staggering when you first see the books and see how much so many of the players are on – then you watch them train and you think, "Wow, they can't be on the money the books say they are, because they are not to that wage level." They'd been at a club that had been teetering on relegation for years, and you could begin to see why that was when you saw the quality of some of the players and the money they were being paid.'

Against that background Grayson needed to restock the squad, but with very little funds at his disposal. In the end, he was able to bring in ten new players, though he paid fees for only three. Some of those recruits would necessarily be a gamble – a case of getting a body in and hoping they would rise to the challenge. But there was a signing Grayson had his heart set on from the start, an attacking winger he was convinced could be of real benefit to Sunderland, and he immediately sought to bring that footballer to the Stadium of Light.

'The one key player I wanted to sign straight away was Aiden McGeady because I knew he was available and I'd had him at Preston and knew he would be outstanding in the Championship. Within ten days we'd managed to get the deal done for £250,000 and it was a snip, really, because he had been quoted at three or four million earlier in the transfer window.

'I paid the money for James Vaughan, who was only about £300,000, and Jason Steele, who came out at about £250,000. When I assessed the squad, I was looking for players who knew what the Championship were about. We tried to avoid League Two players and the risks involved in them stepping up, and also that of young Premier League players who were still learning and stepping down. Of the lads I paid money for, Vaughan and McGeady had played for me at Preston, and Steele had played in the Championship for Blackburn and Middlesbrough, so they knew what it was about – they understood what it meant to play at a big club but they also knew the Championship. I went for Vaughan because I thought he would be a good fit for Sunderland, and that Sunderland fans would like his honesty. I'd worked with him at Huddersfield Town before, and I thought his work rate, his desire, stood out. He was never the most natural of goalscorers – although he'd had a good season at Bury, his stats would suggest he was not a great goalscorer. But what he would do was run through brick walls and chase it, and I thought the supporters would like that – they have an affinity with players that give their all. I think I said it in my first press conference that Sunderland is a working-class city, and they want to see their players giving everything for the shirt. Something I've always tried to have is a spirit and affiliation – putting teams together that reflect what the fans want to see. I mean, I was hard-working as a defender or midfielder. I would give my all and I wanted my teams to reflect myself and what supporters wanted to see. I thought Vaughany would fit into that sort of category and I was hoping he would hold the ball up for others to do the business, like Lewis Grabban did for us. 'It was one of those situations where we had to get players in to make up the numbers and then later players would be coming available through the loan market, and I would look again at players who had performed in the Championship. I wasn't looking for young players because we had plenty of good young players already at the club. We were looking at players who could do a job in the Championship, like Grabban and, later, Jonny Williams, Marc Wilson and Callum McManaman. Tyias Browning and Brendan Galloway from Everton were young Premier League players but they were also two defenders I had worked with the season before at Preston, and I thought they were decent prospects, plus I wanted to create competition for Oviedo in the left-back slot, who had injury problems.

'I don't think we had a senior attacker in the squad when I arrived at the club because they'd all left, so it was good that at least we could get Vaughan and Grabban in for the start of the season.'

By then, though, Grayson had also made a pivotal decision in terms of allowing the sale of former player of the year, keeper Vito Mannone, to Championship side Reading, who were ultimately to survive that season with the Italian making 41 appearances. Whether Mannone would have made a difference to Sunderland's survival prospects that season will always remain a moot point. But what was beyond doubt was that the acquisition of Jason Steele hardly improved Sunderland's strength between the posts – this was arguably to be the worst season in the club's history in terms of the standard of goalkeeping performances. No fan I've spoken to can remember a campaign when a selection of goalkeepers made so many costly blunders.

Grayson explains: 'The chief executive Martin Bain said, "If you sell him you'll get his wages back to get somebody else in, and maybe a little more." And there were a couple of things I had to bear in mind – the first was that he only had a year left on his contract, so we were running the risk of losing a player for nothing rather than getting some money in for a player who would allow us to re-jig. The second thing was that Vito too had been part of that squad that had suffered over a number of years. At the time, I was trying to actively dismantle that squad that had so much baggage. I was trying to get a clean slate with every position that became available to us. Looking back, what I actually wish we had done was sell even more of that squad – even if it was for a lesser value than the club originally wanted. Because, don't get me wrong, we could have sold, Ndong in that transfer window, we could have sold Koné too, and all that lot in that first window – just not for the sale value the club felt they represented at that particular time. In light of how it was all to turn out, it might not have been a bad thing to have taken any money we could get for them and look to use it all for rebuilding more ambitiously, and that might have extended to the goalkeepers.'

It is impossible not to have some sympathy for Grayson as he looked to refresh a shattered and fractured Sunderland squad with a comparative pittance of a transfer budget. Although the club had taken in £30 million in parachute payments, and made almost as much money again from the sale of Jordan Pickford, Grayson's transfer expenditure amounted to little more than £1 million that summer. In contrast, Newcastle United – by whose standard Sunderland would be judged – had spent in the region of £50 million the previous season to ensure they bounced straight back to the Premier League. In the wake of the Magpies' immediate return to the top flight there were many who eulogised the role played by manager Rafa Benítez. But without wanting to minimise the Spaniard's managerial contribution, I think the £50 million helped. Not only was Sunderland's meager transfer spending always likely to hamper them, but clearly the many departures and new arrivals would likely mean it would take time for the players to settle, for a remodelled team to emerge.

That said, no one was expecting pre-season to conclude with a shocking 5-0 drubbing by Celtic at the Stadium of Light, a week before the new campaign got underway – new keeper Steele having a nightmare on a day when the defence was all at sea. That performance and result poured instant cold water on any optimism that might have been building among supporters ahead of the 2017–18 Championship campaign, but Grayson admits he had had a reality check long before that: 'Generally, the results in pre-season weren't bad, but some of the errors were. We went to Bury in our very first game and, although we won, we made schoolboy mistakes which had me thinking that this group was not as good as I expected them to be. Then we went up to St Johnstone and got beat 3-0 up there as well, and it became clear that if we conceded one goal we could concede a second straight afterwards. Speaking to the staff at the time, who had been at the club a while, they said the gist of it was that there was a hangover from relegation in that when they conceded a goal, their heads went down. There were still a lot of players there from the previous season, and it was a common trait that if they conceded their heads went and they conceded another straight away – it could go from 0-0 to 3-0 very quickly. The Celtic game wasn't an eye-opener in that sense, but it reinforced that this was going to be difficult.'

Sunderland, meanwhile, had acquired another goalkeeper. Dutchman Robbin Ruiter had impressed in pre-season games against Bradford and Scunthorpe, so the Black Cats would at least have someone to come in if Steele's Celtic form continued.

Before that became a factor though, there was a bolt from the blue when, within hours of the Celtic defeat, video started to emerge of a seemingly intoxicated Darron Gibson talking to Sunderland fans and being hugely critical of his teammates in a foul-mouthed tirade mainly aimed at the club's foreign legion. The video went viral and the club acted as quickly as it could, with Bain holding an internal inquiry which led to a fine of two weeks' wages for the player, while the shame-faced midfielder made a public apology to his teammates.

'The Darron Gibson situation didn't help us,' nods Grayson. 'Gibbo was one of those players – a bit like Jack Rodwell – who was talented and who you thought, if you could get him playing right, you'd have a good, experienced midfield player on your hands who could be a good asset to the team. After the Celtic game, all you are thinking is, "Right, let's get in in the morning and put that performance to bed." And then I had Martin Bain on the phone asking if I'd seen what was on the internet, and my heart sank when I saw it all. It was the last thing the football club needed, or I needed as a new manager – things like that coming out.

'It's a fact of life, though: you can manage players at the training ground but once they leave your jurisdiction you can't babysit them. You can't babysit 24 players. It's all about player responsibility and what they should be doing and how they conduct themselves. The worst part is it was about his teammates. It was a week before the season started, and I think any manager will tell you that the week before the season starts you want as clear a week as possible, with everyone looking forward to it and no negativity. Well, we'd just suffered a 5-0 defeat and then one of the players, apparently on the drink, is slaughtering his fellow teammates. We tried to sort it and he apologised, but in the back of your head you're thinking, "Is there a lingering resentment there from the players he's criticised? Is there a potential drinking culture in the club that I don't know about?" Because I can't know everything straight away. I can't follow them, I can't put trackers on them – and every manager will tell you the same.

'It was a challenging time because there just seemed to be problem after problem as you went along. You looked at the situation with Gibson after the Celtic game, and things like the ruling by FIFA that Sunderland had to pay £10 million for a player, Ricardo Álvarez, who barely kicked a ball for the club, and it had you shaking your head. There were a lot of things that had clearly been going on.

'As soon as I went in, for example, I was thinking, "Why are there so many people employed by this football club? I get it that it's the Premier League, but do you need four of these and five of these to do this one job?" And I just think that in the previous three or four years at the club there had been a willingness to accept more and more people on the books across the board, to accept we would fly everywhere and be involved in Africa, and so on and so on. Things like that. It just felt that there were too many people taking advantage of the owner's generosity.'

Ellis Short, by this stage, was well on his way to becoming a rare sighting at the club. Famously, Grayson's eventual successor Chris Coleman was to spend six months at Sunderland without ever once meeting the club's owner. Grayson himself fared a little better, but not much, with the American by now making no secret of the fact he was looking to sell the club and not prepared to plough even more money into it.

'I met Ellis Short a couple of times,' he reveals. 'I met him the day I got appointed, and then after the Derby game, and then after the Norwich game when we won, and he was buzzing about the situation. I think that at the end of the day, what you can say about Ellis is that he had put the money in. I'm not saying I'm defending him for that. But the hard facts were he'd invested something like £250 million of his own money into a football club. If you are doing that, you must be daft as a brush, but you are also trying to give something back to Sunderland Football Club. He can't be criticised for not investing in the club, but I just don't think he had any interaction or relationship with the supporters. And he just allowed the responsibility for his money to be wasted by so many individuals that they just took it for granted that they could do whatever they wanted to. I knew what the budget was from when I went in, and you were just thinking, "If I could start afresh without the players but with that budget to spend, I would have thought I was going to heaven and back." I would have been able to get a group of players who would certainly be challenging at the top end, but the budget was almost all taken up by the players who were already on the books.'

Despite the Celtic result, despite the shadow of the Gibson fiasco, Sunderland's new season actually got off to a half-decent start: two draws, two wins.

'Given what had happened against Celtic, the Derby County game was a decent result,' says the 48-year-old. 'We started the game really well, could have been a couple of goals up but weren't, and then Derby went down the other end and scored, and that was to become a common theme in our games. I had handed debuts to six players because I wanted to make a change from the past and knew there were still players who were suffering psychologically from the previous few seasons. I was hoping the new players would help improve the confidence of the players who were already there and change the losing culture. But that proved more difficult to shift than I had anticipated, and Chris Coleman after me experienced pretty much exactly the same thing. Our second game of the season was a Cup game away to Bury and I went strong in terms of my team selection because winning breeds confidence, and I wanted as many wins as I could get as early as I could get them. We beat Bury and that carried into our next game, the 3-1 away win over Norwich.'

At Carrow Road Grabban made it three goals in three games and McGeady got off the mark with a fine finish, which boded well.

'It was a really good team performance at Norwich, some good goals, and that's what we needed – to get that first win away from home. That took us to Sheffield Wednesday, another away game, where we totally dominated the first half after taking an early lead – if we'd scored the second one they wouldn't have come back from that. But they equalised midway through the second-half and, on a Tuesday night game away from home, you find you're coming away disappointed. We had enough chances and we should have won that game without a shadow of a doubt.'

Next up for Sunderland was a visit to Grayson's former club Leeds United, the team he supported as a boy, played for as a teenager and managed from 2008 to 2012.

'At Leeds United we hit the crossbar in the first 15 minutes and we were on top, but then Brendan Galloway made a mistake at left-back and we were 1-0 down. When we went behind, Leeds played really well. They were top of the division at the time and playing with confidence, so no complaints there – but we missed that opportunity to get the first goal.' By this point Grayson was becoming concerned that Sunderland's failure to make the most of their spells of dominance, or maintain their focus throughout the game, was more than just early season rustiness. He started to tinker with the side on a game-by-game basis, juggling different personnel and different formations as he sought to find a winning formula. After he had left the club it would be noted that he could never find a settled, successful side, but that was to overlook the fact that he named an unchanged team for the Black Cats' opening four league games.

'It was a conscious thing to leave the team unchanged for as long as possible,' he says. I wanted to get a settled side because I'm not one for changing it all the time, especially when you have new players trying to form relationships. We thought the players were doing well and we wanted to avoid changing it if it possible. We changed it after the Leeds United defeat and then we took on Barnsley looking to up our game.

'But Barnsley was another match where we totally dominated the opening stages but ended up looking about as beaten as a team could be. We'd looked so comfortable in that game early on without scoring, and then the second half was just a complete collapse.'

When Grayson spoke to the Sunderland media outside the press room at Oakwell it was clear to me that he looked shell-shocked by the speed with which his side had gone from impressive to imploding. Plans he had to see his favourite band Kasabian at the Leeds Festival that night were shelved as he turned his full attention to what was now an emerging crisis. Defeat dropped Sunderland to 19th in the table. A promising start of four points from the first six was now five points from

15, and the 4,000 travelling fans who had made the journey to Barnsley either left early or stayed to sing, '*You're not fit to wear the shirt.*'

The new manager's view from the very start of the season had been that his aim would be to stabilise Sunderland mid-table in the Championship with a view to potentially having them within striking distance of the playoffs by the end of the campaign. Many Sunderland fans, though, didn't share that sense of realism. Their expectations were for nothing less than an immediate return to the Premier League. And while they had been prepared to show patience with a slow start to the season they would not tolerate their side either giving up long before the end of a match or being comprehensively rolled over by a side which had only come up from League One a couple of seasons earlier. Their patience with schoolboy errors from Sunderland players was also wearing thin.

Grayson pinned his hopes on the closing transfer window providing team strengthening and stability.

A disinterested Wahbi Khazri, who produced an eye-catchingly inept display as a second-half substitute against Barnsley, was loaned out, never to play for the club again, while prospectively useful signings Jonny Williams, Callum McManaman and Marc Wilson all came in.

'I thought we had a good transfer window and I said so at the time,' says Grayson. 'The ten that we'd brought in all looked as though they might have something to contribute. They were players who should have been able to perform to a good level in the Championship. I didn't think the squad as a whole were that weak and we still had Duncan Watmore and Paddy McNair coming back in a month or so from injury. I thought it was the nucleus of a decent squad. We brought in three players in on transfer deadline day who looked decent signings. And I was so close to getting in Ross McCormack too – five minutes away – it was paperwork, or something, that we couldn't get across the line with Aston Villa. The move fell away in the last five minutes of deadline day and that was disappointing because he would have played as a good number ten off Vaughan or Grabban, and Vaughan would probably have been our back-up striker. It would have given us more options up front, which we were going to need if we kept shipping goals.'

Two home games immediately after the transfer window closed would normally have been just what the doctor ordered. But Sunderland had not won at home in the whole of 2017 – in fact, they had never so much as even led in a home game since the turn of the year.

'We had two defeats: Sheffield United and Nottingham Forest at home,' nods Grayson. 'Sheffield United, we couldn't get near them, they were playing with a bit of confidence and they were like a team who would come up to the Stadium of Light looking to keep us quiet for the first ten to 15 minutes, waiting for the crowd to get on our backs, and that's how it turned out. They did a job on us.

'The Nottingham Forest game was one of those games where the winner came completely out of the blue – they didn't look like they would score in a month of Sundays. We had missed one or two chances and then they suddenly find a way to get a goal in the last couple of minutes.'

A veneer of respectability was given to the Sheffield United defeat by the 2-1 scoreline but the home team were a clear second best on the night and their goal was a consolation one, scored in the 90th minute off the boot of Jack Rodwell.

Rodwell, who was booed throughout the closing stages by Sunderland fans, was the poster boy for all that was wrong with the club – like the Álvarez fiasco, like the crazy sums paid for

Ndong and Djilobodji, Rodwell's signing represented one of the high watermarks of maximum investment for minimal return. Bought for a £10 million price tag that he never looked remotely like justifying, he was reputedly on wages of £70,000 a week and had been allowed to join without a relegation clause in his contract, meaning that while every one of his teammates had to take a big cut in pay on demotion, Rodwell remained in the money. It might have been forgiveable had he produced scintillating performances, but his touch and passing were dreadful, his movement lethargic, his confidence non-existent and his record of forever being on the losing side in games he played for Sunderland had entered folklore. Later in the season, new manager Chris Coleman would reveal the player, who had asked for a transfer earlier in the year, was not in a mentally fit state to play for the club. Grayson had to endure this situation in silence in term of making Rodwell's problems public, all the time hoping he could benefit from some of the Premier League quality the ex-Everton, Manchester City and England player should have been bringing to the party.

'So, as a manager, you're thinking, "Rodwell, a talented player, surely we can get him going?" A 75 per cent Jack Rodwell, or even a 50 per cent Jack Rodwell, compared to the ability he had shown previously, would be an asset to you in the Championship. But there were early signs that his confidence was affected and that he was insecure. His very first morning when we were on the grass training, when I'm still at the shaking hands with players stage, he comes up to me and shakes my hand and says, "I want to play centre-half. I'm not the midfield player everyone thinks I am." And I thought, "Jeez, I've only just met you for the very first time and you're telling me that!" You thought he might have waited a day or two. I was really taken aback, to be honest, but that was an early sign that he had problems. He wasn't a bad lad – I didn't have a problem with him – and obviously he's gone to Blackburn Rovers now, and they hope they are going to get his career going again, but it couldn't be done at Sunderland. I played him as a defensive midfielder against Sheffield United and he was just a shadow of what he was capable of being. You want your holding midfielder to be making angles, to be getting on the ball, but Jack was marking in that game, so he couldn't get on the ball much and he wasn't contributing.'

The Nottingham Forest game was even more of a disappointment for Sunderland, with ex-Black Cats striker Daryl Murphy scoring an 86th-minute winner after a dreadfully misplaced pass by defender Tyias Browning. It was one of only two shots on target the visitors had all night. Grayson had made four changes to the side which lost to Sheffield United, deploying a 4–1–4–1 formation, with returning Lee Cattermole the holding midfielder, Grabban up front, and Sunderland the better-looking side for most of a dull game. The unforced errors and the goals against the run of play were now the norm, though, in pretty much every Sunderland match.

'It seemed a common trait, in three or four home games in particular, that we would start well, hit a crossbar or post and then suddenly be behind out of nothing,' acknowledges Grayson. 'After it had happened four or five times in games, the supporters must have been thinking, "Here we go again" – because I certainly was. I was thinking, "How can we play so well, make one simple mistake and suddenly keep finding ourselves a goal down?"'

The mould was broken a little in the next match, when Sunderland played well enough at Hull City to be looking good value for a second away win of the season before Vaughan's early goal was cancelled out by another late equaliser from a former

Black Cat, this time David Meyler. Grayson's tactics now came under increasing scrutiny by Sunderland fans, with the manager roundly criticised for going overly defensive too early on in the game, with midfielders McManaman and Williams replaced by Billy Jones and Jack Rodwell, minutes before the leveller.

'We had a couple of injuries and the bench wasn't looking great,' Grayson points out. 'I went with the decision to shore it up. Clearly it didn't work out, but I think most managers, when you've lost three on the trot and you have a lead away from home, would do the same thing with just over ten minutes to go. I would do the same thing again. The problem you had was that you just never knew, with some of the players, what they would do over the course of the whole 90 minutes. For 89 minutes of the game some of them would be very good, but then all of a sudden they would make the most ridiculous mistake.

'It was probably summed up best in my last game at Sunderland with Didier Ndong when we had a corner, which was cleared, and Bolton went on the attack. Didier, who had played really well, chased back 60 or 70 yards to make a fantastic recovery run and challenge – brilliant. And then, having done that, he promptly played a weak back-pass straight to their player, who went on to score! That incident epitomised how we were capable of shooting ourselves in the foot at any given moment.

'As a manager you take responsibility for results going right or wrong because you are in overall charge. But, as I would say to the players in the dressing room, I can't take responsibility for them making a bad pass, or a bad decision, or falling over the ball or spilling a corner at the feet of a defender. And it just felt that there was always going to be a mistake in any game from some individual that would directly prevent us from getting the result we would otherwise deserve from it.'

Nowhere was that more tellingly illustrated than in the 2-1 home loss to Cardiff City which followed Sunderland's unceremonious dumping out of the League Cup by Everton, having got past Carlisle United in the previous round.

'I tried to play quite a strong team in the Cup – Carlisle, Bury – because of the losing culture and any victory, especially so early in the season, could be vital,' said Grayson. 'That's why I selected a strong side for the Cup games. That had gone well enough until we came up against Everton who, even though they had been struggling, just had that Premier League class they needed to push us to one side. If you have suffered defeats over a long period of time, to get a victory takes a weight off your shoulders, and the Cup might have served its purpose for that, but after losing to Everton we wanted to return to Wearside and pick ourselves up immediately against Cardiff City.'

It was not to be.

Lamine Koné produced a lamentable performance against the Bluebirds – caught out for the first goal and then giving away a penalty for the second.

'For me, coming into Sunderland as a manager, Koné was the one you had seen the year before and were aware of the price tag going around for him of £12 to £15 million. So you're hoping he's someone you can get the very best out of for as long as you have him. He didn't look like a £12 million player though. Given his reputation and power and size, you felt he could have been that player, but then again you were looking at situations and you were thinking, "How he's managed to do that? How can you mistime something or produce a header as bad as that?" And I don't want to be critical of players – it was just the simple things – but there were certain things being done which didn't add up to a player who was on the wages or the fee associated with them.

'It wasn't a case of players having blinders on the training pitch but not doing it on matchdays either. Even in training you were thinking, "How can X, Y and Z make that basic mistake in a training session, even though there was no pressure on him?" You wanted to know what it was – what was the reason for it happening with certain individuals?

'But that Cardiff game, that exposed another more basic problem we had, which was that there were times when players simply wouldn't take on board what they were being told. That very morning of the Cardiff game we'd given a presentation to the players saying to watch out for the long Cardiff goal-kicks being flicked on by the big striker Kenneth Zohore because Craig Bryson will try to run in behind, get the second ball and score. The game got underway and, six minutes in, Cardiff's first goal-kick is long, Zohore flicks on, someone decides not to go with Bryson and he waltzes off and scores. And you're thinking to yourself, "We've just told you about this! Why haven't you picked up on it?" That was the frustration we had. As coaching staff you do as much as you can but once the whistle goes, it comes down to player responsibility, and I don't know why they didn't respond.

'Koné, they were talking about £15 to 18 million. Again, you think, "Has he had his head turned?" What was his preparation going into games? But Koné was one of a few players who you knew didn't really want to be there. The problem was, you couldn't not play them on occasions because you were needing to be as strong as possible to win games.'

If Cardiff was bad, the next game, away to Ipswich Town, was worse – Sunderland going down to a 5-2 mauling – although the manager thought the scoreline harsh. Grayson made five changes from the side which lost to Cardiff City, which included restoring error-prone goalkeeper Steele to the starting line-up, who had been replaced in the starting line-up for the past five league games by the error-prone Ruiter.

'I personally think we didn't deserve to lose by that scoreline on the night – we were back in it at 4-2 – but, again, it was a tough night because of the pressure we were starting to come under in the wake of the displays and the results overall. I was changing players and formations just looking for a spark or an injection of confidence to get us on a run to take us up the table. As a manager for ten to 12 years, I've never been one for a rigid formation that I'm always going to play. I'm happy to look at different formations which might suit the players, depending on the situation and the opposition. I've always been one for doing that because I believe in adaptability – when things aren't going well, and you're picking up injuries, you have to be adaptable. Every time you lose, you look at whether you change the formation or the personnel or the system – every manager will be the same.'

Three successive draws finally ended the run of defeats – but by now single points were no use to a Black Cats side threatening to take up permanent residence in the bottom three. First up, Grayson had a return to his former club Preston knowing that his welcome would hardly be a friendly one given the way he had chosen to leave that summer.

'I had been looking forward to the Preston game from when the fixtures first came out, but I was also apprehensive because when you walk out of a football club and it hasn't been the football club's decision you are seen as a bit of a villain. I'd been there over four years and I had a really good relationship with the chairman and the supporters, so I wasn't overly concerned about that sort of thing. I just didn't want to suffer the irony of losing my job at the club I had formerly been at!'

Grayson was reliant on his intimate knowledge of the Preston squad giving him something of an edge in game-planning, but it was a close-run thing.

'I knew the Preston players, I knew what system might work against them, and we played quite well and went 1-0 up,' he says. 'But once again we conceded two goals very quickly, at which point I started getting barracked by the Preston fans singing, "*You're getting sacked in the morning!*" It was funny because when we scored our goal I didn't celebrate out of respect, and then at 2-1 down I'm getting pelters from the home fans – not in a really nasty way, more of a joke, really – but I thought it was harsh.

'Then Aiden McGeady scores a worldy to equalise, and I'm punching the air as if we'd just won the World Cup because of the relief at that moment in time! Geads got a lot of stick from the Preston fans – I'm assuming because he'd said something in the press before the game – and he'd ran the full length of the pitch to cup his ear to them. But I was quite happy with that because it certainly took the spotlight off me for celebrating!'

The second draw was another Stadium of Light disappointment, against a QPR side that had as bad an away record as Sunderland had home record. Perhaps a stalemate was inevitable but, with the die being cast on Sunderland's season, the fans were not prepared to accept that their team could not overcome opposition which was struggling so much on its travels. Significantly, the fans did not turn on the manager but targeted the players themselves after a poor Ndong header had helped hand QPR a lead. Although a McGeady goal was to rescue an error-strewn Sunderland display, supporters had had enough and gave ironic cheers when passes weren't misplaced or when keeper Steele safely gathered.

'I get that the fans were unhappy because we were in a position that we didn't want to be in,' says the Yorkshireman. 'Sunderland fans were thinking top half of the table, and there we were near the bottom. So I get it. We weren't in the bottom three that often, we were just teetering there outside of it, but no one had expected that and I knew we needed results, because that's what goes with the territory. Winning against QPR, where they weren't the strongest or best of teams, would have been expected but we just couldn't get that elusive first goal and victory at home. It was like Groundhog Day, every home game, because we would basically start well, miss a chance and then be a goal down. No wonder the fans were getting pissed off with it, because I was exactly the same: every time there was a basic or unforced error, I was thinking, "What have we done here?" And then you get that mentality where there are ironic cheers when one of the players makes a good pass. It was as if there was a sense of anticipation that, "Here we go again, we are going to get the same disappointment, the same result."'

They weren't wrong.

In fact, in Grayson's next game, Sunderland could have produced arguably their worst result of the season when, from being 3-1 up, they almost contrived to throw the game away against lowly opposition.

'Brentford are one of those teams who are not fashionable but, on their day, they can be as good as any in the Championship – so we didn't underestimate them,' said Grayson. 'We got ourselves into a good, strong position in the game, 3-1 up at the break, and you're thinking, "This could be the turning point and we could kick on." But before you know it, we have conceded, conceded again and are hanging on. In those last few minutes, I was thinking, "I'll take a point." That was just the state of the players mentally at the time, and probably the football club in general, that you are still thinking at 3-1, "Are we going to get a good result here?"'

Sunderland escaped with a draw but neither players nor performances were picking up. The Brentford game underlined that no matter how many goals a Grabban or McGeady got at one end, any one of Steele, Ruiter, Jones, Koné, Browning, Galloway, Ndong or others could be guaranteed to inexplicably throw it away at the other.

'It was getting the balance right,' says Grayson. 'We were playing some quite decent football and were getting goals – no one more so than Grabban. But we also knew we had to score goals to make up for the mistakes we kept making as a back four or a back five. It was good to know we had a goalscorer and we knew that with him and McGeady and one or two other players we would have a chance of scoring goals. The problem was that we were conceding them. As a defender myself, it was particularly disappointing we couldn't get a clean sheet. There was a mistake in them all, mistakes that were certainly avoidable. It wasn't just mistakes that cost us goals, it was mistakes which spoke of a lack of concentration or nerves, or whatever – continual individual errors that no coach can legislate for.

'I remember one game, a player went to pass back to Adam Matthews and ended up missing him by about 15 yards and the ball went out for a throw-in, and you're thinking, "How does that even happen?" If somebody is doing that, you're thinking, "Wow, these really are schoolboy errors." You are thinking, "One: has Matthews not been looking for the ball? And two: how has my player misplaced his pass that much?" When you're making such basic mistakes as we were, there are bigger problems that need tackling mentally, rather than just footballing ability.'

Another home disappointment followed – a 2-1 defeat to Bristol City – and at this point it really did feel like the writing was on the wall for the manager. All the familiar problems were there: the individual errors, the lack of fight or urgency, the poor marking, the rabbit-in-the-headlights goalkeeping as Ruiter and Steele swapped places for the umpteenth time. Uncharacteristically, and perhaps with no other option, Grayson did not defend his players in the wake of yet another characteristically poor playing performance. But these were still the players he was coaching, the players he was setting up for games, the players who did not seem to be responding to his instructions. Sunderland had still to keep a clean sheet in the new season and, in fact, would not do so under Grayson – with the biggest culprits arguably being his two keepers, who regularly dropped clangers. The decision to replace Mannone had not paid off, and the manager accepted that that was a problem he couldn't resolve.

'Any club was going to miss Jordan Pickford and then Vito had gone,' he accepts. 'On paper you looked at Jason Steele and he had a decent pedigree. But then he made one or two mistakes, and that kind of set the standard in terms of his performances, and any mistake he made got punished. You bring in Ruiter, who does well, and signs for the club, but then he started to make mistakes as well, and any mistakes affected him. You got to the stage where you're switching the goalkeepers around – just like your outfield players – hoping for one of the keepers to show that they are undroppable. But the mistakes kept coming. Basic ones. A lot came from confidence as well, because after the mistakes you've made you'll get cheers if you catch things or make a decent pass, and that can be tough for them, mentally. Keepers, especially, have to be mentally tough. I think they were better than they showed at Sunderland, but there wasn't a lot on the market at the time.'

For the first time, the fans began to turn on the manager, the bile which had been bubbling up higher and higher on the message boards now spilling down from the terraces.

Promising midfielder Paddy McNair made a return from injury for his first game of the season against Bristol City and, a month earlier, speedy attacker Duncan Watmore had returned from a serious injury of his own. But the new blood of players who could genuinely have helped the struggling side could only be used sparingly and would not be riding to the rescue of their teammates anytime soon.

'We had to be careful with Watmore and Paddy because we couldn't play them in back-to-back games at that stage of their comebacks,' recalls Grayson. 'That was a shame because Catts was one of the players who was perhaps struggling with a lack of confidence at the time and it would have been good to have taken some pressure off him. There was no lack of trying from any of these players – I think they were genuinely honest lads. Catts was one of those players who had suffered the mental torture of relegation and of every week – week in, week out – in the Premier League being a struggle. It carried over. People like Billy Jones, who was known as a real good recognised Championship player, he looked a shadow of his former self in the Championship.'

It meant that Grayson knew he was going into the next game, which pitted bottom-of-the-table Bolton Wanderers against second-bottom Sunderland, needing a victory if the conclusion was not to crystalise that the Black Cats were indeed going down.

'I had spoken to Martin Bain on the Sunday after the Bristol City game, where the crowd hadn't been big and was even less by the end, and he said he was on my side 100 per cent but that Ellis had been making a few noises,' remembers Grayson. 'So I knew going into the Bolton game, based on what Martin had said and what the results had been, that we needed to get a win, probably, to keep my job. But the Bristol City game had been another that had you scratching your head, because Bobby Reid, who is 5 foot 7 inches, scores the winner for them with a header from a corner. How is he allowed a free header – the smallest person on the pitch? It just summed up the lack of concentration or responsibility among that group of players at the time.'

More than a third of the season had now passed, and instead of pushing for promotion Sunderland were simply struggling to avoid going rock bottom of the division. None of the relegated players was showing Premier League form in the Championship and none of the new signings, bar perhaps McGeady and the on-loan and in-form Grabban, had offered anything to really improve the side. The Bolton game brought all the familiar failings to the fore again, Sunderland flattering to deceive before conceding the first goal. Twice they went behind but this time Grayson received personal abuse from supporters each time Sunderland were chasing the game: long and sustained calls for him to go, along with chants of , *'You're not fit to wear the shirt'* at the players. A late strike by Paddy McNair spared Sunderland's blushes – a 3-3 draw which actually moved the Black Cats up a place in the table – but the mood of Sunderland fans at the final whistle was one of real fury as their grim-faced manager headed down the tunnel with chants of, *'You're getting sacked in the morning'* ringing in his ears.

As it turned out, the supporters were wrong, the club didn't wait that long and, much to his surprise, Grayson was sacked within minutes of the final whistle.

'My practice after a game as a manager was to go into my office, spend a couple of minutes speaking to my staff, and then go in to see the players,' he says. 'I found that that was a good way for me to gather my thoughts and allow the players to settle down before I started talking to them. So, as usual, I went into my office but this time, within 30 seconds of sitting down, Martin Bain walks in. He said, "Look, I know this timing isn't the right thing to do but I've had just Ellis on the line asking me to let you know that you're relieved of your duties." I was gobsmacked. I wasn't surprised at the decision – I was surprised at the timing. I thought they could have had at least waited 15 minutes or 20 minutes, but he said, "I'm under instructions." I had a really good relationship with Martin – I still speak to him quite regularly, socialise with him – and I know he felt uncomfortable and embarrassed about doing it. So I gathered my thoughts and I went into the dressing room as I would normally. The dressing room was quiet. I said to the players, "Look, you can't keep on making stupid mistakes. It's something that has happened all season." I went through a few bits and bobs with them that had happened in the game and then I basically finished by saying, "Anyway, you've been a joy to work with. I've just been sacked." And I walked out. There was a stunned silence because they didn't expect it to be done so quickly, and in the way it was done either. I heard later that our captain, John O'Shea, had stood up in the dressing room – and I really appreciate this, because this has come from other people – and he said, "Why is it? What is it with us that we keep getting good people sacked when it is our responsibility?"'

Meanwhile, in the press room, reporters were trying to digest a brief statement from the club read out by a nervous press officer explaining that the manager had been relieved of his duties and would not be coming up. It is hard to say whether preventing Grayson from coming up was either a smart move by the club to divert any damaging comments from the now ex-manager, or whether it was a hasty byproduct of owner Ellis Short having snapped and made an executive order from the other side of the world. Given the shambles the club was in at this stage, you would imagine it was the latter.

'I would quite happily have come up to face the music because I don't duck my responsibilities,' says Grayson. 'But Martin said, "You can't do the press, and that's when the statement came out very quickly. Me? I stayed in my office. My family came down, my dad went home. I texted my fiancé, Carol, straight away to let her know I'd been sacked, because I didn't want her to see it coming up on the telly. And I ended up going back to my hotel room and having a glass of wine with Snods and chewing the fat until 2 a.m. I was up early the next morning, seven, to get into the training ground, get all my bags, and I basically left at 9.30 a.m. before everyone else came in.'

The sudden sacking meant Grayson's plans to move to the area on a more permanent basis had to be reversed.

'I'd been living in Ramside Hall a couple of nights a week, but I'd go back home and come up Monday morning and be there for 7.30 a.m. at the training ground,' he says. 'Maybe if we didn't have a game I'd go home Tuesday night, have Wednesday at home, and come back Thursday. And then the weekends would vary depending where we were in the country. I would go home if were in the north-west, not too far from the Preston area. That was at first, but then possibly within six weeks or eight weeks of doing that and with things going OK, I got an apartment in Durham, so all the paperwork got done. For some reason the woman who was leasing it, who probably knew something I didn't, agreed to let me have it on just a six-months lease, rather than a year. I thought, "Brilliant" – because

I wouldn't need it in the summer. But then I think I only stayed in it twice before getting the sack, which meant for five months I had a holiday home in Durham which went unused!

'Did it hurt me to be sacked? It hurt my pride. I don't like having criticism, but I accept it – it wasn't something that was making me not sleep at night because I know that it comes with the territory of being a manager. I was sacked at Huddersfield and Leeds, but felt both were unwarranted because although the form hadn't been great, on both occasions they let me go we were still outperforming what our original targets had been at the time.

'At Sunderland I couldn't argue we were reaching the targets originally set but, as a manager, you always back yourself to turn it around at some stage. I think it was the most difficult job I was going to go into, regardless of the outcome, because when I went into Leeds, there wasn't the financial trouble there was at Sunderland; it wasn't rock-bottom at the time, like Sunderland had been, and the expectations weren't so great because Leeds were in League One when I came in there.

'It goes back to the question, "Do I regret taking it?" No, because you want to be the one who goes in and is successful and changes it around. I enjoyed going into work every day. I enjoyed going to the training ground, I enjoyed the staff working below me – all the way to the chefs in the canteen, to the point that when we left there were tears from the people I'd got to know over three or four months who weren't there just for the football results. They knew us as friends rather than their boss, as such, and were upset when we left because they could see how hard we were working behind the scenes from morning to night.

'I enjoyed going to work. I didn't enjoy the results and how we played because it reflected, rightly, on me, on the manager's head.'

Despite the blot on his CV, despite not appreciating how much of a basket case of a club he was taking on at the time, Grayson says he has had no second thoughts about his decision to leave his safe post at Preston – he just wished he could have taken most of his Preston team with him!

'I don't have any regrets about taking the job,' he shrugs. 'I still get asked the question even now, but I don't regret it because I wouldn't have wanted to look back at the end of the season and someone else had got Sunderland back to the Premier League. Yes, I know Derek McInnes turned the job down, but it was still a massive and exciting proposition for someone to take on. That's why Chris Coleman was prepared to step in after I left, hoping he would be the one that lifted the club up again. Everyone knows what Sunderland can be like if you get it right at the club, and that's why it will always have that appeal as a job. There can be a snowball effect and it can get going to an unbelievable degree, and that's why I took it. The easiest thing to do would have been to stay at Preston – I had an owner who trusted me, we were debt free and I had a group of players who were among the most talented group of players I'd ever worked with. That squad was put together for about a million and a half and it's worth about £30 to 40 million now. If I could have taken that group of Preston players to Sunderland we would have done a lot better!' Grayson's successor Chris Coleman, the former Welsh international boss and yet another of the high-profile names Sunderland have managed to attract in recent times, was the club's ninth manager in six years. Unfortunately, despite almost two-thirds of the season remaining, Coleman was unable to resolve the same problems Grayson had encountered.

'Chris came in and I thought he was a good choice, a good experienced manager, but I knew he'd be working under the same constraints as me. He had a couple of months to go until the transfer window, and I could see he was being a bit more defensive, hoping to get results. I heard his press conferences, saying if players didn't want to be there he would drive them to their next club himself – exactly the same as I had been saying. But when it came to shipping them out there were no takers, largely because of the money they were on. And Chris was still trying to deal with players who were suffering a lack of confidence and a hangover and all the baggage that had come up over a number of years.'

Perhaps surprisingly, Grayson believes he would have kept Sunderland in the Championship by the season's end had he not been sacked.

'I'm sure Chris will be disappointed he didn't keep them up because he had something like 30 games whereas I had closer to 15,' he says. 'He had a squad which on paper should have been able to stay up, and he had come into a situation where the goal was now simply survival rather than promotion. When I came in, the aim was to be halfway up the table with the potential of making it to the playoffs. I still think I would have kept Sunderland up, with my experience, and knowing the division like I did, but at the time, just being kept up in the Championship wasn't the expectation. If it had been, then I still think I would have stopped them going down because I knew what the Championship was all about. I'm not being disrespectful to Chris, it's just that I know a lot more about the Championship while he's been away involved with international football. I had enough about me to know what it takes to grind out results, but at the time I was at the club, survival wasn't the goal, it was to be top half at the very least – and that was how I was judged.'

Grayson, though, believes it was a tall order for anyone to save the club that season given the historical problems it was coping with, coupled with Ellis Short's decision not to fund the ten-year project further. The summer Grayson was appointed, Sunderland accumulated close to £40 million in player sales and £30 million in parachute payments but the new manager was given just over £1 million to spend to restock a squad down to the bare bones.

'The biggest thing that was hanging over the football club when I came in was that there was so much animosity towards Ellis Short, and he had decided he no longer wanted to invest. So, as much as it is a horrible thing to suffer relegation at the end of the season I was involved, it probably gave Ellis the opportunity to sell the club, and for players to leave. Ultimately, maybe going down a second time can be of longer-term benefit for the club – we've seen it already in the 2018–19 season with Sunderland winning a couple of home games. Having won at home very quickly, all of a sudden you can find yourself on a run that can snowball. Whether it is League One, Championship or Premier League, wins give you momentum – Chris Coleman didn't get a home win for a long time after his arrival, and that didn't help him.'

Much criticism has been aimed in the direction of expensively employed chief executive Bain, particularly when it came to the Scot making large-scale redundancies and losing some well known and long-serving members of the club. It didn't help that rumours circulated that while the services of such staff were being dispensed with the club was in the process of ordering a company car for Bain which cost six figures to procure. But

Grayson has time for the man who delivered the news to his face that he had been sacked as Sunderland AFC manager.

'I think Martin tried to give me as much as he could to help me do the job,' he suggests. 'He was very open and honest about what we could do in terms of the transfer window and so on. I don't think he could have done much more for me because his hands were tied – Ellis had made it clear he wasn't going to put in more money. Martin was trying to shuffle around this, shuffle around that, trying to get this player out, to get this one in – he let a number of staff go to balance the books. Martin has been criticised for a lot of things, but it wasn't his money – he was restricted by the hand that fed him. I thought he did a decent job in the circumstances, because if he hadn't been able to shuffle certain things around the club could have gone to a much worse state. I'd like to have achieved more personally, but I couldn't leave much influence on Sunderland over the four months I was there, and my feeling now is that it was the right club at the wrong time. If I had taken over now, a year later, I would have been the most suitable person for the club because of my reputation for getting four promotions from League One. I'd also have been able to manage expectancy levels from fans in that division because I'd had to do it at Leeds United previously, who are a comparable club. You always try to leave improvements when you depart a club, on and off the pitch, but you need a period of time to do that – you can't do it within three or four months. You need at least three, maybe four transfer windows to make an impact on a football club, and that was especially true of Sunderland because of the turmoil and uncertainty surrounding players.'

Sacked Grayson could have bounced back into management within days but, after the harrowing experience on Wearside, opted to take a break.

'When I left Sunderland I took a bit of time off,' he nods. 'It was the first Christmas I'd had off in 30-odd years – since I was 16. Within weeks of leaving Sunderland I'd been offered four jobs but I just thought I needed a bit of time out to analyse what I needed to analyse and decide what I wanted to do. It got to February and Bradford City came in for me, looking for promotion from League One, and I went for that, but I probably rushed into my decision in terms of the budget and other situations around the club. I took it to the end of the season and then at the end of the season I didn't think it was for me.

'I want to go and be successful at clubs, but the easy option in football is to take any contract that is put under your nose, so I took a step back and decided to wait on. This is the first time in 32 years I've not started the season with a club when the new campaign got under way. It was strange but it was good as well. It was the first summer in such a long time where I'd not spent my time looking at the phone checking who is available and who is not, whether an agent has rung me, organising pre-season, going through transfer deadline and all those sort of things. I got a bit of a normal life for a change and I've enjoyed it. I like music and this summer I've been to the Isle of Wight festival for four days; I was at York Races before going to the Leeds Festival. I do my work for talkSport, Five Live, Sky and then I'm getting to do things for the League Managers' Association and I'm able to watch games for fun. So I'm taking time away from the coalface, but I've still got an edge to me.

'I've been offered three jobs in the last few weeks, home and abroad, but I don't want to go back to work yet, and I don't think the jobs offered are right for me either.'

The Yorkshireman is relishing his freedom and time out of the managerial rat race. It has allowed him to plan marriage to

Carol in Portugal next year, and given him the freedom to cut short the advanced planning of the ceremony to fly back and see his teenage son Joe make his competitive debut for Blackburn Rovers in a 4-1 League Cup victory over Lincoln City – as he had done the week of our interview. He is also free to continue his fundraising for Prostate Cancer UK, having successfully raised tens of thousands of pounds thanks to his connections with bands like Kasabian and The Killers, including events held in the Queens Hotel, where we are now closing our interview. You sense it will be hard to give up that freedom when the right managerial job comes along, but you also sense that his time in football management is not over yet.

Leeds United fans, who have been gathering in the bar but keeping a respectful distance while the interview is being conducted, surge around him once the voice recorder has been switched off and the notepad put away. There are pats on the back, smiles and photographs taken. He will undoubtedly be a better manager for the experience of being at Sunderland AFC, however much of a brutal lesson it might have been in the short term, and the love and respect of fans is intoxicating.

'It was fire-fighting every single day,' he says. 'I'm not saying I didn't make mistakes in my time there, but I have never had so much to cope with at any other club I've been at in the past as I did at Sunderland. Don't get me wrong, it hasn't been a walk in the park at any of my clubs, but Sunderland was different altogether. There was barely a day that passed there was something you had to deal with off the pitch and then you had to deal with on the pitch. It was constantly, "Gosh this has been a long day at the office" – again. I honestly don't know why as a squad they didn't absorb our messages, because they weren't a bad group of players. They didn't cause me problems in training, they would do what we asked of them, and you couldn't say they weren't playing for me because I'd only been in the job three or four months. Even now, though, I'll see players who think they could and should have done better. It was just a collective failure. It's like when I went to Leeds as manager, from knowing it when I'd been there as a player. I learned at Leeds that you have to be a special type of player to be able to play for certain clubs. I think at Leeds that's the case, and I think Sunderland are the same, where you need to be a strong, determined character with strong mental attributes to be able to play for the club. That's why I tried to change the nucleus of the squad around as much as I could, because of the players who had suffered what had happened. But maybe the ones who came in got affected very quickly by what was going off with the other players and what was happening at the club overall.'

It was a very intense period and one of massive change at the Stadium of Light but Grayson hopes that, almost one year on, things are on the up for a club whose potential he knows all too well but was unable to release.

'It takes time when a club has got into that situation,' he reflects. 'We're only now coming up to the third transfer window since I left, but it is starting to get there in terms of breaking with what I inherited. It's new owners, new manager, new division and new players. Regardless of what division you're in you're getting those players out who are out of contract, you are getting rid of them, or eventually selling off players. You are finally making that break and sometimes it is only when you can really move on from what has gone before that you can really start to think about moving on up again. Hopefully that's what happens at Sunderland now.'

EPILOGUE

Grayson's ill-fated reign at Sunderland was followed by a similarly ill-fated Chris Coleman reign and the club was relegated at the end of the 2017–18 campaign. They went down bottom of the table with 37 points, six adrift of safety; a mere 62 behind champions Wolves. Relegation to the third tier of English football for only the second time in the club's proud history was a hammer blow to Sunderland fans, but it did at least mark the end of Ellis Short's increasingly dysfunctional tenure. It was a source of immense regret that the man who had spent more money on the club than anyone in its history by some distance, ended his time on Wearside as a despised and unloved figure. In the final analysis, though, he had no one to blame but himself. And, as he looked to recoup as much of his outlay as possible during the final couple of seasons, with the club crashing down the divisions, his standing among Sunderland fans suffered accordingly.

New owners Stewart Donald and Charlie Methven took over in the summer of 2018, determined to be far more hands-on, and brought promising young Scottish manager Jack Ross south of the border as one of their first acts. Barely a year after Grayson's departure, Sunderland are trying to rise phoenix-like from the flames of burned dollars, steered by optimistic new ownership and a bright young boss.

Only time will tell how successful Jack Ross can be – history, and the chapters of this book, show how much of a challenge the Sunderland manager's job is.

But if this book and the testimony of the managers within tells us one thing, it is that in order for Sunderland Association Football Club to truly fulfil its potential it has to be united, from backroom to boardroom, in a common cause. Otherwise the club is doomed to repeat the mistakes of recent history.

OTHER BOOKS IN THE SERIES

TALES FROM THE RED & WHITES

Brilliant original stories about
Sunderland Association Football Club
by journalists, fans and former players.

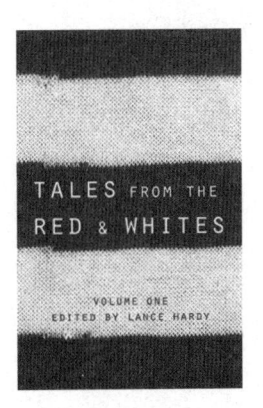

Tales From The Red & Whites Volume 1

The first book of the series features former players Jimmy Montgomery, Gary Rowell and Gary Bennett in addition to contributions from Pete Sixsmith, Mike Grady, Jeff Brown, David Jones, Nick Barnes, Doug Weatherall, Graeme Anderson, Rob Mason and editor Lance Hardy.

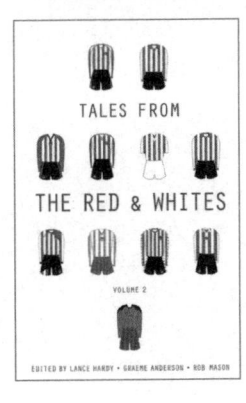

Tales From The Red & Whites Volume 2

This second volume presents a Sunderland XI with a difference, eleven players from various eras – stretching all the way back to the early 1950s – share their memories. From Roker Park to the Stadium of Light; from the Bank of England club to the Premier League; from FA Cup heroes to Third Division champions, and much more besides. Our expert selection panel's interviews offer a fascinating collection of stories that will sit proudly on any Sunderland fan's bookshelf.

All books in the series are available now from
www.talesfrom.com

Nick Barnes' Matchbook

The BBC commentator's beautifully crafted match notes for season 2015/16 in a unique box set design. A collection celebrating a love of football, statistics and art. The A6 size 40 card set in presentation box includes the background to Barnes' creations and a detailed and unique review of every Premier League match of another dramatic season.

All books in the series are available now from
www.talesfrom.com